D1554458

SOUL ECONOMY
BODY, SOUL, AND SPIRIT
IN WALDORF EDUCATION

[XII]

THE FOUNDATIONS OF WALDORF EDUCATION

Rudolf Steiner

SOUL ECONOMY
Body, Soul, and Spirit in Waldorf Education

Lectures presented in Dornach, Switzerland
December 23, 1921 – January 5, 1922

℮ Anthroposophic Press

MAY 1 1 2004

Published by Anthroposophic Press
P.O. Box 799
Great Barrington, MA 01230
www.steinerbooks.org

Translated with permission by Roland Everett from Rudolf Steiner, *Die gesunde Eniwicke-lung des Leiblich-Physischen als Grandlage der freien Enrfalrung des Seelisch-Geistigen* (GA 303) copyright © 1977 Rudolf Steiner–Nachlassverwaltung.

Revised edition by Anthroposophic Press, copyright © 2003
Introduction by William Jensen copyright ©2003

Publication of this work was made possible by a grant from
THE WALDORF CURRICULUM FUND

All rights reserved. No part of this book may be reproduced in any form without the written permission of the publishers, except for brief quotations embodied in critical articles and reviews.

ISBN 0-88010-517-8

Library of Congress Cataloging-in-Publication Data

Steiner, Rudolf, 1861–1925.
  [Gesunde Entwicklung des Leiblich-Physischen als Grundlage der freien Entfaltung des Seelisch-Geistigen. English]
  Soul economy : body, soul, and spirit in Waldorf education / Rudolf Steiner.
     p. cm. — (The foundations of Waldorf education ; 12)
  "Lectures presented in Dornach, Switzerland, December 23, 1921–January 5, 1922."
  Includes bibliographical references and index.
  ISBN 0-88010-517-8 (alk. paper)
  1. Steiner, Rudolf, 1861–1925 — Views on education. 2. Waldorf method of education.
  3. Anthroposophy. I. Title. II. Series.

  LB775.S7G47I3 2003
  370'.1— dc21

                                                              2003006511

Printed in the United States of America

10 9 8 7 6 5 4 3 2 1

CONTENTS

Editor's Introduction

William Jensen

Rudolf Steiner presented more than twenty lecture courses on education and child development, each taking a somewhat different approach to the introduction of his insights and pedagogical methods. The important lectures in this volume were presented in Dornach, Switzerland, to leading educators, including many from England, led by Professor Millicent Mackenzie, a pioneer in education from Cardiff University. As a result of these talks, Steiner went to Oxford, England, later that year, where he expanded on many of the themes begun in these lectures.[1]

The setting for these lectures was the White Hall in the first Goetheanum, where, because of the large attendance and limited space, the audience was split into two groups. Each lecture was presented twice, first to the German speakers and then to those who had traveled from England and

Speaker's rostrum in the White Hall

---

1. Those lectures took place also under the guidance of Professor Mackenzie; they are contained in *The Spiritual Ground of Education* (Anthroposophic Press, 2003), GA 305.

Holland. The repeated second sessions are represented in this volume. Consequently, in these lectures Steiner was speaking mostly to English-speaking educators, many of whom were relatively new to the ideas of spiritual science.

He begins by describing the development and movement of anthroposophy as the necessary foundation for understanding the principles behind Waldorf education. Again and again, he states the need to understand the human being as a whole and emphasizes the importance of basing all education on a deep knowledge of children as continually developing beings of body, soul, and spirit—an approach Steiner refers to in these talks as "soul economy." From this perspective, any enlightened approach to education is always based on the teacher's ability to observe and respond to each stage of a child's development. This method considers the critical importance of doing the right things at the right times as each stage of a child's life unfolds. It also takes into account each child's unique temperament. In a very real sense, then, Steiner's approach does not present methods for the education of children; it shows us how to educate individuals as whole human beings.

During the discussion periods that followed a couple of these lectures, Steiner responded to questions and expanded on certain themes, including his views on the state of Waldorf education and the anthroposophic movement in general. He presented these lectures with the great hope that his ideas on education would soon be understood and practiced well beyond Central Europe, bringing with them a lively impulse for social and spiritual renewal in the world.

INTRODUCTORY NOTE

Rudolf Steiner

Before the conference began, Rudolf Steiner addressed the partici-pants gathered in the White Hall of the Goetheanum:

Ladies and Gentlemen, before beginning this lecture course, allow me to bring up an administrative matter. Originally, this course was meant for a smaller group, but it has drawn such a response that it has become clear that we cannot gather in this tightly-packed hall. It would be impossible, and you would soon realize this if you were to attend both the lectures and the translations. Consequently, I have decided to present the lec-tures twice—the first each day at ten A.M. and again at eleven, for those who wish to hear it translated into English. For tech-nical reasons this is the only way to proceed. Therefore, I will begin the earlier lectures exactly at ten and second at eleven o'clock. I will ask those who came from England, Holland, and Scandinavia to attend the later lectures and everyone else to attend the first.[2]

---

2. Only the repeated lectures were recorded in shorthand. They were presented in two or three parts, each followed by George Adams's English translations. The text of this edition (apart from a few slight revisions) follows the version provided by Marie Steiner for its initial publication.

THE THREE PHASES
OF THE ANTHROPOSOPHIC MOVEMENT

December 23, 1921

First of all I would like to express my great joy at meeting so many of you here in this hall. Anyone whose life is filled with enthusiasm for the movement centered here at the Goetheanum is bound to experience happiness and a deep inner satisfaction at witnessing the intense interest for our theme, which your visit has shown. I would therefore like to begin this introductory lecture by welcoming you all most warmly. And I wish to extend a special welcome to Mrs. Mackenzie, whose initiative and efforts have brought about this course.[1] On behalf of the anthroposophic movement, I owe her a particular debt of gratitude.

I would like to add that it is not just a single person who is greeting you here, but that, above all, it is this building, the Goetheanum itself, that receives you. I can fully understand if some of you feel critical of certain features of this building as a work of art. Any undertaking that appears in the world in this way must be open to judgment, and any criticism made in good faith is appreciated—certainly by me. But, whatever your reactions may be to this building, it is the Goetheanum itself

---

1. Millicent Mackenzie was a professor of education at Cardiff University (1910–1915).

that welcomes you. Through just its forms and artistic compo-
sition, you can see that the aim here was not to erect a building
for specific purposes, such as education, for example. The
underlying spirit and style of this building shows that it was
conceived and erected from the spirit of our time, to serve a
movement and destined to play its part in our present civilization. And because education represents an integral part of
human civilization, it is proper for it to be nurtured here at this
center.

The close relationship between anthroposophic activities and
problems of education will occupy us in greater detail within
the next few days. Today, however, as part of these introductory
remarks, I would like to talk about something that really is a
part of any established movement. In a sense, you have come
here to familiarize yourselves with the various activities centered here at the Goetheanum, and in greeting you most
warmly as guests, I feel it right to begin by introducing you to
our movement.

The aims of this anthroposophic movement, which has been
in existence now for some twenty years, are only gradually
beginning to manifest. It is only lately that this movement has
been viewed by the world at large in ways that are consistent
with its original aims. Nevertheless, this movement has gone
through various phases, and a description of these may provide
the most proper introduction.

Initially, the small circle of its adherents saw anthroposophy
as a movement representing a very narrow religious perspective.
This movement tended to attract people who were not especially interested in its scientific background and were not
inclined to explore its artistic possibilities. Nor were they aware
of how its practical activities might affect society as a whole.
The first members were mainly those dissatisfied with traditional religious practice. They were the sort of people whose

deepest human longings prompted them to search for answers to the problems inherent in the human soul and spirit—problems that could not be answered for them by existing religious movements.

For me it often was quite astonishing to see that what I had to say about the fundamentals of anthroposophy was not at all understood by members who, nevertheless, supported the movement with deep sympathy and great devotion. When matters of a more scientific nature was discussed, these initial members extracted what spoke to their hearts and appealed to their immediate feelings and sentiments. And I can truly say that it was the most peaceful time within the anthroposophic movement, though this was certainly not what I was looking for. Because of this situation, during its first phase the anthroposophic movement was able to join another movement (though only outwardly and mainly from an administrative perspective), which you might know as the Theosophical Society.

Unless they can discern the vital and fundamental differences, those who search with a simple heart for knowledge of the eternal in human nature will find either movement equally satisfactory. The Theosophical Society is concerned primarily with a theoretical knowledge that embraces cosmology, philosophy, and religion and uses the spoken and printed word as its means of communication. Those who are satisfied with their lives in general, but wish to explore the spirit beyond what traditional doctrines offer, might find either movement equally satisfying. But (and only a few members noticed this) once it became obvious that, in terms of cosmology, philosophy, and religion, anthroposophic goals were never intended to be merely theoretical but to enter social life in a direct and practical way according to the demands of the spirit of our times— only then did it gradually become obvious that our movement could no longer work within the Theosophical Society. For in our time (and this will become clear in the following lectures), any movement that limits itself to theories of cosmology, philosophy, and religion is bound to degenerate into intolerable dogmatism. It was the futility of dogmatic arguments that finally caused the separation of the two movements.

It is obvious that no one who is sensible and understands western culture could seriously consider what became the crux of these dogmatic quarrels that led to this split. These quarrels were sparked by claims that an Indian boy was the reincarnation of Christ.[2] Since such a claim was completely baseless, it was unacceptable.

To waste energy and strength on theoretical arguments is not the way of anthroposophy, which aims to enter life directly. When it became necessary to work in the artistic, social, scientific, and—above all—in the educational realm, the true aims of anthroposophy made it necessary to separate from the Theosophical Society. Of course, this did not happen all at once; essentially, all that happened in the anthroposophic movement after 1912 demonstrated that this movement had to fight for its independence in the world, if it was going to penetrate ordinary life.

In 1907, during a Theosophical Society congress in Munich, I realized for the first time that it would be impossible for me to work with this movement. Along with my friends from the German section of the Theosophical Society, I had been given the task of arranging the program for this congress. Apart from the usual items, we included a performance of a mystery play

---

2. This refers to claims by leaders of the Theosophical Society that Christ had reappeared in the person of Krishnamurti, who later on refuted those claims himself. See Rudolf Steiner, *From the History and Contents of the First Section of the Esoteric School, 1904–1914* (Anthroposophic Press, 1998), part 2.

by Edouard Schuré (1841–1929), *The Sacred Drama of Eleusis.* We decided to create a transition from the movement's religious theories to a broader view that would encourage artistic activity. From our anthroposophic perspective, we viewed the performance as an artistic endeavor. But there were people in the movement who tried to satisfy their sometimes egotistical religious feelings by merely looking for a theoretical interpretation. They would ask, What is the meaning of this individual in the drama? What does that person mean? Such people would not be happy unless they could reduce the play to theoretical terms.

Any movement that cannot embrace life fully because of a lopsided attitude will certainly become sectarian. Spiritual science, on the other hand, is not the least inclined toward sectarianism, because it naturally tends to bring ideals down to earth and enter life in practical ways.

These attempts to free the anthroposophic movement from sectarianism by entering the artistic sphere represent the second phase of its history. Gradually, as membership increased, a need arose for the thought of philosophy, cosmology, and religion to be expressed artistically, and this in turn prompted me to write my mystery plays. And these must not be interpreted theoretically or abstractly, because they are intended to be experienced directly on the stage. To bring this about, my plays were performed in ordinary, rented theaters in Munich, from 1910 to 1913. And this led to an impulse to build a center for the anthroposophic movement. The changing situation made it clear that Munich was inappropriate for such a building, and so we were led to Dornach hill, where the Goetheanum was built as the right and proper place for the anthroposophic movement.

These new activities showed that, in keeping with its true spirit, the anthroposophic movement is always prepared to enter every branch of human life. Imagine that a different movement of a more theoretical religious character had decided to build a center; what would have happened? First, its members would collect money from sympathizers (a necessary step, unfortunately). Then they would choose an architect to design the building, perhaps in an antique or renaissance style or in a gothic or baroque or some other traditional style.

However, when the anthroposophic movement was in the happy position of being able to build its own home, such a procedure would have been totally unacceptable to me. Anything that forms an organic living whole cannot be assembled from heterogeneous parts. What relationship could any words, spoken in the spirit of anthroposophy, have had with the forms around a listener in a baroque, antique, or renaissance building? A movement that expresses only theories can present only abstractions. A living movement, on the other hand, must work into every area of life through its own characteristic impulses. Therefore, the urge to express life, soul, and spirit in practical activity (which is characteristic of anthroposophy) demanded that the surrounding architecture—the glowing colors of the wall paintings and the pillars we see—should speak the same language that is spoken theoretically in ideas and abstract thoughts. All of the movements that existed in the world previously were equally comprehensive; ancient architecture was certainly not isolated from its culture, but grew from the theoretical and practical activities of the time. The same can be said of the renaissance—certainly of the gothic, but also of the baroque.

To avoid a sectarian or theoretical ideology, anthroposophy had to find its own architectural and artistic styles. As mentioned before, one may find this style unsatisfactory or even paradoxical, but the fact is, according to its real nature, anthroposophy simply had to create its own physical enclosure. Let me make a comparison that may appear trivial but may, nevertheless, clarify these thoughts. Think of a walnut and its kernel. It is obvious that both nut and shell were created by the same forces, since together they make a whole. If anthroposophy had been housed in an incongruous building, it would be as if a walnut kernel had been found in the shell of a different plant. Nature produces nut and shell, and they both speak the same language. Similarly, neither symbolism nor allegory was needed here; rather, it was necessary that anthroposophic impulses flow directly into artistic creativity. If thoughts are to be expressed in this building, they must have a suitable shell, from artistic and architectural points of view. This was not easy to do, however, because the sectarian tendency is strong today, even among those looking for a broadening of religious ideals. But anthroposophy must not be influenced by people's sympathies or antipathies. It must remain true to its own principles, which are closely linked to the needs and yearnings of our times, as will be shown in the next few days.

And so anthroposophy entered the practical domain—as far as this was possible in those days. At the time, I surprised some members by saying, "Anthroposophy wants to enter all walks of life. Although conditions do not allow this today, I would love to open banks that operate according to anthroposophic principles." This may sound strange, but it was meant to show that anthroposophy is in its right element only when it can fertilize every aspect of life. It must never be seen merely as a philosophical and religious movement.

We now come to the catastrophic and chaotic time of the World War, which produced its own particular needs. In September 1913, we laid the foundation stone of this building. In 1914, when war broke out, we were building the foundation of the Goetheanum. Here I want to say only that, at a time when Europe was torn asunder by opposing nationalistic aspirations, here in Dornach we successfully maintained a place where people from all nations could meet and work together in peace, united by a common spirit. This was a source of deep inner satisfaction. Those war years could be considered as the second phase in the development of our movement.

Despite efforts to continue anthroposophic work during the war, the outer activities of the anthroposophic movement were mostly paralyzed. But one could experience how peoples everywhere gradually came to feel an inner need for spiritual sustenance, which, in my opinion, anthroposophy was able to offer. After 1918, when the war had ended, at least outwardly, there was an enormous, growing interest in spiritual renewal, such as anthroposophy wished to provide. Between autumn 1918 and spring 1919, numerous friends—many from Stuttgart—came to see me in Dornach. They were deeply concerned about the social conditions of the time, and they wanted the anthroposophic movement to take an active role in trying to come to terms with the social and economic upheavals. This led to the third phase of our movement.

It happened that Southern Germany—Württemberg in particular—was open to such anthroposophic activities, and one had to work wherever this was possible. These activities, however, were colored a little by the problems of that particular region, problems caused by the prevailing social chaos. An indescribable misery had spread over the whole of Central Europe at the time. Yet, seen in a broader context, the suffering caused by material needs was small compared to what was happening in the soul realm of the population. One could feel that humanity had to face the most fundamental questions of human existence. Questions once raised by Rousseau, which led to visible consequences in the French Revolution, did not touch the most basic human yearnings and needs as did the questions presented in 1919, within the very realms where we wished to work.

In this context, awareness of a specific social need began to grow in the hearts of my friends. They realized that perhaps the only way to work effectively toward a better future would be to direct our efforts toward the youth and their education. Our friend Emil Molt (who at the time was running the Waldorf-Astoria Cigarette Factory in Stuttgart) offered his services for such an effort by establishing the Waldorf school for his workers' children, and I was asked to help direct the school. People were questioning everything related to the organization of society as it had developed over the past centuries from its tribal and ethnic elements. This prompted me to present a short proclamation concerning the threefold social order to the German people and to the civilized world in general, and also to publish my book *Towards Social Renewal.*[3]

Many other activities connected with the social question also occurred, at first in South Germany, which resulted from this general situation and prevailing mood. It was essential then, though immensely difficult, to touch the most fundamental aspirations of the human soul. Despite their physical and mental agony, people were called upon to search, quite abstractly, for great and sublime truths; but because of the general upheaval they were unable to do so. Many who heard my addresses said to me later, "All this may be correct and even beautiful, but it concerns the future of humanity. We have faced death often during the last years and are no longer concerned about the future; we must live from day to day. Why should we be more interested in the future now than when we had to face the guns every day?" Such comments characterize the prevailing apathy of that time toward the most important and fundamental questions of human development.

---

3. *Towards Social Renewal: Rethinking the Basis of Society* (Rudolf Steiner Press, 2000).

Before the war, one could observe all sorts of educational experiments in various special schools. It was out of the question, however, that we would establish yet another country boarding school or implement a certain brand of educational principles. We simply wished to heal social ills and serve the needs of humankind in general. You will learn more about the fundamentals of Waldorf education during the coming lectures. For now, I merely wish to point out that, as in every field, anthroposophy sees its task as becoming involved in the realities of a situation as it is given. It was not for us to open a boarding school somewhere in a beautiful stretch of open countryside, where we would be free to do as we pleased. We had to fit into specific, given conditions. We were asked to teach the children of a small town—that is, we had to open a school in a small town where even our highest aspirations had to be built entirely upon pragmatic and sound educational principles. We were not free to choose a particular locality nor select students according to ability or class; we accepted given conditions with the goal of basing our work on spiritual knowledge. In this way, as a natural consequence of anthroposophic striving, Waldorf education came into existence.

The Waldorf school in Stuttgart soon ceased to be what it was in the beginning—a school for the children of workers at the Waldorf-Astoria Cigarette Factory. It quickly attracted students from various social backgrounds, and today parents everywhere want to send their children. From the initial enrollment of 140 children, it has grown to more than 600, and more applications are coming in all the time. A few days ago, we laid the foundation stone for a very necessary extension to our school, and we hope that, despite all the difficulties one must face in this kind of work, we will soon be able to expand our school further.

I wish to emphasize, however, that the characteristic feature of this school is its educational principles, based on knowledge of the human being and its ability to adapt those principles to external, given realities. If one can choose students according to ability or social standing, or if one can choose a locality, it is relatively easy to accomplish imaginary, even real, educational reforms. But it is no easy task to establish and develop a school on educational principles closely connected with the most fundamental human impulses, while also being in touch with the practical demands of life.

Thus, during its third phase, our anthroposophic movement has spread into the social sphere, and this aspect will naturally occupy us in greater depth during the coming days. But you must realize that what has been happening in the Waldorf school until now represents only a beginning of endeavors to bring our fundamental goals right down into life's practicalities.

Concerning other anthroposophic activities that developed later on, I would like to say that quite a number of scientifically trained people came together in their hope and belief that the anthroposophic movement could also fertilize the scientific branches of life. Medical doctors met here, because they were dissatisfied with the ways of natural science, which accept only external observation and experimentation. They were convinced that such a limited attitude could never lead to a full understanding of the human organism, whether in health or illness. Doctors came who were deeply concerned about the unnecessary limitations established by modern medical science, such as the deep chasm dividing medical practice into pathology and therapy.

These branches coexist today almost as separate sciences. In its search for knowledge, anthroposophy uses not just methods of outer experimentation—observation of external phenomena synthesized by the intellect—but, by viewing the human being as body, soul, and spirit, it also utilizes other means, which I will describe in coming days. Instead of dealing with abstract thoughts, spiritual science is in touch with the living spirit. And because of this, it was able to meet the aspirations of those urgently seeking to bring new life into medicine. As a result, I was asked to give two courses here in Dornach to university-trained medical specialists and practicing doctors, in order to outline the contribution spiritual science could make in the field of pathology and therapy. Both here in Dornach and in nearby Arlesheim, as well as in Stuttgart, institutes for medical therapy have sprung up, working with their own medicines and trying to utilize what spiritual science can offer to healing, in dealing with sickness and health. Specialists in other sciences have also come to look for new impulses arising from spiritual science; thus, courses were given in physics and astronomy. In this way, anthroposophic spirit knowledge was called upon to bring practical help to the various branches of science.

Characteristic of this third phase of the anthroposophic movement is the fact that gradually—despite a certain amount of remaining opposition—people have come to see that spiritual science, as practiced here, can meet every demand for an exact scientific basis of working and that, as represented here, it can work with equal discipline and in harmony with any other scientific enterprise. In time, people will appreciate more and more the potential that has been present during these past twenty years in the anthroposophic movement.

Yet another example shows how the most varied fields of human endeavor can be fructified through spiritual science, through the creation of a new art of movement we call eurythmy. It uses the human being as an instrument of expression, and it aims toward specific results. So we try to let anthroposophic life—not anthroposophic theories—flow into all sorts of activities—for example, the art of recitation and speech, about which you will hear more in the next few days.

This last phase with its educational, medical, and artistic impulses is the most characteristic one of the anthroposophic movement. Spiritual science has many supporters as well as many enemies—even bitter enemies. But now it has entered the very stage of activities for which it has been waiting. And so it was a satisfying experience during my stay in Kristiania [Oslo], from November twenty-third to December fourth this year to speak of anthroposophic life to educators and to government economists, as well as to Norwegian students and various other groups.[4] All of these people were willing to accept not theories or religious sectarian ideas, but what waits to reveal itself directly from the spirit of our time in answer to the great needs of humanity.

So much for the three phases of the anthroposophic movement. As an introduction to our course I merely wanted to acquaint you with this movement and to mention its name to you, so to speak. Tomorrow, we will begin our actual theme.

Nevertheless, I want you to know that it is the anthroposophic movement, with its deep educational interests, that gladly welcomes you all here to the Goetheanum.

---

4. Two lectures on education were presented in Oslo: "Educational Methods Based on Anthroposophy" (in two parts), in *Waldorf Education and Anthroposophy 1: Public Lectures, 1921–22* (Anthroposophic Press, 1995).

EDUCATION BASED ON KNOWLEDGE OF THE HUMAN BEING
Part 1

December 24, 1921

The art of education (about which we will say a great deal during this course of lectures) is based entirely on knowledge of the human being. If such knowledge is to have a deep foundation, however, it must be based on knowledge of the entire universe, because human beings, with all their inherent abilities and powers, are rooted in the universe. Therefore true knowledge of the human being can spring only from knowing the world in its entirety. On the other hand, one can say that the educational attitudes and ideas of any age reflect the general worldview of that age. Consequently, to correctly assess current views on education, we must examine them within the context of the general worldview of our time. In this sense, it will help to look at the ideas expressed by a typical representative of today's worldview as it developed gradually during the last few centuries. There is no doubt that, since that time, humankind has been looking with great pride at the achievements accomplished through intellectuality, and this is still largely true today.[1]

---

1. The German word *Intellektualismus* as used here implies the parasitic nature of an intellect that proliferates into "intellectuality." — TRANS.

Basically, educated people today have become very intellectualized, even if they do not admit to it. Everything in the world is judged through the instrument of the intellect. When we think of names associated with the awakening of modern thinking, we are led to the founders of modern philosophy and of today's attitudes toward life. Such individuals based all their work on a firm belief in human intellectual powers. Names such as Galileo, Copernicus, and Giordano Bruno come to mind, and we easily believe that their mode of thinking relates only to scientific matters; but this is not the case.

If one observes without prejudice the outlook on life among the vast majority of people today, one finds a bit of natural scientific thinking hidden almost everywhere, and intellectuality inhabits this mode of thinking. We may be under the impression that, in our moral concepts or impulses and in our religious ideas and experiences, we are free from scientific thinking. But we soon discover that, by being exposed to all that flows through newspapers and popular magazines into the masses, we are easily influenced in our thinking by an undertone of natural science.

People simply fail to see life as it really is if they are unaware that today's citizens sit down to breakfast already filled with scientific concepts—that at night they take these notions to bed and to sleep, use them in their daily work, and raise their children with them. Such people live under the illusion that they are free from scientific thinking. We even take our scientific concepts to church and, although we may hear traditional views expressed from the pulpit, we hear them with ears attuned to natural scientific thinking. And natural science is fed by this intellectuality.

Science quite correctly stresses that its results are all based on external observation, experimentation, and interpretation. Nevertheless, the instrument of the soul used for experiments in chemistry or physics represents the most intellectual part of the human entity. Thus the picture of the world that people make for themselves is still the result of the intellect.

Educated people of the West have become quite enraptured by all the progress achieved through intellectuality, especially in our time. This has led to the opinion that, in earlier times, humankind more or less lacked intelligence. The ancients supposedly lived with naive and childish ideas about the world, whereas today we believe we have reached an intelligent comprehension of the world. It is generally felt that the modern worldview is the only one based on firm ground. People have become fearful of losing themselves in the world of fantasy if they relinquish the domain of the intellect. Anyone whose thinking follows modern lines, which have been gradually developing during the last few centuries, is bound to conclude that a realistic concept of life depends on the intellect.

Now something very remarkable can be seen; on the one hand, what people consider the most valuable asset, the most important feature of our modern civilization—intellectuality—has, on the other hand, become doubtful in relation to raising and educating children. This is especially true among those who are seriously concerned with education. Although one can see that humanity has made tremendous strides through the development of intellectuality, when we look at contemporary education, we also find that, if children are being educated only in an intellectual way, their inborn capacities and human potential become seriously impaired and wither away. For some, this realization has led to a longing to replace intellectuality with something else. One has appealed to children's feelings and instincts. To steer clear of the intellect, we have appealed to their moral and religious impulses. But how can we find the right approach? Surely, only through a thorough knowledge of the human being, which, in turn, must be the result of a thorough knowledge of the world as a whole. As mentioned, looking at a representative thinker of our time, we find the present worldview reflected in educational trends. And if one considers all relevant features, Herbert Spencer could be chosen as one such representative thinker.[2]

I do not quote Spencer because I consider his educational ideas to be especially valuable for today's education. I am well aware of how open these are to all kinds of arguments and how, because of certain amateurish features, they would have to be greatly elaborated. On the other hand, Spencer, in all his concepts and ideas, is firmly grounded in the kind of thinking and culture developed during the last few centuries. Emerson wrote about those he considered representative of the development of humankind—people such as Swedenborg, Goethe, and Dante. For modern thinking and feeling, however, it is Herbert Spencer above all who represents our time. Although such thinking may be tinged with national traits according to whether the person is French, Italian, or Russian, Spencer transcends such national influences. It is not the conclusions in his many books on various aspects of life that are important, but the way he reaches those conclusions, for his mode of thinking is highly representative of the thinking of all educated people—those who are influenced by a scientific view and endeavor to live in accordance with it.

Intellectualistic natural science is the very matrix of all he has to say. And what did he conclude? Herbert Spencer, who naturally never loses sight of the theory that humankind evolved gradually from lower life forms, and who then compares the human being with animals, asks this question: Are we educating our youth according to our scientific ways of thinking? And he answers this question in the negative.

---

2. Herbert Spencer (1820–1903). Steiner speaks of his book *Education* (1861).

In his essay on education, he deals with some of the most important questions of the modern science of education, such as, Which kind of knowledge is most valuable? He critically surveys intellectual, moral, and physical education. But the core of all considerations is something that could have been postulated only by a modern thinker, that we educate our children so they can put their physical faculties to full use in later life. We educate them to fit into professional lives. We educate them to become good citizens. According to our concepts, we may educate them to be moral or religious. But there is one thing for which we do not educate them at all: to become educators themselves. This, according to Spencer, is absent in all our educational endeavors. He maintains that, fundamentally, people are not educated to become educators or parents.

Now, as a genuine natural scientific thinker, he goes on to say that the development of a living creature is complete only when it has acquired the capacity of procreating its own species, and this is how it should be in a perfect education; educated people should be able to educate and guide growing children. Such a postulate aptly illustrates the way a modern person thinks.

Looking at education today, what are Spencer's conclusions? Metaphorically, he makes a somewhat drastic but, in my opinion, very appropriate comparison. First he characterizes the tremendous claims of education today, including those made by Pestalozzi.[3] Then, instead of qualifying these principles as being good or acceptable, he asks how they are implemented in practice and what life is actually like in schools. In this context,

---

3. Johann Heinrich Pestalozzi (1746–1827) was a Swiss humanitarian and educationalist. He believed that women are the first teachers of any infant, and promoted education for girls. He wrote numerous books and articles on his educational philosophy.

he uses a somewhat drastic picture, suggesting we imagine some five to six centuries from now, when archeologists dig up some archives and find a description of our present educational system. Studying these documents, they would find it difficult to believe that they represent the general practice of our time. They would discover that children were taught grammar in order to find their way into their language. Yet we know well that the grammar children are taught hardly teaches them to express themselves in a living way later in life. Our imaginary archeologists would also discover that a large portion of students were being taught Latin and Greek, which, in our time, are dead languages. Here, they would conclude that the people of those documents had no literature of their own or, if they did, little benefit would be gained by studying it.

Spencer tries to demonstrate how inadequately our present curricula prepare students for later life, despite all the claims to the contrary. Finally, he lets these archeologists conclude that, since the document could not be indicative of the general educational practice of their time, they must have discovered a syllabus used in some monastic order. He continues (and of course this represents his opinion) by saying that adults who have gone through such educational practice are not entirely alienated from society, behaving like monks, because of the pressures and the cruel demands of life. Nevertheless, according to our imaginary archeologists, when having to face life's challenges, those ancient students responded clumsily, because they were educated as monks and trying to live within an entirely different milieu. These views—expressed by a man of the world and not by someone engaged in practical teaching—are in their own way characteristic of contemporary education.

Now we might ask, What value do people place on their lives after immersion in a natural scientific and intellectualistic attitude toward the world?

With the aid of natural laws, we can comprehend lifeless matter. This leads us to conclude that, following the same methods, we can also understand living organisms. This is not the time to go into the details of such a problem, but one can say that, at our present state of civilization, we tend to use thoughts that allow us to grasp only what is dead and, consequently, lies beyond the human sphere. Through research in physics and chemistry, we construct a whole system of concepts that we then apply to the entire universe, albeit only hypothetically. It is true that today there are already quite a few who question the validity of applying laboratory results or the information gained through a telescope or microscope to build a general picture of the world. Nevertheless, a natural scientific explanation of the world was bound to come and, with it, the ways it affects human feelings and emotions. And if one uses concepts from laboratory or observatory research to explain the origin and the future of the earth, what happens then? One is forced to imagine the primeval nebulae of the Kant-Laplace theory, or, since views have changed since their time, something similar. But this notion of primeval nebulae makes sense only when we apply to it the laws of aeromechanics. Such laws, however, contain nothing of a soul or spiritual character. People who long for such a soul and spiritual element, therefore, must imagine that all sorts of divine powers exist along side the aeromechanical view of the universe, and then these spirit beings must be somehow blended skillfully into the image of the nebulae. The human being, in terms of soul and spirit, is not part of this picture, but has been excluded from that worldview. Those who have gotten used to the idea that only an intellectually based natural science can provide concrete and satisfactory answers find themselves in a quandary when looking for some sort of divine participation at the beginning of existence.

A hypothetical concept of the end of the cosmos is bound to follow the laws of physics. In this context, we encounter the so-called second fundamental law of thermodynamics. According to this theory, all living forces are mutually transformable. However, if they are transformed into heat, or if heat is transformed into living forces, the outcome is always an excess of heat. The final result for all earthly processes would therefore be a complete transformation of all living forces into heat. This destruction through heat would produce a desert world, containing no forces but differences of temperature. Such a theory conjures up a picture of a huge graveyard in which all human achievements lie buried—all intellectual, moral, and religious ideals and impulses. If we place human beings between a cosmic beginning from which we have been excluded and a cosmic end in which again we have no place, all human ideals and achievements become nothing but vague illusions. Thus, an intellectual, natural scientific philosophy reduces the reality of human existence to a mere illusion. Such an interpretation may be dismissed simply as a hypothesis, yet even if people today do not recognize the way science affects their attitudes toward life, the negative consequences are nevertheless real. But the majority are not prepared to face reality. Nor do such theories remain the prerogative of an educated minority, because they reach the masses through magazines and popular literature, often in very subtle ways.

And, against the background of this negative disposition of soul, we try to educate our children, True, we also give them religious meaning, but here we are faced above all with division. For if we introduce religious ideas alongside scientific ideas of life, which is bound to affect our soul attitude, we enter the realm of untruth. And untruth extracts a toll beyond what the intellect can perceive, because it is active through its own inner power. Untruth, even when it remains concealed in the realm of the unconscious, assumes a destructive power over life. We enter the realm of untruth when we refuse to search for clarity in our attitudes toward life. This clarity will show us that, given the prevailing ideas today, we gain knowledge of a world where there is no room for the human being.

Let us examine a scientific discovery that fills us with pride, as it should. We follow the chain of evolution in the animal world, from the simplest and most imperfect forms via the more fully developed animals, right up to the arrival of the human being, whom we consider the most highly developed. Does not this way of looking at evolution imply that we consider the human being the most perfect animal? In this way, however, we are not concerned with true human nature at all. Such a question, even if it remains unconscious, diminishes and sets aside any feeling we might have for our essential humanity.

Again I wish to quote Herbert Spencer, because his views on contemporary education are so characteristic, especially with the latest attempts to reform education and bring it into line with current scientific thinking. In general, such reforms are based on concepts that are alien to the human spirit. Again, Spencer represents what we encounter in practical life almost everywhere. He maintains that we should do away with the usual influences adults—parents or teachers—have on children. According to him, we have inherited the bad habit of becoming angry when a child has done something wrong. We punish children and make them aware of our displeasure. In other words, our reaction is not linked directly to what the child has done. The child may have left things strewn all over the room and we, as educators, may become angry when seeing it. To put it drastically, we might even hit the child. Now, what is the causal link (and the scientific researcher always looks for causal links) between hitting the child and the untidy child? There is none.

Spencer therefore suggests that, to educate properly, we should become "missionaries of causal processes." For example, if we see a boy playing with fire by burning little pieces of paper in a flame, we should be able to understand that he does this because of his natural curiosity. We should not worry that he might burn himself or even set fire to the house; rather, we should recognize that he is acting out of an instinct of curiosity and allow him—with due caution, of course—to burn himself a little, because then, and only then, will he experience the causal connection. Following methods like this, we establish causal links and become missionaries of causal processes.

When you meet educational reformers, you hear the opinion that this principle of causality is the only one possible. Any open-minded person will reply that, as long as we consider the intellectualistic natural scientific approach the only right one, this principle of causality is also the only correct approach. As long as we adhere to accepted scientific thinking, there is no alternative in education. But, if we are absolutely truthful, where does all this lead when we follow these methods to their logical extremes? We completely fetter human beings, with all their powers of thinking and feeling, to natural processes. Thoughts and feelings become mere processes of nature, bereft of their own identity, mere products of unconscious, compulsory participation. If we are considered nothing more than a link in the chain of natural necessity, we cannot free ourselves in any way from nature's bonds.

We have been opposed by people who, in all good faith, are convinced that the ordinary scientific explanation of evolution can be the only correct one. They equate the origin of everything with the primeval nebulae, comprehensible only through the laws of aeromechanics. They equate the end of everything with complete destruction by heat, resulting in a final universal grave. Into this framework they place human beings, who materialize from somewhere beyond the human sphere, destined to find that all moral aspirations, religious impulses, and ideals are no more than illusions. This may seem to be the very opposite of what I said a few minutes ago, when I said that, when seen as the last link in evolution, human beings loses their separate identity and are therefore cast out of the world order. But because human identity remains unknown, we are seen only as a part of nature. Instead of being elevated from the complexities of nature, humankind is merely added to them. We become beings that embody the causal nexus. Such an interpretation casts out the human being, and education thus places the human being into a sphere devoid of humanity; it completely loses sight of the human being as such. People fail to see this clearly, because they lack the courage. Nevertheless, we have reached a turning point in evolution, and we must summon the courage to face basic facts, because in the end our concepts will determine our life paths.

A mood of tragedy pervades such people. They have to live consciously with something that, for the majority of people, sleeps in the subconscious. This underlying mood has become the burden of today's civilization. However, we cannot educate out of such a mood, because it eliminates the sort of knowledge from which knowledge of the human being can spring. It cannot sustain a knowledge of the human being in which we find our real value and true being—the kind of knowledge we need if we are to experience ourselves as real in the world. We can educate to satisfy the necessities of external life, but that sort of education hinders people from becoming free individuals. If we nevertheless see children grow up as free individuals, it happens despite of our education, not because of it.

Today it is not enough just to think about the world; we must think about the world so that our thinking gradually becomes a general feeling for the world, because out of such feelings impulses for reform and progress grow. It is the aim of anthroposophy to present a way of knowing the world that does not remain abstract but enlivens the entire human being and becomes the proper basis for educational principles and methods.

Today we can already see the consequences of the materialistic worldview as a historical fact. Through a materialistic interpretation of the world, humankind was cast out. And the echo of what has thus lived in the thoughts of educated people for a long time can now be heard in the slogans of millions upon millions of the proletariat. The civilized world, however, shuts its eyes to the direct connection between its own worldview and the echo from the working classes. This mood of tragedy is experienced by discerning people who have decided that moral ideas and religious impulses are an illusion and that humanity exists only between the reality's nebulous beginning and its ultimate destruction by heat. And we meet this same mood again in the views of millions of workers, for the only reality in their philosophy is economic processes and problems.

According to the proletarian view of life, nothing is more important than economics—economic solutions of the past, labor and production management, the organization of buying and selling, and how the process of production satisfies the physical needs of people. On the other hand, any moral aspirations, religious ideas, or political ideals are viewed as an illusory ideologies and considered to be an unrealistic superstructure imposed on the reality of life—the processes of material production. Consequently, something that was theoretical and, at best, a semi-religious conviction among certain educated social circles has, among the proletariat, become the determining factor for all human activity. This is the situation that humankind faces today. Under these conditions, people are trying to educate. To do this task justice, however, people must free themselves of all bias and observe and understand the present situation.

It is characteristic of intellectuality and its naturalistic world-view that it alienates people from the realities of life. From this perspective, you only need to look at earlier concepts of life. There you find ways of thinking that could very well be linked to life—thoughts that people of the past would never have seen as mere ideologies. They were rooted in life, and because of this they never treated their thinking as though it were some sort of vapor rising from the earth. Today, this attitude has invaded the practical areas of most of the educated world. People are groaning under the results of what has happened. Nevertheless, humankind is not prepared to recognize that the events in Russia today, which will spread into many other countries, are the natural result of the sort of teaching given at schools and universities. There one educates and while the people in one part of the earth lack the courage to recognize the dire consequences of their teaching, in the other part, these consequences ruthlessly push through to their extremes. We will not be able to stop this wheel from running away unless we understand clearly, especially in this domain, and place the laws of causality in their proper context. Then we shall realize that the human being is placed into a reality tht will leave him no room for maneuvering as long as he tries to comprehend the world by means of the intellect only. We will see that intellectuality, as an instrument, does not have the power of understanding realities.

I once knew a poet who, decades ago, tried to imagine how human beings would end up if they were to develop more and more in a onesided, intellectualistic way.[4] In the district where he lived, there was a somewhat drastic idea of intellectual people; they were called "big heads" (*grosskopfet*). Metaphorically,

---

4. Hermann Rollett (1819–1904).

they carried large heads on their shoulders. This poet took up the local expression, arguing that human development was becoming increasingly centered in the intellect and that, as a result, the human head would grow larger and larger, while the rest of the body would gradually degenerate into some sort of rudimentary organs. He predicted only rudimentary arms, ending in tiny hands, and rudimentary legs with tiny feet dangling from a disproportionately large head—until the moment when human beings would move by rolling along like balls. It would eventually come about that one would have to deal with large spheres from which arms and legs were hanging, like rudimentary appendages. A very melancholic mood came over him when he tried to foresee the consequences of one-sided intellectual development.

Looking objectively at the phenomenon of intellectuality, we can see that it alienates people from themselves and removes them from reality. Consequently, an intellectual will accept only the sort of reality that is recognized by the proletariat—the kind that cannot be denied, because one runs into it and suffers multiple bruises. In keeping with current educational systems (even those that are completely reformed), such people believe that one can draw conclusions only within the causal complex. On the other hand, if they must suffer from deprivation, again they limit their grasp of the situation to the laws of causality. Those who are deprived of the necessities of life can feel, see, and experience what is real only too well; but they are no longer able to penetrate the true causes. While distancing themselves from reality in this way, people become less and less differentiated. Metaphorically, they are, in fact, turning into the poet's rolling sphere. We will need to gain insight into the ways our universities, colleges, and schools are cultivating the very things we abhor when we encounter them in real life, which, today, is mostly the way it is. People find fault with what they see, but little do they realize that they themselves have sown the seeds of what they criticize. The people of the West see Russia and are appalled by events there, but they do not realize that their western teachers have sown the seeds of those events.

As mentioned before, intellectuality is not an instrument with which we can reach reality, and therefore we cannot educate by its means. If this is true, however, it is important to ask whether we can use the intellect in any positive way in education, and this poignant question challenges us right at the beginning of our lecture course.

We must employ means other than those offered by intellectuality, and the best way to approach this is to look at a certain problem so that we can see it as part of a whole. What are the activities that modern society excels in, and what has become a favorite pastime? Well, public meetings. Instead of quietly familiarizing ourselves with the true nature of a problem, we prefer to attend conferences or meetings and thrash it out there, because intellectuality feels at home in such an environment. Often, it is not the real nature of a problem that is discussed, because it seems this has already been dealt with; rather, discussion continues for its own sake. Such a phenomenon is a typical by-product of intellectuality, which leads us away from the realities of a situation. And so we cannot help feeling that, fundamentally, such meetings or conferences are pervaded by an atmosphere of illusion hovering above the realities of life. While all sorts of things are happening down below at ground level, clever discourses are held about them in multifarious public conferences. I am not trying to criticize or to put down people's efforts at such meetings; on the contrary, I find that brilliant arguments are often presented on such occasions. Usually the arguments are so convincingly built up that one cannot help but agree with two or even three speakers who, in fact, represent completely opposite viewpoints. From a certain perspective, one can agree with everything that is said. Why? Because it is all permeated by intellectuality, which is incapable of providing realistic solutions. Therefore, life might as well be allowed to assume its own course without the numerous meetings called to deal with problems. Life could well do without all these conferences and debates, even though one can enjoy and admire the ingenuity on display there.

During the past fifty or sixty years, it has been possible to follow very impressive theoretical arguments in the most varied areas of life. At the same time, if life was observed quietly and without prejudice, one could also notice that daily affairs moved in a direction opposite to that indicated by these often brilliant discussions. For example, some time ago, there were discussions in various countries regarding the gold standard, and brilliant speeches were made recommending it. One can certainly say (and I do not feel at all cynical about this but am sincere) that in various parliaments, chambers of commerce, and so on, there were erudite speeches about the benefits of the gold standard. Discriminating and intelligent experts—and those of real practical experience—proved that, if we accepted the gold standard, we would also have free trade, that the latter was the consequence of the former. But look at what really happened; in most countries that adopted the gold standard, unbearable import tariffs were introduced, which means that instead of allowing trade to flow freely it was restricted. Life presented just the opposite of what had been predicted by our clever intellectuals. One must be clear that intellectuality is alien to reality; it makes the human being into a big head. Hence it can never become the basis of a science of education, because it leads away from an understanding of the human being. Because teaching involves a relationship between human beings—between teacher and student—it must be

based on human nature. This can be done only by truly knowing human nature. It is the aim of anthroposophy to offer
such knowledge.

EDUCATION BASED ON
KNOWLEDGE OF THE HUMAN BEING
Part 2

December 25, 1921

If you take what was presented to you yesterday and study it in greater depth, you will find that today's interpretation of the world cannot lead to a real understanding of the human being. And if you go into further detail in your study of what could be only briefly described here and relate it to specific problems of life, you will find confirmation of all that was postulated in yesterday's lecture.

Now, strangely, exponents of the modern worldview seem unaware of what it means that they cannot reach the specifically human sphere. Nor are they willing to admit that, in this sense, their interpretation of the universe is incomplete. This fact alone is more than enough to justify all the efforts made by spiritual scientific research. We can understand this all the more clearly by observing characteristic examples. When quoting Herbert Spencer, I did not intend to prove anything but only wanted to illustrate modern thinking. Spencer had already formulated his most important and fundamental ideas before Darwinism spread. So-called Darwinism aptly demonstrates how scientific, intellectualistic thinking approaches questions and problems that result from a deep-seated longing in the human soul.

Charles Darwin's *Origin of the Species,* published in 1859, certainly represents a landmark in modern spiritual life.[1] His method of observation and the way he draws conclusions are exemplary for a modern conceptual discipline. One can truly say that Darwin observed the data offered to his sense perceptions with utmost exactitude; that he searched for the underlying laws in a very masterly way; and he considering everything that such observations could bring to his powers of comprehension. Never did he allow himself to be deflected, not to the slightest degree, by his own subjectivity. He developed the habit of learning from the outer world in a way commensurate with the human intellect.

Observing life in this way, Darwin found links between the simplest, least developed organisms and the highest organism on earth—humankind itself. He contemplated the entire range of living organisms in a strictly natural scientific way, but what he observed was external and not part of the essential nature of human beings. Neither the true human being nor human spiritual aspirations were the object of his enquiry. However, when Darwin finally had to face an impasse, his reaction was characteristic; after having formulated his excellent conclusions, he asked himself, Why would it have pleased the Divine Creator any less to begin creation with a small number of relatively undeveloped and primitive organic forms, which would be allowed to develop gradually, than to miraculously conjure fully developed forms right at the beginning of the world?

But what does such a response imply? It shows that those who have made the intellectual and naturalistic outlook their own, apply it only as far as a certain inner sensing will allow and then readily accept these newly discovered boundaries

---

1. Charles Darwin (1809–1882), *The Origin of the Species by Means of Natural Selection* (1859); *The Descent of Man and Selection in Relation to Sex* (1871).

without pondering too much over whether it might be possible to transcend them. In fact, they are even prepared to fall back on traditional religious concepts. In a subsequent book, *The Descent of Man,* Darwin did not fundamentally modify his views. Apart from being typical of the time, Darwin's attitude reveals certain national features, characteristic of Anglo American attitudes and differing from those of Central Europe. If we look at modern life with open eyes, we can learn a great deal about such national traits.

In Germany, Darwinism was initially received with open enthusiasm, which nevertheless spread to two opposite directions. There was, first of all, Ernst Haeckel, who with youthful ardor took up Darwin's methods of observation, which are valid only in nonhuman domains.[2] But, according to his Germanic disposition, he was not prepared to accept given boundaries with Darwin's natural grace. Haeckel did not capitulate to traditional religious ideas by speaking of an Almighty who had created some imperfect archetypes. Using Darwin's excellent methods (relevant only for the non-human realm) as a basis for a new religion, Ernst Haeckel included both God and the human being in his considerations, thus deliberately crossing the boundary accepted by Darwin.

Du Bois-Reymond took up Darwinism in another way.[3] According to his views, naturalistic intellectual thinking can be applied only to the nonhuman realm. He thus remained within its limits. But he did not stop there, unquestioning and guided by his feelings; he made this stopping point itself into a theory. Right there, where Darwin's observations trail off into vagueness, Du Bois-Reymond postulated an alternative, stating that either there are limits or there are no limits. And he found two such limits.

---

2. Ernst Haeckel (1834–1919); see *The Riddle of the Universe* (1899).
3. Emil Du Bois-Reymond (1818–1896); see *Darwin versus Galiani* (1876).

The first limit occurs when we turn our gaze out into the world, and we are confronted with matter. The second is when we turn our gaze inward, toward experiences of our consciousness and find these also finally impenetrable. He thus concluded that we have no way of reaching the suprasensory, and made this into a theory: one would have to rise to the level of "supernaturalism," the realm where religion may hold sway, but science has nothing to do with what belongs to this religious sphere. In this way, Du Bois-Reymond leaves everyone free to supplement, according to personal needs, everything confirmed by natural science with either mystical or traditionally accepted forms of religious beliefs. But he insists that such supernatural beliefs could never be the subject of scientific scrutiny.

A characteristic difference between the people of Central Europe and those of the West is that the latter lean naturally toward the practical side of life. Consequently, they are quite prepared to allow their thoughts to trail off into what cannot be defined, as happens in practical life. Among Central Europeans, on the other hand, there is a tendency to put up with impracticalities, as long as the train of thought remains theoretically consistent, until an either/or condition has been reached. And this we see particularly clearly when fundamental issues about ultimate questions are at stake.

But there is still a third book by Darwin that deals with the expression of feeling.[4] To those who occupy themselves with problems of the soul, this work seems to be far more important than his *Origin of the Species* and *Descent of Man*. Such people can derive great satisfaction from this book—so full of fine observations of the human expression of emotions—by allowing it to work in them. It shows that those who have disciplined themselves to observe in a natural scientific way can also

---

4. *The Expression of the Emotions in Man and Animals* (1872).

attain faculties well suited for research into the soul and spiritual sphere of the human being. It goes without saying that Darwin advanced along this road only as far as his instinct would allow him to go. Nevertheless, the excellence of his observations shows that a training in natural scientific observation can also lead to an ability to go into the suprasensory realm. This fact lies behind the hope of anthroposophic work, which, in any task that it undertakes, chooses not to depart by a hair's breadth from the disciplined training of the natural scientific way of thinking. But, at the same time, anthroposophy wishes to demonstrate how the natural scientific method can be developed, thus transcending the practical limits established by Darwin, crossed boldly by Haeckel's naturalism, and stated as a theory by Du Bois-Reymond. It endeavors to show how the suprasensory world can be reached so that real knowledge of the human being can finally be attained.

The first step toward such higher knowledge does not take us directly into the world of education, which will be our central theme during the coming days. Instead, we will try to build a bridge from our ordinary conceptual and emotional life to suprasensory cognition. This can be achieved if—using ordinary cognition—we learn to apprehend the basic nature of our sense-bound interpretation of the world.

To do this, first I would like you to assume two hypotheses. Imagine that, from childhood on, the world of matter had been transparent and clear to our understanding. Imagine that the material world around us was not impermeable to our sight, but that with ordinary sensory observation and thinking we could fully penetrate and comprehend its nature. If this were the situation, we would be able to comprehend the material aspect of the mineral kingdom. We would also be able to understand the physical aspect of human nature; the human body would become completely transparent to our sight.

If such a hypothesis were reality, however, you would have to eliminate something from your mind that real life needs for its existence; you would have remove from your thinking all that we mean when we speak of love. For what is the basis of love, whether it is love for another person, for humankind in general, or for spiritual beings? Our love depends on meeting the other with forces that are completely different from those that illuminate our thinking. If transparent or abstract thoughts were to light up as soon as we met another being, then even the very first seeds of love would be destroyed immediately. We simply would be unable to engender love. You need only to remember how in ordinary life love ceases when the light of abstract thought takes over. You need only to realize how correct we are to speak of abstract thoughts as cold, how all inner warmth ceases when we approach the thinking realm. Warmth, revealing itself through love, could not come into being if we were to meet outer material life only with the intellect; love would be extinguished from our world.

Now imagine that there is nothing to prevent you from looking into your own inner structure; that, when looking inward, you could perceive the forces and weaving substances within you just as clearly as you see colors and hear tones in the outer world. If this were to happen, you would have the possibility of continuously experiencing your own inner being. However, in this case, too, you would have to eliminate something from your mind that human beings need to exist in the world as it is. What is it that lights up within when you turn your sight inward? You see remembered imagery of what you have experienced in the outer world. In fact, when looking inward, you do not see your inner being at all. You see only the reflection, or memory, of what you have experienced in the world.

On the one hand, if you consider that, without this faculty of memory, personal life would be impossible, and, on the other, consider that to perceive your own inner life you would have to eliminate your memory, then you realize the necessity of the built-in limits in our human organization. The possibility of clearly perceiving the essence of outer matter would presuppose a person devoid of love. The possibility of perpetually perceiving one's own inner organization would presuppose a human being devoid of memory. Thus, these two hypotheses help us to realize the necessity of the two limits placed on ordinary human life and consciousness. They exist for the development of love and because human beings need personal memories for an inner life. But, if there is a path beyond these boundaries into the suprasensory world, an obvious question arise. Can we walk this path without damaging our personal life, on the one hand, and shunning a social life with others, on the other?

Anthroposophy has the courage to say that, with the ordinary established naturalistic approach, it is impossible to attain suprasensory knowledge. At the same time, however, it must ask, Is there any way that, when applied with the strict discipline of natural science, will enable us to enter suprasensory worlds? We cannot accept the notion that crossing the threshold into the supernatural world marks the limit of scientific investigation. It is the goal of anthroposophy to open a path into the suprasensory, using means equally as exact as those used by ordinary science to penetrate the sensory realm. In this way, anthroposophy merely continues along the path of modern science. Anthroposophy does not intend to rebel against present achievements, but it endeavors to bring something that is needed today and something contemporary life cannot provide from its own resources.

If we look at Darwin's attitude as I have presented it, we might be prompted to say, If science can deal only with what is perceptible to the senses, then we have to fall back on religious beliefs to approach the suprasensory, and we simply have to accept the situation as inevitable. Such a response, however, cannot solve the fundamental, urgent human problems of our time.

In this context, I would like to speak about two characteristics of contemporary life, because, apart from supplementing what has been said, they also illuminate educational matters. They may help to illustrate how modern intellectual thinking—which is striving for absolute lucidity—is nevertheless prone to drift into the dark unconscious and instinctive domains.

If you observe people's attitudes toward the world in past ages, you will find that ancient religion was never seen as mere faith—this happened only in later times—but that religions were based on direct experience and insight into spirit worlds. Knowledge thus gained was considered to be as real as the results of our modern natural scientific research. Only in subsequent ages was knowledge confined to what is sense perceptible, and suprasensory knowledge was, consequently, relegated to the religious realm. And so, the illusion came about that anything pertaining to metaphysical existence had to be a matter of faith. Yet, as long as religions rested on suprasensory knowledge, this knowledge bestowed great power, affecting even physical human nature. Modern civilization cannot generate this kind of moral strength for people today. When religion becomes only a matter of faith, it loses power, and it can no longer work down into our physical constitution. Although this is felt instinctively, its importance is unrecognized. This instinctive feeling and the search for revitalizing forces have found an outlet that has become a distinctive feature of our civilization; it is a part of all that we call sports.

Religion has lost the power of strengthening the human physical constitution. Therefore an instinctive urge has arisen in people to gain access to a source of strength through outward, physical means only. As life tends toward polarity, we find that people instinctively want to substitute the loss of invigoration, previously drawn from his religious experiences, by cultivating sports. I have no wish to harangue against sports. Neither do I wish to belittle their positive aspects. In fact, I feel confident that these activities will eventually develop in a healthy way. Nevertheless, it must be said that sports will assume a completely different position in human life in the future, whereas today it is a substitute for religious experience. Such a statement may well seem paradoxical, but truth, today, is paradoxical, because modern civilization has drifted into so many crosscurrents.

A second characteristic of our intellectual and naturalistic civilization is that, instead of embracing life fully, it tends to lead to contradictions that destroy the soul. Thinking is driven along until it becomes entangled in chaotic webs of thought and contradictions, and the thinker remains unaware of the confusion created. For example, a young child in a certain sense will go through the various stages than humankind has passed through, from the days of primitive humanity up to our present civilization, and this fills certain naturalistic intellectuals with admiration. They observe the somewhat turned-up nostrils of a young child and the position of the eyes, which lie further apart than in later life. They observe the formation of the forehead with its characteristic curvature and also the shape of the mouth. All these features remind people of those found in primitive tribes, and so they see young children as "little savages."

Yet, at the same time, sentiments such as those expressed by Rousseau are trying to rise to the surface—sentiments that completely contradict what has just been said.[5] When contemplating

5. Jean Jacques Rousseau (1712–1778), Swiss political philosopher and educationist; *Discourse on the Origin and Foundation of Inequality among Mankind* (1755); *The Social Contract* (1762).

educational aims, some people prefer to "return to nature," both from a physical and a moral aspect. But, being under the influence of an intellectual atmosphere, they soon aim at arranging educational ideas according to the principles of logic, for intellectuality will always lead to logic in thinking. Observing many illogical features in education today, they want to base it on principles of logic, which, in their eyes, are entirely compatible with a child's natural development. Logic, however, does not meet the needs of children at all. One close look at primitive races will make one quickly realize that members of such tribes hardly apply logical thinking to their ways of life.

And so some reformers are under the illusion that they are returning to nature by introducing a logical attitude in educating the young, who are supposed to be little savages, an attitude that is completely alien to a child. In this way, adherents of Rousseau's message find themselves caught in a strange contradiction with an intellectualistic attitude; striving toward harmony with nature does not fit with an intellectualistic outlook. And, as far as the education of the will is concerned, the intellectualistic thinker is completely out of touch with reality. According to this way of thinking, a child should above all be taught what is useful in life. For example, such people never tire of pointing out the impracticability of our modern mode of dress, which does not satisfy the demands of utility. They advocate a return to more natural ways, saying that we should concentrate on the utilitarian aspects of life. The education of girls is especially subjected to sharp criticism by such reformers.

So now they are faced with a paradox; did primitive human beings—the stage young children supposedly recapitulate—live a life of utility? Certainly not. According to archeologists, they developed neither logical thinking nor utilitarian living. Their essential needs were satisfied through the help of inborn instincts. But what captivated the interest of primitive people?

Adornment. They did not wear clothing for practical reasons, but through a longing for self-adornment. Whatever the members of such tribes chose to wear—or not to wear, in order to display the patterns on their skin—was not intended for utility, but as an expression of a yearning for beauty as they understood it. Similar traits can be found in the young child.

Those who perceive these contradictions and imperfections in modern life will be ready to look for their causes. They will increasingly recognize how lopsided and limited the generally accepted intellectualistic, naturalistic way of thinking is, which does not see the human being as a whole at all. Usually only our waking state is considered, whereas in reality the hours spent in sleep are just as much part of human life as those of daytime consciousness. You may object by saying that natural science has closely examined the human sleeping state as well, and indeed there exist many interesting theories about the nature of sleep and of dreams. But these premises were made by people while awake, not by investigators who were able to enter the domains of sleep. If people who are interested in education think in rational and logical ways and in terms of what is practical and useful in life, and if, on the other hand, they feel pulled in the direction of Rousseau's call to nature, they will become victims of strange contradictions. What they really do is pass on to children all that seems of value to themselves as adults. They try to graft onto the child something that is alien to the child's nature. Children really do seek for beauty—though not in the ways suggested by Rousseau—which for them expresses neither goodness nor utility, but simply exists for its own sake.

In the waking state, human beings not only have consciousness but also experience an inner life and actively participate in life. During sleep, on the other hand, people loses their ordinary consciousness, and consequently they examine sleep while awake. A proper study of this phenomenon, however, requires more than abstract theories. Entering sleep in full consciousness is essential for understanding it.

By experiencing both wonder and astonishment when studying the phenomena of sleep, a serious and unbiased investigator is not likely to advance in ways that, for example, Greek philosophy considered important. According to an ancient Greek adage, every philosophy—as a path toward cognition—begins with wonder. But this indicates only the beginning of the search for insight. One must move on. One must progress from wonder to knowledge.

However, the first step toward suprasensory knowledge must be taken not with the expectation of being able to enter the spiritual world directly, but with the intent of building a bridge from the ordinary sensory world to suprasensory knowledge. One way of achieving this is to apply the discipline we use to observe the phenomena of the sensory world to the phenomena we encounter from the realms of sleep and dreams. Modern people have certainly learned to observe accurately, but in this case it is not simply a matter of observing accurately. To gain insight, one must be able to direct observations toward specific areas.

I would like to give you an example of how this can be done when studying dream phenomena, which infiltrate our waking life in strange and mysterious ways.

Occasionally one still encounters people who have remained aware of the essential difference between waking and sleeping, but their awareness has become only a dim and vague feeling. Nevertheless, they are aware that an awake person is an altogether different from one who is asleep. Therefore, someone tells them that sleep is a waste of time and sleepers are idle and lazy, these simple minds will say that, as long as we sleep, we are free from sin. Thus, they try to say that people, whom they consider sinful while awake, are innocent while asleep. A good instinctive wisdom is hidden in this somewhat naive attitude. But to reach clarity, we need to train our own observation. I would like to give you an example.

Surely there are some here—perhaps every one of you—who have had dreams reminiscent of what might have happened to you in daily life. For example, you may have dreamed that you were taken to a river and that you had to get across somehow. So you searched for a boat, which, after a great deal of trouble, you managed to get hold of. Then you had to work hard to row across. In your dream you might have felt the physical exertion of plying the oars, until at last you managed to get across, just as you might have in ordinary life. There are many such kinds of dreams. Their contents are definite reminiscences of our physical, sensory lives. But there are also other kinds of dreams that do not echo waking life. For instance, someone again may dream that it is necessary to get across a river. Wondering how this urge could possibly be fulfilled, the dreamer is suddenly able to spread wings and—presto!—simply fly across and land safely on the opposite bank. This sort of dream is certainly not a memory of something that could happen in waking life, because, to my knowledge, this is hardly the way ordinary mortals transport themselves across a river in real life. Here we have something that simply does not exist in physical life.

Now, if we accurately observe the relationship between sleep and being awake, we discover something very interesting; we find that dreams in which we experience the toil and exhaustion of waking life, which reflect waking life, cause us to awake tired. On waking, our limbs feel heavy and tiredness seems to drag on throughout the day. In other words, if strains and pains of a life of drudgery reappear in our dreams, we awake weakened rather than refreshed. But now observe the effects of the other kind of dream; if you managed to fly—weightless and with hearty enthusiasm, with wings you do not possess in ordinary life—once you have flown across your river, you awake bright and breezy, and your limbs feel light. We need to observe how these differing dreams affect the waking life with the same accuracy we use to make observations in mathematics or physics. We know quite well that we would not get very far in these two subjects without it. Yet dreams do not generally become the object of exact observations and, consequently, no satisfactory results are achieved in this field. And such a situation hardly encourages people to strive for greater powers of insight into these somewhat obscure areas of life.

This is not just a case of presenting isolated glimpses of something that seems to confirm previous indications. The more we ponder over the relevant facts, the more the reciprocal links between sleep and waking life become evident. For example, there are dreams in which you may see some very tasty food that you then enjoy with a hearty appetite. You will find that usually, after having thus eaten in your dreams, you wake up without much appetite. You may not even eat during the following day, as though there were something wrong with your digestion. On the other hand, if in your dream you had the experience of speaking to an angel, and if you entered fully into a dialogue, you will awake with a keen edge to your appetite, which may persist during the whole day. Needless to say, partaking of food in one's dream represents a memory from waking life, for in the spiritual world one neither eats nor drinks. Surely you will accept this without further proof. Therefore, enjoying food in a dream is a reminiscence of physical life, whereas speaking to an angel—an event unlikely to occur to people these days—cannot be seen as an echo of daily life.

Such an observation alone could show even an abstract thinker that something unknown happens to us in sleep—something that nevertheless plays into our daily lives. It is wrong to surmise that it is impossible to gain exact and clear concepts in this realm. Is it not a clear discovery that dreams echoing earthly reality—the kind so popular among naturalistic poets, ever eager to imitate earthly life, never ready to enter the suprasensory realms—have an unhealthy effect on our waking lives? If impressions from ordinary life reappear in dreams, these dreams have an injurious effect upon our health. On the other hand, if unrealistic dream images appear—the kind scornfully dismissed as mystical rubbish by an intellectualistic philistine—they make us feel bright and fresh upon awaking in the morning. It is certainly possible to observe the strange interplay and the reciprocal effects between dreaming and sleeping.

And so we can say that something independent of the human physical condition must be happening during sleep, the effects of which we can observe in the person's physical organism. Dreams cause astonishment and wonder to ordinary consciousness, because they elude us in our waking state. The more you try to collect such examples, the more you will find a real connection between the human sleeping and waking state.

You only need to look closely at dreams to see that they are different from our experiences during waking life. When awake, we are able to link or separate mental images at will, but we cannot do this when dreaming. Dream images are woven as objective appearances beyond the influence of our will. In dreams, the activities of the soul become passive, numb, and immobile.

If we study dreams from yet another aspect, we find that they can reveal other secret sides of human existence. Observe, for instance, your judgment of people with whom you may have a certain relationship. You might find that you keep your full inner feelings of sympathy or antipathy from arising to consciousness, and that your judgment of people is colored by various facts, such as their titles or positions in social life. However, when you dream about such a person, something unexpected may happen; you may find yourself giving someone a good beating. Such behavior, so completely at odds with your attitude in waking life, allows you to glimpse the more hidden regions of your sympathies and antipathies, some of which you would never dare admit, even to yourself, but which the dream conjures up in your soul. Subconscious images are placed before the dreaming soul. They are relatively easy to watch, but if you deeply investigate someone's inexplicable moods of ill temper or euphoria that seem unrelated to outer circumstances, you find that they, too, were caused by dreams, completely forgotten by those concerned. Experiences in sleep and the revelations of dreams work into the unconscious and may lead to seemingly inexplicable moods. Unless we consider this other side of life, the hidden domain of our sleep life, by making exact investigations, we cannot understand human life in its wholeness.

All these reciprocal effects, however, happen without human participation. Yet it is possible to lift what happens subconsciously and involuntarily into a state of clear consciousness equal to that of someone engaged in mathematics or other scientific investigations. When achieving this, one's powers of observation are enhanced beyond the indeterminate relationship between waking and sleeping to the fully conscious states of *imagination, inspiration,* and *intuition.*[6]

---

6. Steiner uses the words *imagination, inspiration,* and *intuition* in very specific ways to describe levels of initiation, or spiritual capacities. Therefore, to distinguish his use of these words from their more common meanings, they are italicized in this volume. For clear descriptions of Rudolf Steiner's use of these terms, see his *Stages of Higher Knowledge* (Anthroposophic Press, 1967) and "Pneumatosophy," (lecture 3), in *A Psychology of Body, Soul, and Spirit* (Anthroposophic Press, 1999).

Only through these three capacities is it possible to attain true knowledge of the human being. What life vaguely hints at through the phenomenon of sleep can be developed in full consciousness by applying methods given by anthroposophy, which strive toward a real knowledge of the universe and the human being.

EDUCATION BASED ON
KNOWLEDGE OF THE HUMAN BEING
Part 3

December 26, 1921

When trying to understand the world through a natural scientific interpretation of its phenomena, whether through cognition or through everyday life, people tend to consider conditions only as they meet them in the moment. Such a statement might seem incorrect to those who merely look at the surface of things, but as we proceed, it will become evident that this is indeed true. We have grown accustomed to investigate the human physical organism with the accepted methods of biology, physics, and anatomy, but (though this may appear wrong at first) in the results we find only what the present moment reveals to us.

For example, we might observe the lungs of a child, of an adult, and of an older person, in their stages from the beginning to the end of life, and we reach certain conclusions. But we do not really penetrate the element of time at all in this way, because we limit ourselves to spatial observations, which we then invest with qualities of time. We are doing the same thing, to use a simile, when we read the time by looking at a clock. We note the position of the hands in the morning, for example, and positions in space indicate the time for us. We may look at the clock again at noon and deduce the passage of time from the spatial changes of its hands. We take our bearing in the course of time from the movements of the clock's hands from point to point in space. This has become our way of judging time in everyday life. But through this method we cannot experience the true nature of time. Yet only by penetrating time with the same awareness we use to experience space can we correctly assess human life between birth and death. I would like to illustrate these theoretical remarks with examples to show the importance of living into the dimension of time, especially if you want to practice the art of education.

Let us take as our example a child who is full of reverence toward adults. Anyone with a healthy instinct would consider such an attitude in a child as something wholesome, especially if such reverence is justified, as indeed it should be on the part of the adult. However, people usually think no further, but merely attribute a feeling of reverence toward adults to certain aspects of childhood and leave it at that. But we cannot recognize the importance of such reverence unless we include the entire course of a human life in our considerations.

As we grows older, we may have the opportunity to observe old people. We may discover that some of them have the gift of bringing soul comfort to those who need it. Often it is not *what* they have to say that acts as balm on a suffering soul, but just the tone of voice or the way they speak. If now you follow this old person's life back to childhood, you find that, as a child, that individual was full of reverence and respect for adults. Naturally, this attitude of reverence will disappear in later life, but only on the surface. Deep down, it will gradually transform, only to reemerge later as the gift of bringing solace and elevation to suffering and troubled minds.

One could also say it this way: If a young child has learned to pray and has learned to develop an inner mood of prayer, this mood will enter the subconscious and transform into the capacity of blessing in the ripeness of old age. When we meet old people whose mere presence radiates blessing upon those around them, you find that in their childhood they experienced and developed this inner mood of prayer. Such a transformation can be discovered only if one has learned to experience time as concretely as we generally experience space. We must learn to recognize the time element with the same awareness with which we experience space. Time must not be experienced only in spatial terms, as when we look at a clock. What I have been trying to illustrate regarding the moral aspects of life needs to become very much a part of our concept of the human being—certainly if we are going to develop a true art of education. I would like to elaborate this in greater detail.

If we compare human beings with the animals, we find that from the moment of birth, animals (especially the higher species) are equipped with all the faculties needed for living. A chick leaving its shell does not need to learn to walk and is immediately adapted to its surroundings. Each animal's organs are firmly adapted to the specific needs of its species. This is not at all true, however, of human beings, who come into this world completely helpless. Only gradually do we develop the capacities and skills needed for life. This is because the most important period in our earthly life is between the end of childhood and the beginning of old age. This central period of maturity is the most important feature of human life on earth. During that time, we adapt our organism to external life by gaining aptitudes and skills. We develop a reciprocal relationship to the outer world, based on our range of experience. This central period, when human organs maintain the ability to evolve and adapt, is completely missing in the life of animals. The animal is born in a state that is fundamentally comparable to an old person, whose organic forms have become rigid. If you want to understand the nature of an animal's relationship to its surroundings, look at it in terms of our human time of old age.

Now we can ask whether an animal shows the characteristics of old age in its soul qualities. This is not the case, because in an animal there is also the opposite pole, which counteracts this falling into old age, and this is the animal's capacity of reproduction. The ability to reproduce, whether in the human or animal kingdom, always engenders forces of rejuvenation. While animal fall prey to the influences of aging too quickly on the one hand, on the other they are saved from premature aging because of the influx of reproductive forces until maturity.

If you can observe an animal or an animal species without preconceived ideas, you will conclude that, when the animal is capable of reproduction, it has reached a stage equivalent to that of old age in a human being. The typical difference in the human being is the fact that both old age and childhood (when the child's reproductive system is slowly maturing) are placed on either end of the human central period, and during this period the human organism remains flexible, enabling human beings to relate and adapt individually to the environment. Through this arrangement, a human being will be a child at the right time, then leave childhood at the right time to enter maturity. And a person leaves maturity when it is time to enter old age.

If you look at human life from this aspect of time, you also understand certain abnormalities. You may encounter people who (if I may put it this way) slip prematurely into old age. I am not thinking so much of the obvious features typically associated with old age, such as grey hair or baldness; even a bald-headed person may still be childish. I am thinking of the more subtle indications, detectable only by more intimate observations. One could call such features the signs of a senile soul life, manifesting in people who should still be in the central period of flexibility and adaptability. But the opposite may also happen; a person may be unable to leave the stage of childhood at the right time and carry infantile features into the central stage of life. In this case, strange things may happen in the life of that person—the symptoms of which we can only touch on today. When we include the time element in our picture of the human being, we can diagnose aberrations in human behavior.

We know that, as we approach old age, we lose flexibility especially in the head. Consequently, all the capacities that we have acquired during life attain more of a soul and spiritual quality. But this is possible only at the expense of the head as a whole assuming certain animal-like qualities. From a physical point of view, an old person goes through conditions similar to those of a newborn animal. To a certain extent one becomes "animalized." Thus old people gain something that they may preserve for the rest of their lives, provided their education was right. Their spiritual, soul experiences of the outer world no longer enter fully into the human organization. The cranium becomes ossified and fixed. Old people thus depend more on soul and spiritual links with the surrounding world. They are no longer able to transform outer events into inward qualities as well as they once did. Thus, a kind of animalization of the upper regions takes place.

It is possible for this animalization of the head structure to occur prematurely—during the middle period of life—but because we remain human despite such a tendency, we do not encounter external symptoms. Rather, we must look for certain changes in the soul realm. If the characteristic relationship of the older person to the outer world manifests prematurely—and this can happen even during childhood—a person's experiences is drawn too much into the physical system, since the general flexibility of the rest of the human organization, typical of the younger age, naturally retains the upper hand. In this case, a person will experience inwardly, and too early, a relationship to the outer world typical of old age. Interaction between inner and outer world would thus be linked too much to the physical organization, bringing about soul properties more like that in the animal world than in normal human beings.

One can say (if you want to express it in this way) that animals have the advantage of a certain instinct over human beings, an instinct that links them more directly and intimately to the environment than is true of the normal human being. It is not simply a myth, but completely reflects the peculiarities of animal life, that certain animals will leave a place that is in danger of a natural catastrophe. Animals are gifted with certain prophetic instincts of self-preservation. It is also true that animals experience far more intensely the changing seasons than do human beings. They can sense the approaching time for migration, because they have an intimate and instinctive relationship with the environment. If we could look into an animal's soul, we would find—although entirely unconsciously—an instinctive wisdom of life that manifests as the animal's ability to live entirely within the manifold processes and forces of nature.

Now, if a person falls victim to encroaching age too early, this animal-like instinctive experience of the surroundings begins to develop, though in a sublimated form because it is lifted into the human sphere. Lower forms of clairvoyance, such as telepathy, telekinesis and so on—described correctly or wrongly—occur abnormally in human life and are simply the result of this premature aging in the central period of life. When this process of aging occurs at the proper time, people experience it in a healthy way, whereas if it appears in the twenties, a person gains clairvoyance of a low order. The symptoms of premature aging represent an abnormality in life that does not manifest outwardly but in a more hidden way. If these forms of lower clairvoyance were studied from the aspect of premature aging, a people would gain far deeper insight into these phenomena. This is possible, however, only when people observe life in a more realistic way. It is not good enough to investigate what we see with our eyes at the present moment. People must learn to recognize indications in these symptoms of a time shift from later to earlier stages of life.

We will see in the next few days how healing processes can occur through exact insight into human nature. It is possible that a kind of animalization could manifest not as an outwardly visible aging process but as a close, instinctive relationship to the environment encroaching on the lower regions of the human being and otherwise characteristic of an animal.

The resulting phenomena of telepathy, telekinesis, and so on do not become less interesting because they are recognized for what they really are—the intrusion of a later stage of life upon an earlier, not manifestations of the spirit world. By developing time consciousness, we can fathom the very depths of human nature. To live in the dimension of time is to survey the course of time until we can see into both the past and future from the present moment.

You can get a sense of how present-day observation (though externally it may appear otherwise) is very remote from this more inward means of observation, which is more concurrent with time and its flow. Inadequate interpretation of what we encounter in life is the result of modern methods of observation. Contemporary scientific explanations and their effects on life are full of anemic interpretations.

Looking at the course of human life, we discover that the opposite of what we just described can also happen when childishness is carried into maturity. It is characteristic of children that they not only experience the external world less consciously than adults, but their experiences are also much more intimately connected with metabolic changes. When children see colors, their impressions strongly affect the metabolic processes; a child takes in outer sensory impressions all the way into the metabolism. It is not a mere metaphor to say that children digest their sensory impressions, because their digestion responds to all of their outer experiences. An old person develops certain animal characteristics within the physical, but a child's entire life is filled with a sensitivity toward the vegetative organic processes that also affect the child's soul life. Unless we are aware of this, we cannot understand a child's nature.

In later years, human beings leave the digestive and metabolic processes more or less on their own; experiences of the external world are more independent of those processes. They do not allow their soul and spiritual reactions toward the outer world to affect the metabolism to the extent that a child does. The response of adults to their surroundings is not accompanied by the same liveliness of glandular secretion as in children.

Children take in outer impressions as if they were edible substances, but adults leave their digestion to itself, and this alone makes them adults under normal circumstances. But there are cases where certain vegetative and organic forces, which are properly at work during childhood, continue to work in an adult, affecting the psyche as well. In this case, other abnormal symptoms are also liable to occur. An example will make this clear. Imagine, for example, a girl who comes to love a dog that has made a deep impression on her nature. If she has carried childishness into later life, this tenderness will work right into the metabolism. Organic processes that correspond to her feelings of affection will be established. In this situation, digestive processes occur not only after eating or as the result of normal physical activities, but certain areas within the digestive system will develop a habit of secreting and

regenerating substances in response to the strong emotions
evoked by the love for the animal. The dog will become indis-
pensable to the well-being of her vegetative system. And what
happens if the dog dies? The connection in outer life is broken; the organic processes continue by force of inertia, but
they are no longer satisfied. Her feelings miss something they
had gotten used to, and inner troubles and strange disturbances may follow. A friend may suggest getting a new dog to
restore the previous state of health, since the inner organic
processes would again find satisfaction through external experiences. We will see later, however, that there are better ways to
cure such an abnormality, but anyone may reasonably try to
solve the problem this way.

There are of course many other examples, less drastic than a
deep affection for a dog. If an adult has not outgrown certain
childhood forces that absorb external impressions into the
digestive system, and if that adult can no longer satisfy this
abnormal habit, certain cravings within the vegetative organism will result. But there are other things that may have been
loved and lost that cannot be replaced; then a person remains
dissatisfied, morose, and psychosomatic. One must try to find
the true causes of the seemingly inexplicable symptoms that
arise from the depths of the unconscious. There are people who
can sense what needs to be done to alleviate suffering caused by
unsatisfied emotions that affect inner organic processes. They
manage to coax and to bring to consciousness what the patient
wants to recall, and in this way they can help a great deal.

Because of the present condition of our civilization, there are
many who have not progressed from childhood to adulthood
in the normal way, and the ensuing symptoms, both light and
serious, have been widely noted. Whereas this led naturally to
conversations in ordinary life among helpful, interested people,
the situation has stimulated—in many respects rightly so—

psychological research, and a new scientific terminology has sprung up. The patient's psyche is examined through investigation of dreams or by freely or involuntarily giving oneself away. In this way, unfulfilled urges arise from the subconscious into consciousness. This new branch of science is called psychology or psychoanalysis, the science of probing the hidden regions of the soul. However, we are not dealing with "hidden regions of the soul," but with the remains of vegetative organic processes left behind and craving satisfaction. When thwarted desires have been diagnosed, one can help patients readapt, and here lies the value of psychoanalysis.

When judging these things, anthroposophy, or spiritual science, finds itself in a difficult position. It has no quarrel with the findings of natural science; on the contrary, spiritual science is quite prepared to recognize and accept whatever remains properly within its realm. Similarly, spiritual science accepts psychoanalysis within its proper limits. But spiritual science tries to see all problems and questions within the widest context, encompassing the entire universe and the whole human being. It feels it is necessary to broaden the arbitrary restrictions laid down by natural science, which even today often investigates in an unprofessional and superficial way. Anthroposophy has no wish and no intention to quarrel and only puts what is stated in a lopsided way into a wider perspective. Yet this approach is distasteful and unacceptable to those who prefer to wear blinders, and, consequently, furious attacks are made against anthroposophy. Spiritual science must defend itself against an imbalanced attitude, but it will never be aggressive. This has to be said regarding the present currents of thought, as we find in psychoanalysis.

A person may draw the last period of life too much into middle age and, with it, experience abnormal relationships with the external world, manifesting as lower forms of clairvoyance, such as telepathy. In this case, one's horizon extends beyond the normal human scope in an animal-like fashion. It is important to distinguish the two opposing situations, since a person may also move in the other direction by pushing what properly belongs to childhood into later periods of life. As a result, one becomes enmeshed too strongly with the physical organism, with the result that organic surges swamp the psyche, causing disturbances and inner abnormalities. Such a person suffers from a relationship that is too close to one's own organic system. This relationship has been diagnosed by psychoanalysis, which should nevertheless direct its attention toward the human organs to understand the roots of this problem.

If we desire a comprehensive knowledge of the human being, it is absolutely necessary to include the entire human life between birth and death in our considerations. It is essential to focus on the effects of passing time and to inwardly live with and experience those effects. Spiritual science pursues knowledge of the whole human being by penetrating the suprasensory, using its own specific methods and fully considering the time element, which is generally ignored completely in our present stage of civilization. *Imagination, inspiration* and *intuition*, which are the specific methods of spiritual scientific work, must be built on an experience of time.

Imagination, inspiration and *intuition*, the ways leading to suprasensory cognition, should not be seen as faculties beyond ordinary human life but as a continuation, or extension, of ordinary human capacities. Spiritual science dismisses the bias that maintains we can attain this sort of cognition only through some special grace; spiritual science holds that we can become conscious of certain faculties lying deep within us and that we have the power to train them. The usual kind of knowledge gotten through modern scientific training and in ordinary practical life must certainly be transcended.

What happens when we try to comprehend the world around us—not as scientifically trained specialists but as ordinary people? We are surrounded by colors, sounds, varying degrees of warmth, and so on, all of which I would like to call the tapestry of the sensory world. We surrender to these sensory impressions and weave them without thoughts. If you think about the nature of memories rising in your soul, you will find that they are the result of sensory impressions woven into our thoughts. Our whole life depends on imparting this texture of sensory impressions and thoughts to our soul life. But what really happens? Look at the diagram. Let the line *a* to *b* represent the tapestry of the sensory world around us, consisting of colors, sounds, smells, and so on. We give ourselves up to our observation, this tapestry of the senses, and weave its impressions with our thinking (indicated here by the wavy line).

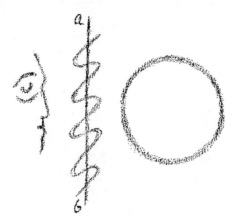

When living in our senses, we unite all our experiences with our thoughts. We interpret the sensory stimuli through thinking. But when we project our thoughts into our surroundings, this tapestry becomes a barrier for us, a metaphorical canvas upon which we draw and paint all our thoughts, but which we cannot penetrate. We cannot break through this incorporeal wall with ordinary consciousness. As the thoughts are stopped by this canvas, they are inscribed upon it.

The only possibility of penetrating this wall is gained by raising one's consciousness to the state of *imagination* through systematic and regular meditation exercises. It is equally possible to undergo an inner training in meditation as a method of research in an outwardly directed study of chemistry or astronomy. If you read my book *How to Know Higher Worlds* and the second part of *An Outline of Esoteric Science,* you can convince yourselves that, if you want to reach the final goal, the methods for such meditative exercises are certainly not simple and less time-consuming than those needed to study astronomy or chemistry. On the other hand, it is relatively easy to read books giving information about such exercises and, using one's common sense, examine the truths of spiritual scientific research. You do not have to take these on authority. Even if you cannot investigate the spiritual world yourself, it is possible to test given results by studying the specific methods employed.

Meditative practice is based on freeing ourselves from outer sensory impressions. In meditation, we do not surrender to sensory impressions, but to the life of thinking. However, by dwelling again and again in meditation on a given thought or mental image—one that is easily and fully comprehensible—we gradually bring our life of thought to such a strength and inner substance that we learn to move in it with the same certainty we have in our sensory impressions. You have all experienced the difference between the striking effects of outer sensory impressions and the rather limp and pale world of our thoughts during ordinary consciousness. Sensory impressions are intense and alive. We give ourselves up to them. Thoughts, on the other hand, turn pale and become abstract and cold. But the very core of meditating is learning, through regular practice, to imbue thoughts with the same intensity and life that normally fills our sensory experiences. If we succeed in grasping a meditation with the same inner intensity that we experience through the stimulus of a color, for example, then we have enlivened, in the right way, the underlying thoughts of a meditation. But all this must happen with the same inner freedom employed in the normal weaving of thoughts or ordinary sense perceptions. Just as we do not allow ourselves to be taken over by nebulous moods or mystical dreaming, or become fatuous visionaries when observing the external world, we must not lose our firm ground when meditating in the right way. The same sane mood with which we perceive the world around us must also take hold when we meditate.

This attitude of taking outer sensory perceptions as an example for one's conduct when meditating is characteristic of the anthroposophic method. There are plenty of vague mystics who disparage sensory perceptions as inferior and advise leaving them behind. They claim that, when you meditate, you should reach a state of mystic dreaming. The result, of course, is a condition of half sleep, certainly not meditation. Spiritual science pursues the opposite goal, considering the quality, intensity, and liveliness of sensory perception as an example to be followed until the meditator moves inwardly with the same freedom with which one encounters sensory perceptions. We need not fear we will become dried up bores. The meditative content (which we experience objectively in meditative practice) saves us from that. Because of the inner content that we experience while freeing ourselves from ordinary life, there is no need to enter a vague, trance-like state while meditating.

Correct meditation allows us to gain the ability to move freely in our life of thinking. This in turn redeems the thoughts from their previous abstract nature; they become image-like. This happens in full consciousness, just as all healthy thinking takes place. It is essential that we do not lose full consciousness, and this distinguishes meditation from a hallucinatory state. Those who give themselves up to hallucinations, becoming futile enthusiasts or visionaries, relinquish common sense; on the other hand, those who wish to follow the methods advocated here must make sure common sense accompanies all their weaving thought imagery. And what does this lead to? Though fully awake, we experience the pictorial quality of the dream world. The significant difference between *imagination* and dream images is that we are completely passive when experiencing the imagery of dreams. If they arise from the subconscious and enter our waking state, we can observe them only after they have occurred. When practicing *imagination*, on the other hand, we initiate them ourselves; we create images that are not mere fantasy, but differ in intensity and strength from the fantasy as do dream images. The main point is that we initiate the images ourselves, and this frees us from the illusion that they are a manifestation of the external world. Those given up to hallucinations, however, always believe that what comes to them represents reality, because they know that they did not create what they see. This is the cause of the deception. Those who practice *imagination* through meditation cannot possibly believe that the images they create represent external reality. The first step toward suprasensory cognition depends on freeing ourselves from the illusion that the images we have created—having the same intensity as those of the dream world— are real. This, however, is obvious, because the meditator remains fully aware of having initiated them in complete freedom. Only the insane would mistake them for outer reality.

Now, in the next step in meditation we acquire the ability to allow these images to vanish without a trace. This is not as easy as one might expect, because, unless the one meditating has created them in full freedom, the images become quite fascinating and fix themselves on the mind like parasites. One has to become strong enough to let such pictures disappear at will. This second step is equally important as the first. In ordinary life, we need the ability to forget; otherwise we would have to go through life with the total of all our memories. Similarly, the complete extinction of meditative images is as important as their initial creation.

When we have thoroughly practiced these exercises, we have done something to our soul life that might be compared to the strengthening of muscles through repeated bending and stretching. By learning to weave and form images and then to obliterate them—and all this is done in complete freedom of the will—we have performed an important training of the soul. We will have developed the faculty of consciously forming images that, under normal circumstances, appear only in dreams, during a state that escapes ordinary consciousness and is confined to the time between falling asleep and awaking. Now, however, this condition has been induced in full consciousness and freedom. Training in *imagination* means training the will to consciously create images and to consciously remove them from the mind. And through this, we acquire yet another faculty.

Everyone has this faculty automatically—not during sleep, but at the moments of awaking and falling asleep. It is possible that what was experienced between these two points in time comes to us as remnants of dreams, often experienced as though they come from the beyond. Naturally, it is equally possible that what we encounter on awaking surprises us so much that all memories of dreams sink below the threshold of consciousness. In general, we can say that, because dream imaginations are experienced involuntarily, something chaotic and erratic that normally lies beyond consciousness finds its way to us. If, while fully awake, we develop the ability of creating and of obliterating *imaginations,* we may reach a condition of emptied consciousness. This is like a new awakening, then, from beyond the tapestry of the sensory world; spiritual entities pass through the tapestry to reach us on paths smoothed by the meditation content (see the circle in the diagram). While thus persevering in emptied consciousness, we push through the barrier of the senses, and images come to us from beyond the sensory world, carried by *inspiration.* We enter the world beyond the sensory world. Through *imagination,* we prepare for *inspiration,* which involves the ability to experience consciously something that happens unconsciously at the moment of awaking. Right at the moment of awaking, something from beyond our waking soul life enters consciousness, so that something beyond the conscious sensory world enters us if, through *imagination,* we have trained our soul as described.

In this way, we experience the spiritual world beyond the world of the senses. The faculties of suprasensory cognition are extensions of those naturally given to us in ordinary life. It is one of the main tasks of spiritual science to train and foster the development of these higher faculties. And grasping the time element in human life is fundamental to such development.

If you look at the preparatory exercises for *imagination, inspiration,* and *intuition* as given in *How to Know Higher Worlds* or *An Outline of Esoteric Science,* you find that everything said there aims at one thing: learning to experience the flow of time.[1] The human being goes through the various stages of experience in the world, first as a child, then as a

---

1. In these books, especially in the first two chapters of *How to Know Higher Worlds,* Steiner provides essential exercises intended to build an inner foundation for the soul development he describes here.

mature person, and finally as an old person; otherwise, one may suffer from an abnormal overlap of one stage into the other. It is not *imagination* itself, but the meditative preparation, that should give the possibility of developing the full potential and of learning how to give ourselves to the world out of the fullness of life. To this end harmony must be brought about between the specific contributions to the world of childhood, middle age, and old age. These must flow together harmoniously into a worldview capable of reaching the spiritual world. Human beings in their wholeness, which includes the domain of time, must be actively engaged in work in the world. To achieve a worldview that reaches beyond the barriers of the sensory world, human beings must preserve the freshness of experience proper to youth; the clarity of thought and the freedom of judgment proper to the central period of life; and the power of loving devotion toward life that can reach perfection in old age. All these qualities are a necessary preparation for the proper development of *imagination, inspiration,* and *intuition.*

HEALTH AND ILLNESS
Part 1

December 27, 1921

As described in the previous lecture, cognition through *imagination* can be attained by lifting into consciousness what is active subconsciously and involuntarily in dreaming. To be more precise, it is the activity behind our dreaming and not the dreaming itself with its content that is lifted into consciousness, since if this were to happen, we should remain in the realm of unreality. (For the moment I will leave this activity behind our dreaming undefined.) It is this activity—lifted into consciousness by controlled will power—that becomes the basis for cognition through *imagination,* and this conscious activity is very different from that of dreaming. In dream activity, because we are not active participants, we have the feeling that our experiences are real. But when we lift the activity that produces dreams into consciousness, we realize very well that we are seeing images we ourselves made. It is this awareness that saves us from falling into hallucinations instead of doing research through spiritual science.

This first meditative activity of creating images must now be superseded by a second step that involves obliterating those images, thus leading to empty consciousness. If you have been able, in full consciousness and under full control, to enhance your soul powers in this way, you will have in fact entered the spiritual world. You will then be able to engage in an activity that, being solely soul and spirit, is independent of the physical body; you no longer perceive with your physical organs. While thinking becomes freed from the body, your conscious experience becomes purely spiritual.

Yesterday I showed that, for spiritual scientific investigators, dreamlike experience is not to be seen as a model for spiritual perception. Only fully controlled experiences, similar to those of our sensory perceptions, are valid. Obviously there is no possibility of sensory perception in suprasensory cognition. Nevertheless, we can see definite capacities in our ability to move freely when surrounded by sensory perceptions and in our independence from our personal makeup while perceiving. An example will clarify my meaning.

Let us look at one of our most characteristic and representative sensory organs, the human eye. We recognize the relative independence of this organ by the way it rests in its cavity, attached to the remaining organism by insubstantial links. Forgetting for the moment what happens in the act of seeing, we find another, more external process. Near the eye are the lachrymal glands, which, while we are awake, continually secrete a liquid composed mainly of salt water. This liquid flushes the whole eyeball, especially the part exposed to the outer air when the eye is open. Through this glandular activity, the eye is constantly bathed so that dust entering the eye from the outside is washed away through tear ducts entering the nose. This process, which forms part of the normal function of our organ of sight, is hidden from ordinary consciousness.

Now this wisely ordained (though completely unconscious) activity of the lachrymal glands can be accelerated by the various stimuli of pressure or cold, for example, or through exhaustion, either in the eye or in the organism in general. The lachrymal glands thus become more active, and the cause of secretion and the secretion of tears itself begins to enter our consciousness. However, a further increase of this activity may occur in a very different way; when sadness makes us weep, tears flow as a result of a purely emotional stress or because our feelings have been deeply moved. Here we see how, under normal circumstances, the lachrymal liquid is constantly secreted in complete unconsciousness, and how outer irritants will lead to an increase in our consciousness of this activity. But when a person cries because of soul distress, this lachrymal activity is lifted into the sphere of consciousness only through soul or moral issues, not through physical causes.

This simple fact can help to illustrate what happens when, through meditation, we are able to lift ourselves into a body-free state of consciousness, in which we can live entirely in soul and spiritual experiences. If you shed tears because you receive a letter that makes you unhappy, you must admit that the cause of your tears has nothing to do with your physical eyes. Nevertheless, it affects your physical eyes. The fact that tears are not connected with the physical act of reading the letter is easily proved if someone else reads the letter to you and you experience the same tearful consequences. Something nonphysical has set an organic process in motion.

Now imagine you have gained such mastery over yourself that you can suffer great sorrow without shedding any tears. Of course, this does not imply that your anguish would be any less intense than when you weep. In this situation, soul experiences do not directly affect the bodily functions. This example may illustrate how, through self-development, we can achieve a state of soul and spirit, emancipated from the physical organism. It may help you to form some idea of how *imagination, inspiration,* and *intuition* as methods of spiritual science can open the gates into the suprasensory world. If you take the proper steps, you will be able to describe experiences from beyond the tapestry of the senses, experiences that may be seen as an enhanced continuation of what a person experiences in normal life. This, however, is possible only through the practice of specific soul and spiritual exercises.

If now, through continued spiritual training, you have reached the stage where you can suppress previous imaginations of your own creation, and if in the ensuing stage of emptied consciousness you are able to experience real soul and spiritual content, the first thing that comes to meet you is a tableau sort of image of your earthly life, approximately from birth until the present. You will be unable to see your physical body in that picture, because it vanishes when you reach body-free perception. And there before you, ready to meet your soul, is everything you have experienced, everything that belongs to your stream of memory, which normally remains unconscious, with only individual images occasionally arising. It confronts you as an entity, as a kind of time organism full of its own inner movement.

If you look at the physical body as it appears spatially, you find that its members are interdependent, all together making up the whole. What happens in the head has a certain relationship with the stomach and vice versa. All the processes in an organism are interrelated. The same is true of an organism existing in time; later events depend on earlier ones, and the past lives in the present. At such a moment, you are all at once confronted by a tableau of your whole life.

Now, if you are able to consciously suppress the tableau of these memory pictures—not just the body but the entire life tableau—you reach the stage where you are able to perceive experiences prior to birth, or rather, prior to conception. The realm of soul and spirit that you inhabited before entering this earthly existence remains part of your inner being, even during life on earth. It works and lives in us in a way similar to the way hydrogen lives with oxygen after they form water. One cannot examine hydrogen separately from the oxygen while they form water; similarly, one cannot examine the human soul and spirit separately while we live on earth. Just as the oxygen must first be isolated from water before we can examine the remaining hydrogen, the soul and spiritual parts of the human being must first be isolated. When this happens, we are led not into the present time but into our pre-earthly existence. Thus, you really can perceive what has descended from the spirit world to assume earthly form. The realm where we lived before entering earthly life is revealed to us.

It is understandable if some are unprepared to go to such lengths to investigate the eternal human being. Certainly, everyone is free not to follow these paths. But to think it is possible to examine the human soul and spirit using ordinary methods of cognition is like believing naively that we could examine hydrogen while it forms a part of water, without first isolating it. One must recognize that ordinary consciousness is unable to enter the realm of soul and spirit. If you are unprepared to accept the results of spiritual investigation, you will have to remain silent about suprasensory realities. And in this case, you will have to be content with involvement only within material existence. The truth may be irksome to some, but there are certain facts in life that one must simply accept.

Continuing along this path of spiritual training, we gradually reach knowledge through *inspiration*. We become inspired by something that does not normally enter consciousness but permeates our being as does the oxygen we breathe in from the outer air. In full consciousness, we are filled with *inspirational* cognition and the experience of our pre-earthly life, just as in respiration we are filled with physical oxygen. We breathe with our soul and spiritual being, rising to the stage of *inspiration*. This word was not chosen arbitrarily, but with the nature of this type of cognition in mind.

Inspirational cognition has yet another characteristic. You will find more about it in *How to Know Higher Worlds*.[1] In order to develop this higher cognition, another faculty is necessary: presence of mind. It is this faculty that enables us to act spontaneously during any given life situation. In order not to miss the right moment, we may have to act without waiting until we have time to assess an issue properly. We should really use these moments in life to practice swift and decisive action, learning to quickly grasp the moment, because whatever comes through *inspiration* passes in a flash. As soon as it appears, it has already vanished. One must be able to catch such fleeting moments with the utmost attentiveness.

The ordinary world of the senses appears to us be spread out in space. But when we are confronted by our life tableau, we see it existing in time. However, during *inspirational* cognition, we are outside the realm of time. We depend on being able to perceive in the flash of a moment; time loses its meaning as soon as we experience *inspiration*.

If we penetrate this life tableau, we find something far more real than the ordinary memory pictures can give us. The images of memory are neutral and lack inner strength; they are there, and we are free to take them up, but in themselves they have no strength. When viewing our life tableau, on the other hand, we see that it is full of its own life and strength and contains the very forces that form the human being. These are the suprasensory, formative forces that are active, for example, in forming the brain of a young child before the final structure has been finished. It is these formative forces that we begin to recognize, for

---

1. On this subject, see also Rudolf Steiner, *A Way of Self-Knowledge* (Anthroposophic Press, 1999), especially the meditations in part 2.

they are contained within this life tableau. We do not apprehend something abstract, but a full reality, encompassing the course of time and full of power. It is the refined nonmaterial body of forces that we also call the ether body, or body of formative forces. This body presents only momentarily a well-defined appearance in space, for it is in constant motion. If we were to try to paint a picture of it, we would paint something unreal, because the ether body is in a constant flow. Its subsequent stage would be very different again, just as a former stage was different. This ether body is a time organism through and through, and is the basis for the growing processes and the forces active in the human metabolism.

Once we have advanced far enough in *imaginative* cognition, consciously living in the realm of soul and spirit beyond the physical, and once we have progressed far enough to see our life tableau—or ether body—at will, then we have truly experienced a complete transformation of our cognition. We find that experiences in the etheric world are similar to, and yet very different from, what happens in the world of artistic activity. To experience this, one has to develop a more creative way of thinking, one very different from abstract naturalistic thinking. Although in certain respects this kind of thinking resembles that of a creative artist, in other ways it is quite different. An artist's creations have to reach a certain finality within the realm of fantasy. The artist's creativity remains bound to the physical; it is not freed from corporeality. But the activity practiced in *imaginative* cognition is freed entirely from the physical and, therefore, is capable of grasping spiritual reality. For example, when we look at the *Venus de Milo,* we hardly have the feeling that this statue will move and walk toward us; an artistic creation does not embody outer realities. If you saw the devil painted on canvas, you would not be afraid that he was coming after you. The important thing is the way an artist, bound to physical reality, deals with material reality. But artists do not plunge into the reality of soul and spirit. What has been achieved in *imaginative* cognition, on the other hand, is immersed in ultimate reality, the reality of spiritual processes.

Now someone might argue that pure cognition should be kept separate from artistic activities. It is easy to prove by logic that cognizing means moving from one concept to the next in logical sequence and that, if we enter the sphere of art, we are in fact transgressing the realm of cognition. One can argue for a long time about the laws of cognition. But if nature herself is an artistic creator, she will never reveal herself to mere logical thinking. Logic alone will never reach her true being. Therefore, however much logic might prove that cognizing should not be confused with artistic activities, we cannot enter the reality of the etheric world without an artistic mode of cognition. What matters is the way things are and not what the laws of cognition should be. Even when certain suppositions are logically tenable, they may only prevent us from reaching our goal. Therefore it is proper to maintain that an artistic element must become part of our efforts if we wish to raise our ordinary cognition to the level of *imagination*.

When we reach the stage of *inspiration*, we may again compare our experiences with something they resemble, yet differ from greatly: moral experiences and the comprehension of moral ideas. Viewed qualitatively, *inspirations* are like moral ideas. Yet they are totally different, since any moral ideal we may have does not, in itself, have the power to realize itself on its own; in themselves, moral ideals are powerless. We must make them effective through our own physical personality, placing them in the world by means of our physical existence. Otherwise, they remain only thoughts. But this cannot be said of an *inspiration*. Though qualitatively similar to moral ideas, or moral impulses, *inspiration* manifests as a reality, existing in its own right. It is a powerful force that works like the elemental forces in nature. Thus we enter a world that, whereas we have to imagine it as similar to the world of moral ideas, has reality because of its primal power.

If one can take a stand in the world of soul and spirit, having advanced far enough in the state of *inspiration,* then something else is still needed to experience its content. We have to carry something into this realm that does not exist at all in our abstract world of thoughts: complete devotion to our chosen objective. It is impossible to come to know a being or power in the spiritual world unless we surrender lovingly and completely to what we encounter during the state of *inspiration.* At first, *inspiration* remains only a manifestation of the spiritual world. Its full inner nature reveals itself only when, with loving devotion, we pour ourselves out into its substance. And only after experiencing the reality of soul and spirit in this way—full of life and with heightened consciousness—do we enter the realm of *inspiration.*

And this is *intuitive* cognition. Shadow forms of *intuition* can be found in ordinary life, where they exist in religious feelings and moods. However, a religious feeling remains a purely inner experience that does not lift us into outer spirituality. *Intuition,* on the other hand, is an experience of objective spiritual reality. In this way, *intuition* is similar and yet again very different from a purely religious experience.

If you want to arrange these levels of higher knowledge in a more or less systematic order, we can say, first of all, that in ordinary life we have knowledge of the material world, which we could call naturalistic knowledge. Then we come to knowledge gained through *imagination,* which has a kind of artistic nature. The next step is knowledge attained through *inspiration,* which is, in essence, a moral one. Finally we reach knowledge through *intuition,* which is like religious experiences, but only in the sense just described.

These suprasensory experiences of an artistic, moral, and religious sort work on and transform the whole human being. Although ordinary consciousness knows nothing of them, they nevertheless form part of the human being. Therefore suprasensory knowledge gained through *imagination, inspiration,* and *intuition* enables us to know the whole human being. And because these powers streaming from the spiritual world into earthly existence work in an especially strong way in children, higher cognition, in particular, allows us to understand the nature of a child. It is important, however, to recognize how suprasensory forces are related to physical forces.

This can be illustrated particularly well if we take memory as an example, because active memory definitely depends on the functioning of physical organs. Even commonplace experiences can demonstrate how our body must play its part when we use our powers of memory. For instance, we may wish to memorize part of a play or a poem, only to find that the lines simply refuse to become imprinted on the mind. Yet, after sleeping on them overnight, we may suddenly remember them without difficulty. This happens because, during the sleep, our body has regenerated so that we are able to use its renewed vitality the following morning for the task of remembering the lines.

One can also prove anatomically and physiologically that, through paralysis or the separation of certain areas within the nervous system, specific areas of memory may be wiped out. In other words, we can see that memory depends on the functioning of the physical organization and that physical organs are active during the process of remembering. However, this kind of memory activity is completely different from what we experience in heightened consciousness through *imagination, inspiration,* and *intuition.* For these suprasensory experiences simply must not be involved in any way in the functions of physical organs. This tells us why such experiences cannot be remembered in the ordinary way; they do not impress themselves into ordinary memory.

Anyone engaged in spiritual scientific research must allow ordinary memory to run its course alongside what one experiences in the suprasensory realm. Ordinary memory must remain intact. In a way, a student of anthroposophy has to maintain a second personality that represents ordinary life and is always present. But the researcher knows full well that there is this other, first personality engaged in suprasensory knowledge that will not allow itself to become imprinted on the memory. In ordinary life we can retain only a memory image of a fish we have seen, not the fish itself. In suprasensory cognition, we have direct perceptions—not mental images—and thus we cannot carry them in our memory. Consequently one has to return to them again and again. However, it is possible to remember the process we used to gain suprasensory cognition, and if we repeat those efforts, suprasensory sight will reemerge, albeit only passively, since it cannot live in the memory. It can be attained only through renewed inner activity. The fact that these higher faculties are beyond the reach of memory is a characteristic of suprasensory cognition. One can regain it, but only by following a route similar to the one traveled earlier. One can remember the path taken previously, but not the suprasensory experience itself.

It is this fact that distinguishes suprasensory experiences from those of ordinary life. It must be emphasized again and again, however, that a healthy memory goes hand in hand with true suprasensory experiences. If you lose the stream of common memory while engaged in suprasensory experiences, you will pour your subjective personality into them. Then you would not be a student of spiritual scientific research but live in hallucinations and personal visions. It is important to understand that all forms of hallucinations should be strictly excluded from suprasensory cognition and that such cognition must be developed along with a normal, healthy soul life. Anyone who argues that *imagination* and *inspiration* attained through anthroposophy might simply be hallucinations does not understand the nature of the spiritual scientific path and talks only out of ignorance.

It is essential to recognize this difference between suprasensory cognition and memory, since both are real in life. Suprasensory substance gained through *imagination* and *inspiration* has its own separate existence, and we can become aware of it through our own effort. Memory, on the other hand, is not just the result of our own effort, because the subconscious also plays a role. What we experience through *imagination* remains in the spirit world, as though it comes to unite with us. But memory flows right through us, entering the physical body and causing it to participate; it penetrates the physical human being. Comparing memory with *imagination* helps us appreciate the difference between everything related to the physical body and the suprasensory forces that live in us eternally, even between birth and death. But, because this eludes ordinary consciousness, it must be shown through spiritual scientific investigation.

We come to know the whole human being only by immersing ourselves in this relationship between the suprasensory aspect of the human being and physical existence. If we penetrate the knowledge gained through suprasensory cognition, we come to know the child and the growing human being in such a way that we can develop a true art of education. This example of the relationship between the suprasensory human being and the activity of memory helps shed light on this problem.

Let us imagine that a teacher is introducing a subject to a class. First he approaches it in a somewhat general way and may have the impression that all was going well. But after a time, he notices that a child in the class is becoming pale. Pallor is not always obvious and might easily go unnoticed by those not trained in exact observation. Ideally, however, teachers should remain fully aware of each student's condition.

The symptoms I will describe could have many causes. But when teachers deepen their knowledge of the human being through anthroposophic training, they awaken and enhance their ordinary pedagogical instincts so they are able to diagnose and address other causes as well. If a science of education establishes fixed and abstract rules, it affects teachers as though they were constantly stepping on their own feet while trying to walk; it robs them of all creative spontaneity. When teachers always have to wonder how to apply the rules prescribed by educational science, they lose all ingenuity and their proper pedagogical instincts. On the other hand, the educational principles based on spiritual science have the opposite effect. They do not allow inborn pedagogical sense to wither away but enliven and strengthen the teacher's whole personality. At least, this is the intention of the practical educational principles that spring from anthroposophy.

However varied external symptoms may be (life, after all, is full of surprises), our imaginary teacher, whose pedagogical sense has been stimulated and sharpened by anthroposophy, might suddenly realize that this child is growing pale because he was overfed with memory content. Of course, there might be many other reasons for such a symptom, which a gifted teacher would also be able to discover. I am giving you this example, however, to illustrate one of the fundamental tasks of spiritual science: to make people aware of how the human soul and spirit interacts with the physical, material nature of the human being. Anthroposophy does not want to simply reveal spiritual knowledge; most of all, it endeavors to open people's eyes to the way living spirit works and reveals itself in matter.

Such knowledge enables us to deal correctly with the practical problems of life, and it places us firmly in the world where we have to fulfill our tasks.

If this pallor, caused by the overburdening of the student's memory, is not recognized in time, a perceptive teacher will notice a further change in the child—this time psychological—as an anxiety complex develops. Again, this symptom may not be conspicuous and might be detected only by teachers for whom intense observation has become second nature. And, finally, overtaxing a student's memory can eventually have the effect of retarding the child's growth forces; even physical growth can be affected.

Here you have an example of how soul and spirit interact with what is physical. It shows us how important it is for teachers to know how to deal with children's tendencies toward health and sickness. Of course, illnesses have to be treated by medical doctors, but educators are always confronted by inherent trends toward health or sickness in children, and they should learn to recognize these tendencies. They should also be aware of how illnesses can come out later in life and how, often, they can be traced back to what happened in school. Such knowledge makes teachers far more circumspect in choosing their teaching methods. In the example given, the teacher would certainly avoid placing too much stress on the student's memory, and he might see a healthier complexion return to the child's face. He could bring about such a change by showing his student something beautiful that would give pleasure. The next day he might again show the child something beautiful or a variation of the previous object, thus bypassing mere memory.

A teacher may also discover the opposite symptoms in a child. For example, a teacher notices a girl whose face appears permanently flushed, even if only slightly. She may discover that this change is not at all the result of embarrassment, but represents a shift in the girl's health. Again, this symptom may be so slight that it would go unnoticed by a less perceptive teacher. And this condition could have many other causes, and these would not escape our teacher's notice either. It could be that this student has a tendency to blush because the teacher did not appeal sufficiently to the child's memory. Realizing this, she would try to rectify this condition by giving the student more memorizing to do. If not addressed, this irregularity could intensify and spread to the girl's psyche, where it would manifest in mild but significant outbursts of temper.

This connection between slackness in memorizing and slight but unhealthy fits of temper is certainly a possibility. The general repercussions of such a condition would be injurious to a student's health. In such cases, the mutual effects between soul and spirit on the one hand, and the body on the other, could lead to breathing and circulatory problems. Thus, teachers who are unaware of such links may unwittingly plant illnesses in their students, and these can remain dormant for many years and then, triggered by other causes, lead to serious illnesses. For this reason, any teacher worthy of the title should be aware of these connections and characteristics in human nature.

As mentioned previously, acute illnesses must be dealt with by medical doctors, but during their developmental stages, children are always moving either toward health or illness. The art of education demands that teachers be conversant with these indications and have the ability to perceive them, even in their more subtle manifestations.

To illustrate this point even more drastically, I will give you one more example that, I realize, may be open to argument, but life presents us with a great number of situations. Consequently, the case I will describe may also be the result of completely different causes. If you live with what anthroposophy offers to teaching, you become used to looking around for the most varied causes when confronted with a particular problem. But the following connections between symptom and cause are certainly possible.

Let us imagine that a boy in a class has followed the lessons attentively and to the satisfaction of the teacher. However, one day he suddenly appears somewhat blasé; he is no longer inclined to pay attention, and much of the subject matter seems to pass unnoticed. Depending on the experience and outlook of the boy's teacher, he might even resort to corporal punishment or some other form of correction to bring about greater participation. However, if this teacher is aware of the interplay between spirit and matter that manifests in health and illness, he would approach this in a very different way. He might say to the boy, "You shouldn't allow your finger- and toe-nails grow too long. You ought to cut them more often." Outer signs of growth, such as fingernails and toenails, are also permeated by soul and spirit. And if fingernails and toenails grow too long, these growth forces become blocked. Being held back in this way, those forces are no longer able to flow into the nails. This obstruction to the flow of growth forces, which is removed when the nails are cut, similarly affects the soul and spiritual counterpart and manifests as difficulties in concentration. The ability to pay attention can be developed only with a free and unlimited flow of the life forces that permeate the whole organism. In most cases, this kind of change in powers of concentration may pass unnoticed. I give this example to show that anthroposophic principles and methods of education in no way neglect the physical aspects of life. Nor do they lead to a vague kind of spirituality; spirit is taken fully into account, so that life can be understood and treated appropriately.

Educators who gradually learn to understand human nature can learn how to deal correctly with matters related to their students' health and illness.

HEALTH AND ILLNESS
Part 2

December 28, 1921

It was not my intention in yesterday's lecture to single out certain types of illnesses nor to specify differing degrees of health, nor is it my aim to do so today as we continue this subject. I merely wish to point out how important it is for teachers to learn to recognize both healing and harmful influences in the lives of their students. True educators, above all else, must have acquired real understanding of the entire human organization. They must not allow abstract educational theories or methods to cause them deviate from their natural or (as we could also call it) natural, intuitive understanding. Abstract theories will only hamper teachers in their efforts. They must be able to look at the children without preconceived ideas.

There is a saying often heard in Central Europe (perhaps this is also known in the West): "There is only one health, but there are numerous illnesses." Many people believe in this saying, but it really does not stand up to scrutiny. Human beings are so individualized that we all, including children, have our own specific states of health, representing individual variations of the general notion of health. One might just as well coin the saying, "There are as many kinds of health and illness as there are people in the world." This alone indicates how we must always consider the individual nature of each person. But this is possible only when we have learned to see human beings in their wholeness.

In every human being, soul and spiritual forces continually interact with physical forces, just as hydrogen and oxygen interact in water. We cannot see hydrogen and oxygen as separate elements in water, and similarly we cannot ordinarily see the human soul and spirit as separate from the physical and material aspects of a human being when we look at someone. To recognize the true relationship between the soul and spiritual aspect and the physical nature of a human being, one must first get to know them intimately, but we cannot do this through just our ordinary means of knowledge. Today we are used to seeing the human being from two points of view. One involves the study of physiology and anatomy, in which our image is not based on the living human being at all, but upon the human corpse, with the human soul and spirit excluded. The other point of view comes from psychology, the study of our inner life. But psychologists can form only abstractions, thin and cold concepts for our naturalistic and intellectualistic era. Such researchers warm up only when they try to plumb the depths of human emotions and will impulses. In their true essence, however, these are also beyond their grasp; in a vague way, they see only waves surging up from within.

It is obvious that cold, thin, and pale concepts of the human psyche will not give us a true sense of reality. What I am about to say might seem strange from the modern point of view, but it is true nevertheless. People today adopt a materialistic attitude, because for them spirit has become too attenuated and distant; as a result, when people observe the human inner life, it no longer has any sense of reality. The very individuals who live with the most abstract thoughts have become the most materialistic people during our cultural epoch. Contemporary thinking—and thinking is a spiritual activity—turns people into materialists. On the other hand, those who are relatively untouched by today's scientific thinking, people whose minds turn more toward outer material events, are the ones who sense some of the mystery behind external processes. Scientific thinking today leaves little room for life's mysteries. Its thoughts are thin and transparent and, for the most part, terribly precise; consequently, they are not grounded in the realities of life. The material processes of nature, on the other hand, are full of mysteries. They need more than the clarity of intellectual thoughts, since they can evoke a sense of wonder, in which our feelings also become engaged.

Those who have not been influenced by today's sterile thinking and have remained aloof from the rigorous discipline of a scientific training are more open to the mysteries of the material processes of nature. But here there is a certain danger; in their longing to find spirit in nature, they look for the spiritual as if it, too, were only matter. They become spiritualists. Modern scientific thinking, on the other hand, will not produce people who are directed to the spiritual, but people who are materialists. A natural openness toward the material world, however, easily produces a spiritualistic approach, and here lies a strange contradiction typical of our time. But neither the materialistic view nor the spiritualistic view can provide a true picture of the human being. This is accomplished only by discriminating how—in every organ of the human being—the soul and spiritual element interacts with the material nature of the human being.

People do talk about soul and spirit today, and they talk about our physical aspect. They then philosophize about the relationship between these two aspects. Experts have presented detailed theories, which may be ingenious but never touch reality, merely because we find reality only when we perceive the complete interpenetration of the soul and spiritual element and the physical, material element of the whole human being. If we look at the results of today's investigations, both in physiology and in psychology, we always find them vague and colorless.

Today, when people look at another person, they have the feeling they are confronted by a unified whole, because the other person is neatly wrapped up in skin. One generally fails to realize that this seeming singularity is the result of the cooperation of the most diverse organs. And if we say that this unity must not be assumed, opponents quickly arise and accuse us of destroying the idea that the human being is unified, which they consider fundamental. However, their concept of human oneness is still just an abstract thought unless they can harmonize the manifold members of the human being into a single organization.

When people look inward, they sum up all that lives within them with the little word *I*. Eminent people such as John Stuart Mill worked hard to formulate theories about the nature of this inner feeling of identity, which we express with the word *I*.[1] Just stop and think, however, how vague this idea of a pointlike *I* really is. You will soon see that you no longer grasp concrete reality with this concept. In German, only three letters form this little word (*ich*), and in English even fewer. People seldom manage to get beyond the outer meaning of these letters, and consequently today's knowledge of the human being remains vague, regardless of whether you look at the inner life or the physical constituents.

It is the ability to see the spiritual and physical working together that enriches our efforts at comprehending the nature of the human being. There are many today who are inwardly

---

1. John Stuart Mill (1806–1873), English empiricist philosopher and social reformer. He was leader of the Benthamite utilitarian movement and helped form the Utilitarian Society. His essay "On Liberty" is his most popular work.

satisfied by Goethe's words, "Matter in spirit, spirit in matter." It is good if these words make people happy, since they certainly express a truth. But for anyone who has the habit of seeing spirit and matter working together everywhere, these words express a mere triviality; they extol the obvious. The fact that so many receive this somewhat theoretical dictum with such acclaim just goes to show that they no longer experience its underlying reality. Theoretical explanations usually hide the loss of concrete inner experience. We find an example of this in history when we look at theories about the holy communion, theories that were widely discussed beginning at the very point in time when people had lost their ability to experience its reality. In general, theories are formed to explain what is no longer experienced in practice.

The attitude of mind expressed so far will be helpful to those who wish to practice education as an art. It will enable you to acquire a concrete image of the manifold members of the human being instead of having to work with some vague notion of human oneness. An image of the human being as an organic whole will emerge, but in it you can see how the various members work together in harmony. Such a picture inevitably leads to what I have indicated in my book *Riddles of the Soul:* the discovery of the three fundamental human aspects, each different from the others in both functions and character.[2] Externally, the head as an organization appears very different from, say, the organism of the limbs and metabolic system. I link these two latter systems together, because the metabolism shows its real nature in the activity of a person's limbs. In morphological terms, we can see the digestive system as a kind of continuation (though perhaps only inwardly) of a person in movement. There is an intimate relationship between the limbs

---

2. *Riddles of the Soul,* Spring Valley, NY: Mercury Press, 1996.

and the digestive systems. For instance, the metabolism is more lively when the limbs are active. This relationship could be demonstrated in detail, but I am merely indicating it here. Because of their close affinity, I group these two systems together, although, when each one is seen individually, they also represent certain polarities.

Now let us look at the human shape, beginning with the head. For the moment, we will ignore the hair, which, in any case, grows away from the head and, because it is a dead substance, remains outside the living head organization. Human hair is really a very interesting substance, but further details of this would only lead us away from our main considerations.

The head is encased in the skull, which is formed most powerfully at the periphery, whereas the soft, living parts are enclosed within. Now compare the head with its opposite, the limb system. Here we find tubular bones enclosing marrow, which is typically not considered as important for the entire organism as the brain mass in the skull. On the other hand, here we find the most important parts—the muscles—attached on the outside, and from this point of view we see a polarity characteristic of human nature. This polarity consists of the nerves and senses, centered primarily (though not exclusively) in the head, and the metabolism localized in the metabolic and limb systems.

Despite this polarity, the human being is of course a unity. At this point, however, we must not be tempted to make up diagrams that divide the human being into three parts (as though these parts could exist separately), which we then define as the nervous-sensory system, a second part, which will be discussed shortly, and, finally, the metabolic and limb organization. It is not like this at all. Metabolic as well as muscular activities constantly take place in the head, and yet we can say that the head is the center of the organization of nerves and senses. Conversely, the organization of digestion and limbs are also permeated by forces emanating from the head, but we can nevertheless call it the seat of the "metabolic-limb system."

Midway between these two regions, we find what we can call the rhythmic system of the human being, located in the chest, where the most fundamental rhythms take place: breathing and blood circulation. Each follows its own speed; the rhythm visible in a person's breathing is slower, and the blood circulation, felt as the pulse, is faster. This "rhythmic organization" acts as a mediator between the other two poles. It would be tempting to go into further detail, but since we have gathered to study the principles and methods of Waldorf education, I must refrain. However, if you can see the chest organization from the point of view just indicated, you find in every one of its parts—whether in the skeletal formation or in the structure of the inner organs—a transition between the head organization and the metabolic-limb system. This is the image that emerges when we observe human beings according to their inner structure rather than foggy notions about human unity. But there is more, for we are also led to understand the various functions within the human being, and here I would like to give you an example. One could mention countless examples, but this must suffice to show how important it is for real educators to follow the directions indicated here.

Imagine that a person suffers from sudden outbursts of temper. Such eruptions may already occur in childhood, and then a good teacher must find ways of dealing with them. Those who follow the usual methods of physiology and anatomy might also consider the psychological effects in this person. Furthermore they may include the fact that, along with extreme anger, there is an excess of gall secretion. However, these two aspects—the physical and psychological—are not generally seen as two sides of the same phenomenon. The soul-spiritual aspect of anger and the physically overactive secretion of bile are not seen as a unity. In a normal person, bile is of course a necessary for the nutritive process. In one who is angry, this gall activity becomes imbalanced and, if left alone, such a person will finally suffer from jaundice, as you all know.

If we consider both the soul-spiritual and the physical aspects, we see that a tendency toward a certain illness may develop, but this alone is still not enough to assess human nature, because, while bile is being secreted in the metabolism, an accompanying but polar opposite process occurs in the head organization. We are not observing human nature fully unless we realize that while bile is secreted, an opposite process is taking place at the same time in the head organization. In the head, a milk-like sap, produced in other parts of the body, is being absorbed. In an abnormal case, if too much bile is secreted into the metabolism, the head organization will try to fill itself with too much of this fluid; consequently, once the temper has cooled down, one feels as if one's head were bursting. And whereas an excess of bile will cause this milky sap to flow into the head, once the temper has cooled down this person's face may turn somewhat blue. If we study not just the external forms of bones and organs but also their organic processes, we certainly can find a polarity between the nervous-sensory organization centered in the head and the limb-metabolic system. Between these lives the rhythmic system with its lung and heart activities, which always regulate and mediate between the two outer poles.

If we keep our images flexible and avoid becoming too simplistic by picturing the various organs in a static way—perhaps by making accurate, sharp illustrations—we are certain to be captivated by the multifarious relationships and constant interplay within these three members of the human being. If we look at the rhythmic activity of breathing, we see how during inhalation the thrust is led to the cerebrospinal fluid. While receiving these breathing rhythms, this fluid passes the vibrations right up into the brain fluid, which fills the various cavities of the brain. This "lapping" against the brain, so to speak, caused by rhythmic breathing, stimulates the human being to become active in the nervous-sensory organization. The rhythms caused by the process of breathing are constantly passed on via the vertebral canal into the brain fluid. Thus the stimuli activated by breathing constantly strive toward the region of the head.

If we look downward, we see how rhythmic breathing, in a certain sense, becomes more "pointed" and "excited" in the rhythm of the pulse and how the blood's circulation affects the metabolism with each exhalation—that is, while the brain and cerebrospinal fluid push downward. If we look with lively, artistically sensitive understanding at the breathing process and blood circulation, we can follow the effects of the pulsing blood upon both the nervous-sensory organization and the metabolic-limb system. We see how, on the one side, the processes of breathing and blood circulation reach up into the brain and the region of the head, and, on the other, in the opposite direction into the metabolic-limb system. If we gradually gain a living picture of the human being in this way, we can make real progress in our research. We can form concepts that accord fully with the nature of the human central system. Such concepts must not be so simple that we can make them into diagrams; schemes and diagrams are always problematic when it comes to understanding the constant, elemental weaving and flowing of human nature.

In the early days of our anthroposophic endeavors, when we were still operating within theosophical groups (permit me to mention this), we were faced again and again with all sorts of diagrams, generously equipped with plenty of data. Everything seemed to fit into elaborate, neat schematic ladders, high enough for anyone to climb to the highest regions of existence. Some members seemed to view such diagrammatic ladders as a kind of spiritual gym equipment, with which they hoped to reach Olympic heights; everything was neatly enclosed in boxes. These things made one's limbs twitch convulsively. They were hardly bearable for those who knew that, to get hold of our constantly mobile human nature in a suprasensory way, we must keep our ideas flexible and alive. Fixed habits of thinking made us want to flee. What matters is that, in our quest for real knowledge of the human being, we must keep our thinking and ideation flexible, and then we can advance yet another step.

Now, as we try to build mental images of how this rhythm between breathing and blood circulation becomes changed and transformed in the upper regions, we are led to the following idea, which I will sketch on the blackboard—not as a fixed scheme but merely as an indication (see drawing). Let the thick line represent the mental image of some sort of rope, which will help us imagine, roughly, the processes in our breathing and blood circulation. This is one way we can get hold of what exists beyond the physical blood in a much finer and imponderable substance of the "etheric nerves."

Now, using our imagination, we can go further by looking from the chest organization upward, feeling inwardly compelled, as it were, to "fray" our images and transform them into fine threads that interweave and form a delicate network. Thus we can grasp through mental images—turned upward and modified—something that occurs externally and physically. We find that we simply have to fray these thick cords into threads. Imagining this process, we gradually experience the white, fibrous brain substance under the grey matter. In our mental images we become as flexible as the very processes that pervade human nature.

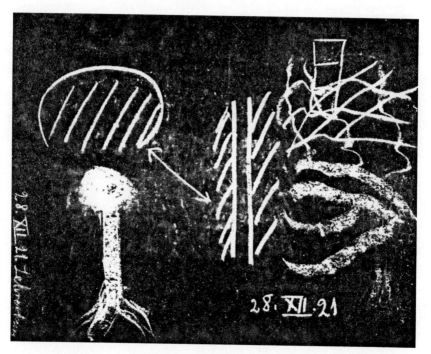

Directing your image making in the opposite direction, downward, you will find it impossible to split up or fray your mental images into fine threads to be woven into some sort of texture, as seen externally in the nervous system; such threads simply vanish, and you lose all traces of them. Otherwise, you would be led astray into forming images that no longer correspond to external reality. If you follow the brain as it continues downward into the spinal cord through the twelve dorsal vertebrae—through the lumbar and sacral vertebrae and so on—you find that the nerve substance, which now is white on the outside and grey inside, gradually dissolves toward the region of the metabolism. Somehow it becomes impossible to imagine the nerves continuing downward. We cannot get a true and comprehensive picture of the human being unless our images are able to transform; we must keep our images flexible.

If we look upward, our mental pictures change from those we find when looking down. We can recreate in images the flexibility of human nature, and this is the beginning of an artistic activity that eventually leads researchers to what we find externally in the physical human being. So we avoid the schism caused by looking first at the outer physical world and forming abstract concepts about it. Rather, we dive right into human nature. Our concepts become lively and stay in harmony with what actually exists in the human being. There is no other way to understand the true nature of the human being, and this is an essential prerequisite in the art of education.

To know the human being, we have to become inwardly flexible, and then we can correctly discover these three members of the human organization and how they work together to create a healthy equilibrium. We will learn to recognize how a disturbance of this equilibrium leads to all kinds of illnesses and to discriminate, in a living way, between the causes of health and illness in human life. If you look at the creation of the human being with the reverence it deserves, you will not oversimplify this intricate human organization by calling it a natural unity. And, when looking at the chest region, if you imagine coarse, rope-like shapes that become more refined as you approach the region of the head, until they fray into simple threads, you begin to reach the material reality. You find your imagination confirmed outwardly by the physical nerve fibers and by the way they interweave.

This is especially important when we consider the entire span of human life, because these three members of the human organization are interrelated in different ways during the various stages of life. During childhood the soul-spiritual element works into the physical organization in a completely different way than it does during the later stages. It is essential that we pay enough attention to these subtle changes. However, if we are willing to develop the kind of mental images indicated here, we gradually learn to broaden and deepen previous concepts.

It seem I offended many readers of my book *The Spiritual Guidance of the Individual and Humanity* when I pointed out that children have a kind of wisdom that adults no longer possess.[3] I certainly do not wish to belittle adult wisdom and abilities, but just imagine what would happen if, at an early stage when the brain and the other organs are still relatively unformed, our whole organization had to come about and form itself by relying solely on our personal wisdom. I am afraid we would turn out rather poorly. Certainly, children form their brains and other organs entirely subconsciously, but there is great wisdom at work nonetheless.

When you consider the whole of human life as described in previous lectures, you can recognize this wisdom, especially if you have a sense for what children's dreams can tell you. Adults tend to dismiss these dreams as childish nonsense, but if you can experience their underlying reality, children's dreams, so different from adult dreams, are in fact very interesting. Of course, children cannot express themselves clearly when speaking about their dreams, but there are ways of discovering what they are trying to say. And then we find that, through images of spirit beings in their dreams, children dimly experience the sublime powers of wisdom that help shape the brain and other physical organs. If we approach children's dreams with a reverence in tune with their experience, we see a pervading cosmic wisdom at work in them. From this point of view (forgive this somewhat offensive statement), children are much wiser, much smarter than adults. And when teachers enter the classroom,

---

3. *The Spiritual Guidance of the Individual and Humanity,* Hudson, NY: Anthroposophic Press, 1992.

they should be fully aware of this abundance of wisdom in the children. Teachers themselves have outgrown it, and what they have gained instead—knowledge of their own experience—cannot compare with it in the least.

Adult dreams have lost that quality; they carry everyday life into their dreams. I have spoken of this from a different perspective. When adults dream, they carry daytime wisdom into their life at night, where it affects them in return. But when children dream, sublime wisdom flows through them. Though unaware of what is happening, children nevertheless retain a dim awareness upon awaking. And, during the day, when they sit in school, they still have an indistinct sense of this cosmic wisdom, which they cannot find it in the teacher. Teachers, on the other hand, feel superior to children in terms of knowledge and wisdom. This is natural, of course, since otherwise they could not teach. Teachers are conscious of their own wisdom, and from this point of view, they certainly are superior. But this kind of wisdom is not as full and sublime as that of the child.

If we put into words what happens when a young child, pervaded by wisdom, meets the teacher, who has lost this primordial wisdom, the following image might emerge. The abstract knowledge that is typical of our times, and with which teachers have been closely linked for so many years of life, tends to make them into somewhat dry and pedantic adults. In some cases, their demeanor and outer appearance reveal these traits. Children, on the other hand, have retained the freshness and sprightliness that spring from spiritual wisdom.

Now, when teachers enter the classroom, children have to control their high spirits. Teachers feel that they are intelligent and that their students are ignorant. But in the subconscious realms of both teachers and students, a very different picture emerges. And if dreams were allowed to speak, the picture again would be quite different. Children, somewhere in their subconscious, feel how stupid the teacher is. And in their subconscious, teachers feel how wise the children are.

All this becomes a part of the classroom atmosphere and belongs to the imponderables that play a very important role in education. Because of this, children cannot help confronting their teachers with a certain arrogance, however slight, of which they remain completely unaware. Its innate attitude toward the teacher is one of amusement; they cannot help feeling this flow of wisdom pervading their own bodies and how little has survived in the teacher. Instinctively, children contrast their own wisdom with that of their teachers, who enter the classroom somewhat stiff and pedantic—the face grown morose from living so long with abstract intellectual concepts, the coat so heavy with the dust of libraries that it defies the clothes brush. Mild amusement is the uppermost feeling of a child at this sorry sight.

This is how the teacher is seen through the eyes of a child, however unaware the child may be. And we cannot help seeing a certain justification in this attitude. After all, such a reaction is a form of self-protection, preserving the child's state of health. A dream about teachers would hardly be an elevating experience for young students, who can still dream of the powers of wisdom that permeate their whole being.

In a teacher's subconscious regions, an opposite kind of feeling develops that is also very real, and it, too, belongs to the imponderables of the classroom. In the child, we can speak of dim awareness, but in the teacher, there lurks a subconscious desire. Though teachers will never admit this consciously, an inner yearning arises for the vital forces of wisdom that bless children. If psychoanalysts of the human soul were more aware of spiritual realities than is usually the case, they would quickly discover the important role that children's fresh, vital growth and other human forces play in a teacher's subconscious.

These are some of the invisible elements that pervade the classroom. And if you are able to look a little behind the scenes, you will find that children turn away from the teacher because of a certain disenchantment. They dimly sense an unspoken question: In this adult, who is my teacher, what became of all that flows through me? But in teachers, on the other hand, a subconscious longing begins to stir. Like vampires, they want to prey on these young souls. If you look a little closer, in many cases you can see how strongly this vampire-like urge works beneath an otherwise orderly appearance. Here lies the origin of various tendencies toward ill health in young children. One only needs to look with open eyes at the psychological disposition of some teachers to see how such tendencies can result from life in the classroom.

As teachers, we cannot overcome these harmful influences unless we are sustained by a knowledge of the human being that is imbued with love for humankind—knowledge both flexible and alive and in harmony with the human organism as I have described it. Only genuine love of humankind can overcome and balance the various forces in human nature that have become onesided. And such knowledge of the human being enables us to recognize not just the way human nature is expressed differently in various individuals, but also its characteristic changes through childhood, maturity, and old age. The three members of the human being have completely different working relationships during the three main stages of life, and each member must adapt accordingly.

We need to keep this in mind, especially when we make up the schedule. Obviously, we must cater to the whole being of a child—to the head as well as the limbs—and we must allow for the fact that, in each of the three members, processes that spring from the other two continue all the time. For example, metabolic processes are always occurring in the head.

If children have to sit still at their desks to do head work (more on this and classroom desks later), if their activities do not flow into their limbs and metabolism, we create an imbalance in them. We must balance this by letting the head relax—by allowing them to enjoy free movement later during gym lessons. If you are aware of the polar processes in the head and in the limbs and metabolism, you will appreciate the importance of providing the right changes in the schedule.

But if, after a boisterous gym lesson, we take our students back to the classroom to continue the lessons, what do we do then? You must realize that, while a person is engaged in limb activities that stimulate the metabolism, thoughts that were artificially planted in the head during previous years are no longer there. When children jump and run around and are active in the limbs and metabolism, all thoughts previously planted in the head simply fly away. But the forces that manifest only in children's dreams—the forces of suprasensory wisdom—now enter the head and claiming their place. If, after a movement lesson, we take the children back to the classroom to replace those forces with something else that must appear inferior to their subconscious minds, a mood of resentment will make itself felt in the class. During the previous lesson, sensory and, above all, suprasensory forces have been affecting the children. The students may not appear unwilling externally, but an inner resentment is certainly present. By resuming ordinary lessons right after a movement lesson, we go against the child's nature and, by doing so, we implant the potential seeds of illness in children. According to a physiologist, this is a fact that has been known for a long time. I have explained this from an anthroposophic perspective to show you how much it is up to teachers to nurture the health of children, provided they have gained the right knowledge of the human being. Naturally, if we approach this in the wrong way, we can, in fact, plant all sorts of illnesses in children, and we must always be fully aware of this.

As you may have noticed by now, I do not glorify ordinary worldly wisdom, which is so highly prized these days. That sort of wisdom hardly suffices for shaping the inner organs of young people for their coming years. If we have not become stiff in our whole being by the time we mature, the knowledge we have impressed into our minds through naturalistic and intellectual concepts—which is thrown back as memory pictures—all that would eventually flow down into the rest of our organism. However absurd this may sound, a person would become ill if what belongs in the head under ordinary conditions were to flow down into limb and metabolic regions. The head forces act like poison when they enter the lower spheres. Brain wisdom, in fact, becomes a kind of poison as soon as it enters the wrong sphere, or at least when it reaches the metabolism. The only way we can live with our brain knowledge—and I use this term concretely and not as a moral judgment—is by preventing this poison from entering our metabolic and limb system, since it would have a devastating effect there.

But children are not protected by the stiffness of adults. If we press our kind of knowledge into children, our concepts can invade and poison their metabolic and limb system. You can see how important it is to recognize, from practical experience, how much head knowledge we can expect children to absorb without exposing them to the dangers of being poisoned in the metabolic-limb organization.

So it is in teachers' hands to promote either health or illness in children. If teachers insist on making students smart intellectually according to modern standards, if they crams children's heads with all sorts of intellectuality, they prevent subconscious forces of wisdom from permeating those children. Cosmic wisdom, on the other hand, is immediately set in motion when children run around and move more or less rhythmically. Because of its unique position between head and limb-metabolism, rhythmic activity brings about physical unity with the cosmic forces of wisdom. Herbert Spencer was quite correct when he spoke of the negative effects of a monastic education aimed at making the young excel intellectually. He pointed out that in later years those scholars would be unable to use their intellectual prowess, because during their school years they had been impregnated with the seeds of all sorts of illnesses.

These matters cannot be weighed by some special scales. They are revealed only to an open mind and to the kind of flexible thinking achieved through anthroposophic training; this kind of thinking must stay in touch with practical life.

So much for the importance of teachers getting to know the fundamentals that govern health and illness in human beings. Here it must be emphasized again that, to avoid becoming trapped by external criteria and fixed concepts, you must learn to recognize the ever-changing processes of human nature, which always tend toward either health or illness. Teachers will encounter these things in their classes, and they must learn to deal with them correctly. We will go into more detail when we focus on the changing stages of the child and the growing human being.

Children before
the Seventh Year

December 29, 1921

Anyone called on to look after a very young child—either as a parent or in any other capacity of child care—will experience the great responsibility this task involves. Such people feel morally obligated to lay the best foundations for the child's future development. Therefore it grieves me deeply that our Waldorf school in Stuttgart can accept only children who have reached the official school age, and it would give me the greatest satisfaction if we could take in the younger children as well.[1] In addition to other difficulties, our goal of opening a nursery has been thwarted by a lack of funds, as happened with so many other anthroposophic activities. This continual shortage of money leaves us with at least the hope that, if we can win support from the general public, we will eventually be able to build a nursery class as an integral part of our Waldorf school.

Very young children are the least accessible to us. The gates to the soul life are absolutely closed to the outer world, and outer influences cannot touch it. Those who take care of infants of this age are powerless when they struggle and cry; these children do what they want. Thus, observant adults must accept the fact that the will of

---

1. A child had to be five years old to attend school. The Waldorf school opened a kindergarten at Easter 1926.

children is beyond their control—even during later stages and occasionally the latest stages of life.

You may know that early in 1894, well before publishing other anthroposophic works, I published *Die Philosophie der Freiheit* [*Intuitive Thinking As a Spiritual Path*]. This book was intended to give the world a true assessment of the human quality that develops, within the social context, the impulse toward individual freedom. If you accept its message—the matter of freedom, on the one hand, and destiny, on the other—you can see that it is relevant even to a baby.

If you listen to what lives in the human heart, you find that real human happiness on earth depends on the awareness of human freedom, an appreciation of human values, and a feeling for human dignity. Anthroposophy shows us that—apart from what a person may have developed even before birth or conception while still in the spiritual world and apart from what one will meet again after death—the very purpose of earthly incarnation involves enlivening the impulse toward freedom. This impulse depends completely on plunging into an earthly body. This freedom can be realized only during physical incarnation; we can attain freedom only while living on earth, and when we enter other worlds, we can take with us only the degree of freedom we have attained here on earth.

If you approach young children with such feelings (and feelings are the most potent source for those engaged in the art of education), this question will always be present in your mind as you take charge of an infant: What must I do to enable this child to develop the fullest consciousness of human freedom at maturity? And with this question, a new truth begins to dawn. The outer conditions of life are already clearly pointing at it, and, through anthroposophic insight, it can be understood with inner certainty. It is the fact that, despite one's freedom, each person has a destiny, or to use the Eastern term, karma.

Let us imagine that, later in life, a man meets a person he has known before, and that this person has a profound influence on the life of this man. Perhaps such people might even begin a partnership for life. At first it may seem to them as if their meeting were simply chance. But when they look back over the years of their lives—even with no knowledge of spiritual science—this man may well discover the strange fact that, during the years before this meeting, he had unconsciously taken numerous steps that eventually led to this other person. Though at first it appeared to be mere chance, hindsight revealed an inherent pattern and underlying plan. Looking back over his life, Goethe's old friend Nobel spoke these meaningful words from the depths of his soul: "If, in later years, we survey our early life, everything seems to fall into a definite pattern; everything fits together." Since our will is woven into all our actions, we can see everywhere how destiny confronts us in the events of life. One could quote many others who, through observing ordinary life, reached the same conclusion. When we look at life's external events, we find confirmation of the hidden truths of karma.

Anyone in charge of young children—especially those who work in children's homes—who is aware of the activity of destiny, must ask, Have I been specifically chosen for the important task of guiding and educating these children? And other questions follow: What must I do to eliminate as far as possible my personal self, so I can leave those in my care unburdened by my subjective nature? How do I act so I do not interfere with a child's destiny? And, above all, How can I best educate a child toward human freedom? If you come to understand what happens in a child between birth and the change of teeth—during the first seven years—you will realize how vulnerable young children are and how deeply we can affect their being (I will speak later about the period of embryonic development). The change of teeth represents a decisive turning point in the life of children. Close observation reveals that, after the seventh year, an entirely new interrelationship emerges between the child's thinking, feeling, and willing.

We have become accustomed to applying certain concepts gained from observing physical processes to the life of the human being. For instance, in natural processes, when we notice the sudden emergence of heat that was imperceptible in a previous state and had not been introduced externally, we say that latent heat is being released. Just as latent heat can be set free by material processes, similarly, soul and spirit forces are set free after the change of teeth, forces that have thus far been bound up with the organism and instrumental for its growth. Freed from processes of growth and nourishment, however, these forces go to work in the child's soul; they are transformed into soul forces.

Natural science today forms abstract concepts about the relationship between body and soul; theories are invented to explain the effects of one on the other. One speaks of a psycho-physical parallelism and so on. Instead of making exact observations, one philosophizes. But all this leads nowhere. If you want to fathom the secrets of human nature, you have to observe it with the same precision used to observe the phenomena of outer nature. Then you will discover that, after approximately the seventh year, forces that were engaged in building the physical organism of the child are now transformed into soul forces that will determine a child's relationship to the outer world.

If we wish to find out what the soul of a child is like between birth and the seventh year, we must observe the child's development from the seventh year on. Then, in the child's soul, we can see the very same forces that were active in the physical organization. And we will find that the hidden, organic activity that molds and shapes the child's brain and the rest of the organism has a very special significance. Through birth, or conception, children carry into their physical organization what they brought from the worlds of soul and spirit. When children are fully engaged in building up the physical organs in this way, they must be left free to do so, and consequently the doors leading to the outer world remain closed. It is essential that we refrain from interfering in our clumsy ways with these inner activities in children, because they are doing what they have to do and are thus inaccessible to outer will forces.

We must also realize, however, that despite the preoccupation of children with their processes of growth, everything we do around them nevertheless makes deep and distinct impressions on them. I will go into further detail later, but we must not forget that everything at work within the child's soul after the seventh year was directly involved in the process of building organs up to that age. This means that until the seventh year, the impressions coming from the outer world directly affect their physical constitution—the lungs, stomach, liver, and other organs. In children at this age, the soul has not yet become free of the physical organization, where it is still actively engaged. Because of this, all of the impressions they receive from us through our general conduct have a decisive effect on their future constitution of health or illness.

You came expecting to learn something about our educational principles, but it is the practical application of these principles that is most important. What really matters in education are the mood and soul attitude that teachers carry in their hearts toward the human being. We cannot truly serve the art of education unless we approach the growing human being with real insight. One could even say that teachers are free to approach subjects in their own individual ways, since, in any event, they must prepare their subject material according to what they have learned from life. The important thing is that teachers each carry within themselves a true picture of the human being; if this picture is present to their inner eyes, they will do the right thing, although outwardly each teacher may act in very different ways.

I visited parallel classes as the spiritual guide of the Waldorf school (the large numbers already require parallel classes), and when I saw how the teachers each treat the same subject in very individual ways, I never object or insist that they all follow the same set courses. Even when two versions of the same subject appear contradictory externally, each may nevertheless be correct in its own way. In fact, if one teacher were to copy another, the results could be entirely wrong. There is a good reason that our school is called the "Free Waldorf School." This is not just because of our independence from the state system, but the name very much reflects the atmosphere of freedom that pervades its entire makeup.

During the previous lecture I pointed out that a suprasensory contemplation of the human being will reveal to us—apart from the physical body—another, finer body that we call the ether body, or body of formative forces. This ether body provides not just the forces that sustain nourishment and growth; it is also the source of memory faculties and the ability to create mental images and ideas. It does not become an independent entity until the change of teeth, and its birth is similar to the way the physical body is born from one's mother. This means that, until the change of teeth, the forces of the ether body work entirely in the processes of a child's organic growth, whereas after that time—while still remaining active in this realm to a great extent—those forces partially withdraw from those activities. The released forces of the ether body then begin to work in the soul realm of mental images and memory, as well as in many other nuances of a child's soul life.

The change of teeth is a unique event. The forces needed to push out the second teeth existed prior to this event, but now they are no longer needed. Once the second teeth have appeared, this particular activity of the ether body becomes redundant. The final activity of pushing out the second teeth is an external manifestation of the sort of activity that is happening within a child's organism. At the end of the first seven-year period, most of these ether forces are released to flow into a child's soul and spiritual nature.

One can recognize these seven-year periods throughout the entire human life, and each again can be seen in three clearly differentiated shorter periods. If we observe the gradual withdrawal of some of these ether forces until approximately the seventh year, we see how during the first two and a half years after physical birth the ether body frees itself from the head region; in the next two and a half years, it frees itself from the chest region; and finally, until the change of teeth, it frees itself from the child's metabolic-limb system. Thus we see three phases in the gradual withdrawal of ether forces. And we clearly recognize how, while the ether body is still connected with the head region, a child rejects any intentional influence coming from outside.

What children learn during this first two-and-a-half-year period is extremely important for their whole life. They do so through an incoming activity and from what they have brought with them from prenatal existence. Just consider how children learn to speak and walk during this first short period. These are two human faculties that are closely connected with maintaining self-confidence, both from a personal and a social point of view. These two important faculties are developed while the ether body is still engaged in shaping the brain and radiating into the rest of the organism. If these ether forces radiate too strongly into the organism and disturb the infant's delicate processes of metabolism, breathing, and blood circulation—if they become too powerful within a baby's organism—scarlet fever and similar childhood illnesses may occur even at this young age. Basically, because of all this activity within children at this stage, they remain inaccessible to conscious approaches directed by the will and demands from the outside. They want to be left to work on their own organism.

Being inaccessible to the outer world during the first two and a half years is one significant factor. Another is the fact that children have a fine, instinctive perception for everything going on around them, especially what is happening in people with whom they have established a certain rapport. Anyone caring for such a child naturally belongs to this category. I am not speaking of a child's ability to use the senses as an older person does. It is not a matter of what children see with their eyes, but a general perception of the most intimate kind that takes in what is happening in their surroundings. This perception, however, excludes anything that seeks to impose itself from outside, against which children will defend themselves instinctively during those first two and a half years.

To get a better understanding of children's susceptibility to the outer world when their sensory perceptions are still deeply immersed in feeling, it may help to look at animals, the creatures immediately below the human being, because they show a similar, acute sensitivity toward the outer world. I am not contradicting what I said about senility in a previous lecture; one must simply observe accurately. Animals are especially sensitive to their surroundings. I do not know whether those who have come from England or other European countries have ever heard of the horses that, a few years before the war, created a sensation by appearing to do simple mathematical calculations. In Berlin, there was the famous horse of Mr. von Osten, and in Elberfeld there were several horses that could do numeric calculations. Well, I cannot say anything about the Elberfeld horses, but I did make the acquaintance of von Osten's horse in Berlin, and I was able to observe the close relationship between this horse and its master. It is true that the horse stamped its legs—three times three is nine—which, for a horse, is a very respectable achievement.

All kinds of theories were advanced to explain the horse's reactions to questions from von Osten. There was one university lecturer—a most erudite man—who even wrote a whole book on this horse. He wrote, "Of course the horse cannot calculate, but whenever Mister von Osten says, 'Three times three,' he accompanies his words by barely noticeable facial expressions. He sort of mimes, and when he pronounces the word *nine,* the horse is capable of observing these facial expressions and stamps accordingly." His was certainly a learned treatise. He continued, "I myself was unable to detect the miming on von Osten's face and therefore I cannot guarantee that my theory is correct. But it must have been there and the horse was able to observe it." It seems to me that the author merely states that he, a university lecturer, considered the horse more capable of observation than he was himself. In my opinion, the crucial point was von Osten's procedure, for he had large pockets filled with sweets that he shoved into the horse's mouth, thus maintaining an uninterrupted flow of sensation and gratification. The result was an intimate relationship between master and horse. Everything was immersed in a feeling of sympathy, which made the horse extremely receptive, in keeping with its animal nature, to all that came from its master, even his thoughts and shades of feeling, but hardly the play of mysterious expressions on his face. The processes of calculation going on in von Osten's mind were transferred to the horse via the taste of sweetness. This phenomenon does not become any less interesting when interpreted this way, but it can teach us a great deal about the relationship of living beings. It cannot be explained hypothetically by observing the facial expressions a horse can detect, though not a university lecturer.

During the first two and a half years, children have a similar rapport with the mother or with others they are closely connected with as long as their attitude and conduct make this possible. Then children become perfect mimics and imitators. This imposes a moral duty on adults to be worthy of such imitation, which is far less comfortable then exerting one's will on children. Children take in all that we do, such as the ways we act and move. They are equally susceptible to our feelings and thoughts. They imitate us, and even if this is not outwardly noticeable, they nevertheless do this by developing tendencies for imitation that, through their organic soul forces, they press down into the physical organism. Therefore, education during these first two and a half years should be confined to the self-education of the adults in charge, who should think, feel, and act in a way that, when perceived by children, will cause them no harm. Fundamentally, the stage of imitation continues until the change of teeth, and thus children will be strongly influenced by their environment later on as well.

The following example may demonstrate this. Two disconsolate parents once came to me, saying, "Our child has always been good, but now she has stolen money." Was this really true? At a superficial glance, yes, for she had taken money out of the cupboard where it was always kept by her mother. The child then bought sweets with the money and even gave some to other children. I reassured the parents that their child had not stolen at all, but that she had merely imitated her mother, who regularly took money from the cupboard to buy things. There was never any intention of stealing; this concept did not yet exist in the child's mind. But children are imitators and will do what mother does. If we wish to avoid confusion, it is up to adults to realize this and act differently in front of the children.

Neither will children learn to walk through our efforts to make them stand and do all sorts of movements. Such instruction belongs in gym much later on. If we intervene by making children stand and walk prematurely, we may do irreparable damage to the nerve processes, which may persist for their whole life. If children see adults in an upright position, as imitator they try to raise themselves to the same position when the time comes. We must always see the human being during the initial stages as an imitator and arrange our child rearing accordingly.

This can certainly be very trying at times, and we all know that there are babies who seem to be yelling all day and, apart from the ear-splitting noise, inflict all kinds of other provocations on the adult. True, there are situations that have to be dealt with, even drastically, to avoid serious damage by a child. But such measures do not really belong to the field of education. Admittedly, it is hard to put up with a screaming child, but when we behave as described, our conduct gradually sinks into the deeper layers of a child's soul and spiritual forces (which are still closely connected to organic processes) and eventually brings about more positive results.

If we observe small children without preconceived ideas, we find that their screaming and other unpleasant features come from their physical organization. Although the inherent forces in the behavior of intense crying remain with the child, the habit of crying will gradually pass. Such forces are very intense. If we influence the child correctly by setting the proper example and acting morally, the forces behind a baby's crying will reveal themselves as intensely moral forces in later life. A strong morality later in adult life is an expression of those same forces that lived in the intense crying of a young child. On the other hand, if those close to a child have an immoral attitude—even if only in thoughts—these forces will reappear later as intensely immoral forces. And we must be careful not to harm the development of children while they are learning to speak. This easily happens when we make them say words we choose; this, too, is an imposition of our will on the child. It is best to speak naturally in front of children (as long as we speak in a moral way) so that they have opportunities to hear us. In this way, children find their own way into language.

Now you can appreciate the real point of what has been said so far—that we must not be tempted by a false kind of instinct to make baby talk for the child's benefit. This is not an instinct but something we may have acquired through misguided customs. Nurses or others dealing with young children should never speak to them in an artificial or childish way. We really do a great wrong when we change our normal way of speaking to "suit" a child, for children always want to imitate us as we really are, not as we pretend to be. They reject anything that approaches them as an expression of another person's will, such as childish and naive baby talk. Children have to put up with it, but they have a deep inner resentment toward such an approach. The effects of such well-intended folly is so far-reaching that it may come to light in later years as a weakened digestion. When an older person is diagnosed as having a weak digestion, it might be nothing but the result of the wrong approach by an over-zealous but misguided nurse during that person's early childhood.

These are the main points regarding the first third of the first seven-year period, and they need to be kept in mind.

At the age of two and a half, the head organization in children is developed far enough so that the forces of the ether body that have been working on it may be released. This gradual withdrawal continues into the area of the chest until about the fifth year, when breathing and blood circulation have also reached a certain stage of completion. Thus, by the time children learn to speak and walk, the formative forces released from the head (now acting now as soul and spiritual forces) join those being released in the chest region. This change can be recognized externally by the emergence of an exceptionally vivid memory and wonderful imagination, which children develop between two and a half and five. However, you must take great care when children develop these two faculties, since they are instrumental in building the soul. Children continue to live by imitation, and therefore we should not attempt to make them remember things we choose. At this stage it is best to leave the evolving forces of memory alone, allowing children to remember whatever they please. We should never give them memory exercises of any kind, otherwise, through ignorance, we might be responsible for consequences we can see only when viewing the entire course of human life.

Sometimes we meet people who, around the age of forty or later, complain of shooting pains or rheumatism. This may certainly have various causes, but if we carry our research far enough, we may find that the rheumatism was caused by a premature overloading of the memory during early childhood. The pattern of life is indeed very complex, and only by trying to recognize its many hidden links can we engender the love that is the true basis of growing human beings.

Whatever one's attitude may be, as educators we must respond to the imagination and fantasy of children, which tries to express itself outwardly when they play with toys or join in games with other children. The urge to play between the ages of two and a half and five is really just the externalized activity of a child's power of fantasy. And if we have the necessary ability of observation for such matters, we can foretell a great deal about the future soul life of children merely by watching them play. The way young children play provides a clear indication of their potential gifts and faculties in later life. The most important thing now is to meet their inborn urge to play with the right toys. People in the past responded to this need according to their own particular understanding.

Perhaps this also happened in the West, but at one time a regular epidemic spread throughout Central Europe of giving children boxes of building bricks, especially at Christmas. From separate cubic and quadrilateral stones, children were expected to build miniature architectural monstrosities. This sort of thing has a far-reaching effect on the development of imagination in children, since it leads to an atomistic, materialistic attitude—a mentality that always wants to put bits and pieces together to form a whole. In dealing with practical life, it is far better to give full freedom to children's flexible and living powers of imagination than to nurture intellectual capacities that, in turn, encourage the atomistic nature of modern thinking. Imagination in children represents the very forces that have just liberated themselves from performing similar creative work within the physical formation of the brain. This is why we must avoid, as much as possible, forcing these powers of imagination into rigid, finished forms.

Imagine two nurses who are looking after a child between two and a half and five years of age. One of them—she may be very fond of the little girl in her charge—gives her a "beautiful" doll, one that has not only painted cheeks and real hair but eyes that close and a moveable head. I believe there are dolls that can even speak. Well, she gives this doll to the little girl, but since it is finished in every detail, there is nothing left for the child's imagination to create, and her yearning for creative flexibility remains unsatisfied. It is as if its forces of imagination were put into a straitjacket. The other nurse, who has a little more understanding for the inner needs of the child, takes an old piece of cloth that is of no use for anything else. She winds a thread around its upper end until something resembling a head appears. She may even ask the little girl to paint two black dots on the face or perhaps more, for the eyes, nose, and mouth. Now, because the child's imagination is stimulated, because she can create instead of having to put up with fixed and finished forms, the child experiences a far more lively and intimate response than she does toward the so-called beautiful doll. Toys, as much as possible, should leave the power of fantasy free in children. And since intellect is not the same as fantasy or imagination, the activity of assembling many parts is really not in harmony with the type of fantasy that is characteristic of children at this age.

Anything that evokes an inner feeling of liveliness and flexibility is always suitable for young children. For example, there are children's books with cut-outs and nicely colored figures that can be moved by pulling strings attached below, so they will do all kinds of things, such as embracing or thrashing each other. These always stimulate children to invent whole stories, and thus they are very wholesome objects of play. Similarly, games with other children should not be too formal but should leave plenty of scope for children's imagination.

All these suggestions spring from a knowledge of the human being, based on reality and allowing educators to acquire the necessary understanding, especially in terms of the practical side of life.

When children approach the fifth year, the ether forces of the body—which have thus far been building the breathing and the blood circulation—now become available for other activities. Likewise, up to the change of teeth, ether forces will struggle free and, after completing their task within the metabolic-limb system, become redundant. At that time, new spiritual soul forces gradually awaken and emerge fully after the seventh year (we will study this in more detail later). However, these forces already shine with a dawning light in this third and final period, which concludes the first seven-year period of human life.

When ether forces from the chest area reappear as soul and spiritual forces, children are becoming amenable to exhortations and to a sense of authority. Previously, unable to understand what they should or should not do, they could only imitate, but now, little by little, they begin to listen to and believe what adults say. Only toward the fifth year is it possible to awaken a sense of right and wrong in children. We can educate children correctly only by realizing that, during this first seven-year period until the change of teeth, children live by imitation, and only gradually do they develop imagination and memory and a first belief in what adults say.

Faith in the adult induces a feeling of authority, especially for teachers with whom children have a very close relationship. However, at this stage, children are too young for any formal education. It pains me to know that the sixth year has been fixed as the official school age. Children should not enter elementary school before their seventh year. I was always glad to hear, therefore (and I don't mind if you consider this uncivilized), that the children of some anthroposophists had no knowledge of writing and reading, even at the age of eight. Accomplishments that come with forces that are available later on should never be forced into an earlier stage, unless we are prepared to ruin the physical organism.

In the next few days I will show you how we try to treat our children without inflicting harm on them when they enter the Waldorf school. Tomorrow I will begin by introducing you to the Waldorf school, though only by speaking of it.

THE WALDORF SCHOOL

December 30, 1921

Looking back at the past several meetings of this conference, I feel it is necessary to digress a little from our planned program and tell you something about the practical aspects of Waldorf education. From what you have heard so far, you may have gathered that the key to this form of education, both in its curriculum and in its methods, is the understanding of the human constitution of body, soul, and spirit as it develops throughout life. In order to follow this principle, it was necessary to take a new look at education in general, with the result that the Waldorf school is, in many ways, run very differently from traditional schools.

The first point we had to consider was how to make the most of the available time for teaching, especially in regard to the development of the student's soul life. The usual practice is to split up the available time into many separate lessons, but this method does not bring enough depth and focus to the various subjects. For example, suppose you want to bring something to your students that will have lasting value for them, something they can take into later life. I will use the example of a subject taught in almost every school: history. Imagine that you want to introduce the era of Queen Elizabeth I, including the main events and people usually described to children. A teacher could do this by talking about the facts of that historical period in history lessons, and it might take, say, half a year. But you can also do this in a different way. After methodical preparation at home, a teacher can cultivate within a fine feeling for the salient facts, which then become a kind of framework for this period. The teacher allows these to work upon the soul, thus enabling the students to remember them without much difficulty. All additional material will then fall into place more or less naturally. If one masters the subject in this way, we can say without exaggerating that, in only three to four lessons, it is quite possible to give students something that might otherwise take half a year, and even in greater depth so that the students retain a lasting impression of the subject.

If you do a detailed survey of all that children are supposed to learn in school today, you will agree with the method I just described. In our present state of civilization, what our children are supposed to learn by the age of fourteen is such an accumulation of material that it is really beyond their capacity to absorb it all. No school is truly successful in teaching this much, but this fact is usually ignored. People merely pretend that the present system works, and the curricula are set accordingly.

The aim of Waldorf education is to arrange all of the teaching so that within the shortest possible time the maximum amount of material can be presented to students by the simplest means possible. This helps children retain an overall view of their subjects—not so much intellectually, but very much in their feeling life.

It is obvious that such a method makes tremendous demands on teachers. I am convinced that, if teachers apply this method (which I would call a form of teaching based on "soul economy"), they will have to spend at least two or three hours of concentrated preparation for each half hour they teach. And they must be willing to do this if they want to avoid harming their students. Such preparation may not always be practical or possible, but if the teacher wants to succeed in carrying a comprehensive and living presentation of the subject into the classroom, such private preparation is fundamental. It does make great demands on teachers, but such obligations are intrinsic to this calling and must be accepted in the best way possible.

Before we could practice this basic educational principle in our newly established Waldorf school, it was necessary to create a suitable curriculum and a schedule. Today I would like to outline this curriculum and its application, but without going into details, since this will be our task during the coming days.

And so, having prepared themselves as just described, the teachers enter the school in the morning. The students arrive a little earlier in the summer, at eight o'clock, and a little later in the winter. When they assemble in their classrooms, the teachers bring them together by saying a morning verse in chorus with the whole class. This verse, which could also be sung, embraces both a general human and a religious element, and it unites the students in a mood of prayer. It may be followed by a genuine prayer. In our "free" Waldorf school, such details are left entirely up to each teacher.

Then begins our so-called main lesson, which lasts nearly two hours; in traditional schedules, these are often broken up into smaller periods. But the principle of soul economy in teaching makes it necessary to alter the conventional schedule. Thus, during the first two hours of the morning, students are taught the same subject in "block" periods, each lasting four to six weeks. It is left to the class teacher to introduce a short break during the main lesson, which is essential in the younger classes. In this way, subjects like geography or arithmetic are taught for four to six weeks at a time. After that, another main lesson subject is studied, again for a block period, rather than as shorter lessons given at regular intervals through the year.

Thus one introduces the various main lesson subjects according to the principles we agreed on, which include a carefully planned economy of the children's soul life. At all costs, one must avoid too much stress on the mind and soul of the child. Children should never feel that lessons are too difficult; on the contrary, there should be a longing in the child to keep moving from one step to the next. Students should never experience an arbitrary break in a subject; one thing should always lead to another. During the four to six weeks of a main lesson block, the class teacher will always try to present the material as a complete chapter—an artistic whole—that children can take into later life. And it goes without saying that, toward the end of the school year before the approaching summer holidays, all the main lesson subjects taught during the year should be woven together into a short, artistic recapitulation.

Just as we provide children with clothing with enough room for their limbs to grow freely, as teachers we should respond to their inner needs ·by giving them material not just for their present stage but broad enough for further expansion. If we give children fixed and finished concepts, we do not allow for inner growth and maturing. Therefore all the concepts we introduce, all the feelings we invoke, and all will impulses we give must be treated with the same care and foresight we use to clothe our children. We should not expect them to remember abstract definitions for the rest of their lives. At the age of forty-five, your little finger will not be the same as it was when you were eight, and likewise, concepts introduced at the age of eight should not remain unchanged by the time students reach the age of forty-five. We must approach the child's organism so that the various members can grow and expand. We must not clothe our material in fixed and stiff forms so that, when our students reach forty-five, they remember it exactly as it was presented in their eighth or ninth year. This, however, is possible only if we present our subject with what I call "soul economy." During the remaining hours of the morning, the other lessons are taught, and here foreign languages play the most important part. They are introduced in grade one, when the children first enter the Waldorf school in their sixth and seventh year. Foreign languages are presented so that the children can really go into them, which means that, while teaching a language, the teacher tries to avoid using the children's native language.

The foreign language teacher naturally has to take into account that the students are older than they were when they first learned their own language and will arrange the lessons accordingly. This is essential to keep in harmony with the student's age and development. The children should be able to get into the language so that they do not inwardly translate from their native tongue into the foreign language whenever they want to say something. Jumping from one language to the other should be avoided at all costs. If, for example, you want to introduce a particular word such as *table* or *window,* you would not mention the corresponding word in the child's native language but indicate the object while saying the word clearly. Thus children learn the new language directly before learning to translate words, which might not be desirable at all. We have found that, during the early stages, if we avoid the usual grammar and all that this entails, children find their way into a new language in a natural and living way. More details will be given when we speak about the various ages, but for now I wanted to give you a general picture of the practical arrangements in the Waldorf school.

Another very important subject for this stage is handwork, which includes several crafts. Because the Waldorf school is coeducational, boys and girls share these lessons, and it is indeed a heartwarming sight to see the young boys and girls busy together engaged in knitting, crocheting, and similar activities. Experience shows that, although boys have a different relationship to knitting than do girls, they enjoy it and benefit from such activity. Working together this way has certainly helped in the general development of all the students. In craft lessons that involve heavier physical work, girls also participate fully. This is the way manual skills are developed and nurtured in our school.

Another subject taught during morning sessions could be called "worldview." Please understand that a Waldorf school— or any school that might spring from the anthroposophic movement—would never wish to teach anthroposophy as it exists today. I would consider this the worst thing we could do. Anthroposophy in its present form is a subject for adults and, as you can see from the color of their hair, often quite mature adults. Consequently, spiritual science is presented through literature and word of mouth in a form appropriate only to adults. I should consider the presentation to students of anything from my books *Theosophy* or *How to Know Higher Worlds* the worst possible use of this material; it simply must not happen. If we taught such material, which is totally unsuitable for schoolchildren (forgive a somewhat trivial expression used in German), we would make them want "to jump out of their skin." Naturally, in class lessons they would have to submit to whatever the teacher brings, but inwardly they would experience such an urge. Anthroposophy as such is not to be taught in a Waldorf school. It's important that spiritual science does not become mere theory or a worldview based on certain ideas; rather, it should become a way of life, involving the entire human being. Thus, when teachers who are anthroposophists enter school, they should have developed themselves so that they are multifaceted and skillful in the art of education. And it is this achievement that is important, not any desire to bring anthroposophy to your students.

Waldorf education is meant to be pragmatic. It is meant to be a place where anthroposophic knowledge is applied in a practical way. If you have made such a worldview your own and linked it to practical life, you will not become theoretical and alienated from life but a skilled and capable person. I do not mean to say that all members of the anthroposophic movement have actually reached these goals—far from it. I happen to know that there are still some men among our members who cannot even sew on a trouser button that fell off. And no one suffering from such a shortcoming could be considered a full human being. Above all, there are still members who do not fully accept the contention that you cannot be a real philosopher if you cannot apply your hands to anything—such as repairing your shoes—if the need arises. This may sound a bit exaggerated, but I hope you know what I am trying to say.

Those who must deal with theoretical work should place themselves within practical life even more firmly than those who happen to be tailors, cobblers, or engineers. In my opinion, imparting theoretical knowledge is acceptable only when the other person is well versed in the practical matters of life; otherwise, such ideas remain alien to life. By approaching the classroom through anthroposophic knowledge, teachers as artists should develop the ability to find the right solutions to the needs of the children. If teachers carry such an attitude into the classroom, together with the fruits of their endeavors, they will also be guided in particular situations by a sound pedagogical instinct. This, however, is seldom the case in the conventional education today.

Please do not mistake these remarks as criticism against any teachers. Those who belong to the teaching profession will be the first to experience the truth of what has been said. In their own limitations, they may well feel they are the victims of prevailing conditions. The mere fact that they themselves had to suffer the martyrdom of a high school education may be enough to prevent them from breaking through many great hindrances. The most important thing while teaching is the ability to meet constantly changing classroom situations that arise from the immediate responses of one's students. But who in this wide world trains teachers to do that? Are they not trained to decide ahead of time what they will teach? This often gives me the impression that children are not considered at all during educational deliberations. Such an attitude is like turning students into papier-mâché masks as they enter school, so that teachers can deal with masks instead of real children.

As mentioned before, it is not our goal to teach ideology in the Waldorf school, though such a thought might easily occur to people when hearing that anthroposophists have established a new school. Our goal is to carry our understanding gained through spiritual science right into practical teaching.

This is why I was willing to hand over the responsibility for religion lessons to those who represent the various religions. Religion, after all, is at the very core of a person's worldview. Consequently, in our Waldorf school, a Roman Catholic priest was asked to give Roman Catholic religion lessons to students of that denomination, and a Protestant minister teaches Protestant religion lessons. When this decision was made, we were not afraid that we would be unable to balance any outer influence brought into the school by these priests, influence that might not be in harmony with what we were trying to do. But then a somewhat unexpected situation arose. When our friend Emil Molt established the Waldorf school, most of our students were from the homes of workers at his factory.[1] Among them were many children whose parents are atheists, and if they had been

1. Emil Molt (1876–1936), industrialist who initiated the first Waldorf school for his worker's children in Stuttgart.

sent to another school, they would not have received religious instruction at all. As such things often happen when dealing with children and parents, gradually these children also wanted to receive some form of religion lessons. And this is how our free, nondenominational, religion lessons came about. These were given by our own teachers, just as the other religious lessons were given by ministers. The teachers were recognized by us as religious teachers in the Waldorf curriculum. Thus, anthroposophic religious lessons were introduced in our school. These lessons have come to mean a great deal to many of our students, especially the factory workers' children.

However, all this brought specific problems in its wake, because anthroposophy is for adults. If, therefore, teachers want to bring the right material into anthroposophic religious lessons, they must recreate it fresh, and this is no easy task. It means reshaping and transforming anthroposophic material to make it suitable for the various age groups. In fact, this task of changing a modern philosophy to suit young people occupies us a great deal. It means working deeply on fundamental issues, such as how the use of certain symbols might affect students, or how one deals with the imponderables inherent in such a situation. We will speak more about this later on.

I am sure you can appreciate that one has to make all kinds of compromises in a school that tries to base its curriculum on the needs of growing children in the light of a spiritual scientific knowledge of the human being. Today it would be quite impossible to teach children according to abstract educational ideas, subsequently called the "principles of Waldorf education." The result of such a misguided approach would be that our graduates would be unable to find their way into life. It is too easy to criticize life today. Most people meet unpleasant aspects of life every day and we are easily tempted to make clever suggestions about how to put the world in order. But it completely inappropriate to educate children so that,

when they leave school to enter life, they can only criticize the sense-
lessness of what they find. However imperfect life may be according
to abstract reason, we must nevertheless be able to play our full part
in it. Waldorf students—who have probably been treated more as
individuals than is usually the case—have to be sent out into life;
otherwise, having a Waldorf school makes no sense at all. Students
must not become estranged from contemporary life to the extent
that they can only criticize what they meet outside.

This I can only touch on here. From the very beginning, we
had to make the most varied compromises, even in our curriculum and pedagogical goals. As soon as the school was founded,
I sent a memorandum to the educational authorities and
requested that our students be taught according to the principles of Waldorf education, from the sixth or seventh year until
the completion of their ninth year, or the end of the third class,
without any outside interference. I meant that the planning of
the curriculum and the standards to be achieved, as well as the
teaching methods, were to be left entirely in the hands of our
teaching staff, the "college of teachers," which would bear the
ultimate responsibility for the running of the school.

In my letter to the authorities, I stated that, on completion of
the third school year, our students would have reached the same
standards of basic education as those achieved in other schools,
and thus would be able to change schools without difficulty. This
implies that a child with a broader educational background than
the students in this new class will nevertheless be able to fit into
any new surroundings, and that such a student will not have lost
touch with life in general. For us, it is not only important that
teachers know their students well, but that there is also a corresponding relationship between the entire body of teachers and all
the students of the school, so that students will feel free to contact
any teacher for guidance or advice. It is a real joy, every time one
enters the Waldorf school, to see how friendly and trusting the

students are, not only with their class teachers but with all the teachers, both in and out of class.

Similarly, I said that our teaching between the end of the ninth and twelfth years—from the end of class three to the end of class six—is intended to achieve standards comparable with those of other schools and that our students would be able to enter seventh grade in another school without falling behind.

We do not wish to be fanatical and, therefore, we had to make compromises. Waldorf teachers must always be willing to cope with the practical problems of life. And if a student has to leave our school at the age of fourteen, there should be no problems when entering a high school or any other school leading to a university entrance examination. So we try to put into practice what has been described.

Now, having established our school through the age of fourteen, every year we are adding a new class, so that we will eventually be able to offer the full range of secondary education leading to higher education. This means that we have to plan our curriculum so that young people will be able to take their graduation exams. In Austria, this exam is called a "maturity exam," in Germany *"Abitur,"* and other countries have other names. In any case, our students are given the possibility of entering other schools of higher education. There is still no possibility that we will open a vocational school or university.[2] Whatever we might try to do in this way would always bear the stamp of a private initiative, and, because we should never want to hold official examinations, no government would grant us permission to issue certificates of education without test

---

2. The German word used here is *Hochschule* (lit. "high school"), which is for those who have finished secondary education (but who have not necessarily taken the graduation exam) and wish to learn a trade or skill, whether manual labor, secretarial or bookkeeping, trades, or household management.

results. Thus, we are forced to compromise in our Waldorf plan, and we are perfectly willing to acknowledge this. What matters is that, despite all the compromises, a genuine Waldorf spirit lives in our teaching, and this as much as possible.

Because we wanted a complete junior school when we opened our Waldorf school, we had to receive some students from other schools, and this gave us plenty of opportunity to witness the fruits of the "strict discipline" that characterizes other schools. At this point, we have a little more than two years of "Waldorf discipline" behind us, which, to a large extent, consists of our trying to get rid of the ordinary sort of school discipline. For example, just a few weeks ago we laid the foundation stone for a larger school building; until now, we have had to make do with provisional classrooms. To my mind, it seemed right that all our children would take part in this stone-laying ceremony. And, as so often happens in life, things took a little longer than anticipated, and by the time we were just getting ready for the actual ceremony, our students were already in the building. First I had to meet teachers and several others, but the children were there already. The adults had to meet in our so-called staff room. What could we to do with all those children? The chair of the college of teachers simply said, "We'll send them back to their classrooms. They have now reached a stage where we can leave them unattended without bad consequences. They won't disturb us."

So, despite the dubious "discipline" imported from other schools, and despite having rid ourselves of so-called school discipline, it was possible to send the students to their class-rooms without any disturbance. Admittedly, this peace was somewhat ephemeral; overly sensitive ears might have been offended, but that did not matter. Children who disturb overly sensitive ears are usually not overly disciplined. At any rate, the effects of imponderables in the Waldorf school became apparent in the children's good behavior under these unusual circumstances.

As you know, various kinds of punishments are administered in most schools, and we, too, had to find ways to deal with this problem. When we discussed the question of punishment in one of our teacher meetings, one of our teachers reported an interesting incident. He had tried to discover the effects of certain forms of punishment on his students. His students had experienced our kind of discipline for some time, and among them there were a few notorious rascals. These little good-for-nothings (as such students are called in Germany) had done very poor work, and they were to be punished according to usual school discipline and given detention. They were told to stay after lessons to do their arithmetic properly. However, when this punishment was announced in class, the other students protested that they, too, wanted to stay and do extra arithmetic because it is so much fun. So you see, the concept of punishment had gone through a complete transformation; it had become something the whole class enjoyed. Such things rarely happen if teachers try to make them happen directly, but they become the natural consequences of the right approach.

I am well aware that the problem of school discipline occupies many minds today. I had the opportunity to closely observe the importance of the relationship between a teacher and his students, a relationship that is the natural outcome of the disposition of both teacher and students. One could go so far as to say that whether students profit from their lessons or how much they gain depends on whether the teacher evokes sympathy or antipathy in the students. It is absolutely open to discussion whether an easygoing teacher—one who does not even work according to proper educational principles—may be more effective than a teacher who, intent on following perfectly sound but abstract principles, is unable to practice them in the classroom.

There are plenty of abstract principles around these days. I am not being sarcastic when I call them clever and ingenious; their merits can be argued. But even when slovenly and indolent teachers enter the classroom, if they nevertheless radiate warmth and affection for their students, they may give their students more for later life than would a highly principled teacher whose personality evokes antipathy. Although the students of a genial but untidy teacher are not likely to grow into models of orderliness, at least they will not suffer from "nervous" conditions later on in life. Nervousness can be the result of antipathy toward a teacher—even one using excellent educational methods—who is unable to establish the right kind of contact with the students.

Such points are open to discussion, and they should be discussed if we take the art of education seriously. I once had to participate in a case like this, and my decision may evoke strong disapproval among some people. During one of my visits to the Waldorf school, I was told of a boy in one of the classes who was causing great difficulties. He had committed all kinds of misdemeanors, and none of his teachers could deal with him. I asked for the boy to be sent to me, because first I wanted to find the root of the trouble. You will admit that in many other schools such a boy would have received corporal punishment or possibly something less drastic. I examined the boy carefully and concluded that he should be moved into the next class above. This was to be his punishment, and I have not heard any complaints since. His new class teacher confirmed that the boy has become a model student and that everything seems to be in order now. This, after all, is what really matters. The important thing is that one goes into the very soul and nature of such a child. The cause of the trouble was that there was no human contact between him and his teacher, and because he was intelligent enough to cope with the work of the next class (there was no comparable class in his case), the only right thing was to move him up. Had we put him down into the next lower class, we would have ruined that child.

If one bears in mind the well-being and inner development of a child, one finds the right way teaching. This is why it is good to look at specific and symptomatic cases. We have no intention of denying that, in many ways, the Waldorf school is built on compromise, but as far as it is humanly possible, we always try to educate from a real knowledge of the human being.

Let us return to the curriculum. The morning sessions are arranged as described. Because it is essential for our students to be able to move on to higher forms of education, we had to include other subjects such as Greek and Latin, which are also taught in morning lessons. In these ancient languages soul economy is of particular importance. The afternoon lessons are given over to more physical activities, such as gym and eurythmy, and to artistic work, which plays a very special part in a Waldorf school. I will give further details of this in the coming days.

We try, as much as possible, to teach the more intellectual subjects in the morning, and only when the headwork is done are they given movement lessons, insofar as they have not let off steam already between morning lessons. However, after the movement lessons they are not taken back to the classroom to do more headwork. I have already said that this has a destructive effect on life, because while children are moving physically, suprasensory forces work through them subconsciously. And the head, having surrendered to physical movement, is no longer in a position to resume its work. It is therefore a mistake to think that, by sandwiching a gym lesson between other more intellectual lessons, we are providing a beneficial change. The homogeneous character of both morning and afternoon sessions has shown itself beneficial to the general development of the students. If we keep in mind the characteristic features of human nature, we will serve the human inclinations best.

I mentioned that we found it necessary to give some kind of anthroposophic religious lessons to our students. Soon afterward, arising from those lessons, we felt another need that led to the introduction of Sunday services for our students. This service has the quality of formal worship, in which the children participate with deep religious feelings. We have found that a ritual performed before the children's eyes every Sunday morning has greatly deepened their religious experience.

The Sunday service had to be enlarged for the sake of the students who were about to leave our middle school. In Germany, it is customary for students of this age to be confirmed in a special ceremony that signifies the stage of maturity at which they are old enough to enter life. We have made arrangements for a similar ceremony that, as experience has shown, leaves a lasting impression on our students.

In any education based on knowledge of the human being, needs become apparent that may have gone unnoticed in more traditional forms of education. For instance, in Germany all students receive school reports at the end of each school year, because it is considered essential to give them something like this before they leave for summer holidays. In this case, too, we felt the need for innovation. I have to admit that I would find it extremely difficult to accept the usual form of school reports in a Waldorf school, simply because I could never appreciate the difference between "satisfactory" and "near-satisfactory," or between "fair" and "fairly good," and so on. These grades are then converted into numbers, so that in Germany some reports show the various subjects arranged in one column, and on the opposite side there is a column of figures, such as 4 ½, 3, 3–4, and so on. I have never been able to develop the necessary understanding for these somewhat occult relationships. So we decided to find other ways of writing our school reports.

When our students leave for holidays at the end of the school year, they do receive reports. They contain a kind of mirror image, or biography, of their progress during the year, which has been written by their class teachers. We have found again and again that our children accept these reports with inner approval. They can read about the impression they have created during the years, and they will feel that, although the description was written with sympathetic understanding, they do not tolerate any whitewashing of the less positive aspects of their work. These reports, which are received with deep inner satisfaction, end with a verse, composed especially for each child. This verse is a kind of guiding motive for the coming years. I believe our kind of reports have already proved themselves and will retain their value in the future, even though in some parts of Germany they have already been referred to as "ersatz" reports.

Students have responded to life in the Waldorf school in an entirely positive way. To show how much they like their school, I should like to repeat something I recently heard from one of our mothers, for such an example helps to illustrate more general symptoms. She said, "My boy was never an affectionate child. He never showed any tender feelings toward me as his mother. After his first year in the Waldorf school—while still quite young—his summer holidays began. When they were nearly over and I told him that soon he would be going to school again, he came and kissed me for the first time." Such a small anecdote could be considered symptomatic of the effects of an education based on knowledge of the human being and practiced in a human and friendly atmosphere. Our school reports also help to contribute towards this atmosphere.

As an introduction to life in the Waldorf school, I felt it necessary to digress a little from our planned program. Tomorrow we shall continue with a more detailed account of the child's development after the change of teeth. Meanwhile, I wanted to include here a description of what by now has become the outer framework of practical life in the Waldorf school.

CHILDREN FROM
THE SEVENTH TO THE TENTH YEAR

December 31, 1921

An important and far-reaching change takes place when children begin to lose their milk, or baby, teeth. This is not just a physical change in the life of a human being, but the whole human organization goes through a transformation. A true art of education demands a thorough appreciation and understanding of this metamorphosis. In our previous meetings, I spoke of the refined body of formative forces, the ether body. These forces are in the process of being freed from certain functions during the time between the change of teeth and puberty. Previously, the ether body worked directly into the physical body of the child, but now it begins to function in the realm of a child's soul. This means that the physical body of children is held from within in a very different way than it was during the previous stage. The situation then was more or less as described by those of a materialistic outlook, who see the foundation of the human psyche in the physical processes of the human body. They see the soul and spirit of children as emanating from the physical and related to it much as a candle flame is related to the candle. And this is more or less correct for a young child until the change of teeth. During the early years, the soul and spiritual life of the child is completely connected to the physical and organic processes, and all of the physical and organic processes have a soul and spiritual quality. All of the shaping and forming of the body at that age is conducted from the head downward. This stage concludes when the second teeth are being pushed through. At this time, the forces working in the head cease to predominate while soul and spiritual activities enter the lower regions of the body—the rhythmic activities of the heart and breath. Previously, these forces, as they worked especially in the formation of the child's brain, were also flowing down into the rest of the organism, shaping and molding and entering directly into the physical substances of the body. Here they gave rise to physical processes.

All this changes with the coming of the second teeth, and some of these forces begin to work more in the child's soul and spiritual realm, affecting especially the rhythmic movement of heart and lungs. They are no longer as active in the physical processes themselves, but now they also work in the rhythms of breathing and blood circulation. One can see this physically as the child's breathing and pulse become noticeably stronger during this time. Children now have a strong desire to experience the emerging life of soul and spirit on waves of rhythm and beat within the body—quite subconsciously, of course. They have a real longing for this interplay of rhythm and beat in their organism. Consequently, adults must realize that whatever they bring to children after the change of teeth must be given with an inherent quality of rhythm and beat. Everything addressed to a child at this time must be imbued with these qualities. Educators must be able to get into the element of rhythm to the degree that whatever they present makes an impression on the children and allows them to live in their own musical element.

This is also the beginning of something else. If, at this stage, the rhythm of breathing and blood circulation is not treated properly, harm may result and extend irreparably into later life. Many weaknesses and unhealthy conditions of the respiratory and circulatory systems in adult life are the consequences of an improper education during these early school years. Through the change in the working of children's ether body, the limbs begin to grow rapidly, and the life of the muscles and bones, including the entire skeleton, begins to play a dominant role. The life of muscles and bones tries to become attuned to the rhythms of breathing and blood circulation. At this stage, children's muscles vibrate in sympathy with the rhythms of breathing and blood circulation, so that their entire being takes on a musical quality. Previously, the child's inborn activities were like those of a sculptor, but now an inner musician begins to work, albeit beyond the child's consciousness. It is essential for teachers to realize that, when a child enters class one, they are dealing with a natural, though unconscious, musician. One must meet these inner needs of children, demanding a somewhat similar treatment, metaphorically, to that of a new violin responding to a violinist, adapting itself to the musician's characteristic pattern of sound waves. Through ill treatment, a violin may be ruined for ever. But in the case of the living human organism, it is possible to plant principles that are harmful to growth, which increase and develop until they eventually ruin a person's entire life.

Once you begin to study the human being, thus illuminating educational principles and methods, you find that the characteristics just mentioned occupy roughly the time between the change of teeth and puberty. You will also discover that this period again falls into three smaller phases. The first lasts from the change of teeth until approximately the end of the ninth year; the second roughly until the end of the twelfth year; and the third from the thirteenth year until sexual maturity.

If you observe the way children live entirely within a musical element, you can understand how these three phases differ from one another. During the first phase, approximately until the end of the ninth year, children want to experience everything that comes toward them in relation to their own inner rhythms—everything associated with beat and measure. They relate everything to the rhythms of breath and heartbeat and, indirectly, to the way their muscles and bones are taking shape. But if outer influences do not synchronize with their inner rhythms, these young people eventually grow into a kind of inner cripple, although this may not be discernible externally during the early stages.

Until the ninth year, children have a strong desire to experience inwardly everything they encounter as beat and rhythm. When children of this age hear music (and anyone who can observe the activity of a child's soul will perceive it), they transform outer sounds into their own inner rhythms. They vibrate with the music, reproducing within what they perceive from without. At this stage, to a certain extent, children have retained features characteristic of their previous stages. Until the change of teeth children are essentially, so to speak, one sense organ, unconsciously reproducing outer sensory impressions as most sense organs do. Children live, above all, by imitation, as already shown in previous meetings. Consider the human eye, leaving aside the mental images resulting from the eye's sensory perceptions, and you find that it reproduces outer stimuli by forming afterimages; the activity leading to mental representation takes hold of these aftermages. Insofar as very young children inwardly reproduce all they perceive, especially the people around them, they are like one great, unconscious sense organ. But the images reproduced inwardly do not remain mere images, since they also act as forces, even physically forming and shaping them.

And now, when the second teeth appear, these afterimages enter only as far as the rhythmic system of movement. Some of the previous formative activity remains, but now it is accompanied by a new element. There is a definite difference in the way children respond to rhythm and beat before and after the change of teeth. Before this, through imitation, rhythm and beat directly affected the formation of bodily organs. After the change of teeth, this is transformed into an inner musical element.

On completion of the ninth year and up to the twelfth year, children develop an understanding of rhythm and beat and what belongs to melody as such. They no longer have the same urge to reproduce inwardly everything in this realm, but now they begin to perceive it as something outside. Whereas, earlier on, children experienced rhythm and beat unconsciously, they now develop a conscious perception and understanding of it. This continues until the twelfth year, not just with music, but everything coming to meet them from outside.

Toward the twelfth year, perhaps a little earlier, children develop the ability to lead the elements of rhythm and beat into the thinking realm, whereas they previously experienced this only in imagination.

If, through understanding, you can perceive what happens in the realm of the soul, you can also recognize the corresponding effects in the physical body. I have just spoken of how children want to shape the muscles and bones in accordance with what is happening within the organs. Now, toward the twelfth year, they begin to be unsatisfied with living solely in the elements of rhythm and beat; now they want to lift this experience more into the realm of abstract and conscious understanding. And this coincides with the hardening of those parts of the muscles that lead into the tendons. Whereas previously all movement was oriented more toward the muscles themselves, now it is oriented toward the tendons. Everything that occurs in the realm of soul and spirit affects the physical realm. This inclusion of the life of the tendons, as the link between muscle and bone, is the external, physical sign that a child is sailing out of a feeling approach to rhythm and beat into what belongs to the realm of logic, which is devoid of rhythm and beat. This sort of discovery is an offshoot of a real knowledge of the human being and should be used as a guide for the art of education.

Most adults who think about things in ways that generalize, whether plants or animals (and as teachers you must introduce such general subjects to your students), will recall how they themselves studied botany or zoology, though at a later age than the children we are talking about. Unfortunately, most textbooks on botany or zoology are really unsuitable for teaching young people. Some of them may have great scientific merit (though this is usually not the case), but as teaching material for the age that concerns us here, they are useless. Everything that we bring to our students in plant or animal study must be woven into an artistic whole. We must try to highlight the harmonious configuration of the plant's being. We must describe the harmonious relationships between one plant species and another. Whatever children can appreciate through a rhythmic, harmonious, and feeling approach must be of far greater significance for Waldorf teachers than what the ordinary textbooks can offer. The usual method of classifying plants is especially objectionable. Perhaps the least offensive of all the various systems is that of Linné.[1] He looked only at the blossom of a plant, where the plant ceases to be merely plant and reaches with its forces into the whole cosmos. But these

---

1. Carolus Linnaeus (Carl von Linné, 1707–1778), Swedish botanist who expounded a system of classification based on plant sex organs.

plant systems are unacceptable for use at school. We will see later what needs to be done in this respect.

It is really pitiful to see teachers enter the classroom, textbook in hand, and teach these younger classes what they themselves learned in botany or zoology. They become mere caricatures of a real teacher when they walk up and down in front of the students, reading from a totally unsuitable textbook in an attempt to remember what they were taught long ago. It is absolutely essential that we learn to talk about plants and animals in a living and artistic way. This is the only way our material will be attuned to the children's inner musical needs. Always bear in mind that our teaching must spring from an artistic element; lessons must not merely be thought out. Even when it is correct, an abstract kind of observation is not good enough. Only what is imbued with a living element of sensitive and artistic experience provides children with the soul nourishment they need.

When children enter class one, we are expected to teach them writing as soon as possible, and we might be tempted to introduce the letters of the alphabet as they are used today. But children at this age—right at the onset of the change of teeth—do not have the slightest inner connection with the forms of these letters. What was it like when we still had such a direct human relationship to written letters? We need only look at what happened in early civilizations. In those ancient times, primitive people engraved images on tablets or painted pictures, which still had some resemblance to what they saw in nature. There was still a direct human link between outer objects and their written forms. As civilization progressed, these forms became increasingly abstract until, after going through numerous transformations, they finally emerged as today's letters of the alphabet, which no longer bear any real human relationship to the person writing them.

In many ways, children show us how the people of earlier civilizations experienced the world; they need a direct connection with whatever we demand of their will. Therefore, when introducing writing, we must refrain from immediately teaching today's abstract letters. Especially at this time of changing teeth, we must offer children a human and artistic bridge to whatever we teach. This implies that we have children connect what they have seen with their eyes and the results of their will activity on paper, which we call writing. Experiencing life actively through their own will is a primary need for children at this stage. We must give them an opportunity to express this innate artistic drive by, for example, allowing them to physically run in a curve on the floor (see image). Now, when we show them that they have made a curve with their legs on the floor, we lift their will activity into a partially conscious feeling. Next we ask them to draw this curve in the air, using their arms and hands. Now another form could be run on the floor, again to be written in the air.

Thus the form that was made by the entire body by running was then reproduced through the hand. This could be followed by the teacher asking the children to pronounce words beginning with the letter *L*. Gradually, under the teacher's guidance, the children discover the link between the shape that was run and drawn and the sound of the letter *L*.

Once children experience their own inner movement, they are led to draw the letters themselves. This is one way to proceed, but there is also another possibility. After the change of teeth children are not only musicians inwardly, but, as an echo from earlier stages, they are also inner sculptors. Therefore, we can begin by talking to the children about a fish, gradually leading artistically to its outer form, which the children then draw. Then, appealing to their sense of sound, we direct their attention from the whole word *fish* to the initial sound "F," thus relating the shape of the letter to its sound.

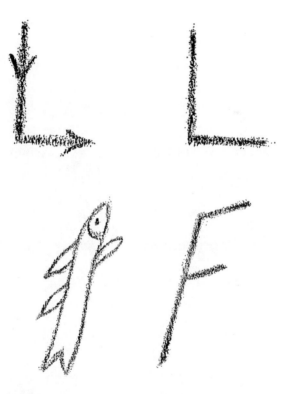

This method, to a certain extent, even follows the historical development of the letter *F.* However, there is no need to limit ourselves to historical examples, and it is certainly appropriate to use our imagination. What matters is not that children recapitulate the evolution of letters, but that they find their way into writing through the artistic activity of drawing pictures, which will finally lead to modern, abstract letter forms. For instance, one could remind the children of how water makes waves, drawing a picture like this first one, and gradually changing it into one like the second.

By repeating something like "washing waves of water—waving, washing water" while drawing the form, we connect the sound of the letter *W* with its written form. By beginning with the children's own life experience, we go from the activity of drawing to the final letter forms.

Following our Waldorf method, children do not learn to write as quickly as they would in other schools. In the Waldorf school, we hold regular meetings for parents without their children present, and parents are invited to talk with the teachers about the effects of Waldorf education. In these meetings, some parents have expressed concern over the fact that their children, even at the age of eight, are still unable to write properly. We have to point out that our slower approach is really a blessing, because it allows children to integrate the art of writing with their whole being. We try to show parents that the children in our school learn to write at the appropriate age and in a far more humane way than if they had to absorb material that is essentially alien to their nature—alien because it represents the product of a long cultural evolution. We must help parents understand the importance of the children's immediate and direct response to the introduction of writing. Naturally, we have to provide students with tools for learning, but we must do this by adapting our material to the child's nature.

One aspect, so often left out today, concerns the relationship of a specific area to life as a whole. In our advanced stage of civilization, everything depends on specialization. Certainly, for a time this was necessary, but we have reached a stage where, for the sake of healthy human development, we must keep an open mind to spiritual investigation and what it can tell us about the human being. To believe that anthroposophists always rail against new technology is to seriously misunderstand this movement and its contribution to our knowledge of the human being. It is necessary to see the complexities of life from a holistic perspective. For example, I do not object at all to the use of typewriters. Typing is, of course, a far less human activity than writing by hand, but I do not remonstrate against it. Nevertheless, I find it is important to realize its implications, because everything we do in life has repercussions. So you must forgive me if, to illustrate my point, I say something about typewriting from the point of view of anthroposophic spiritual insight. Anyone unwilling to accept it is perfectly free to dismiss this aspect of life's realities as foolish nonsense. But what I have to say does accord with the facts.

You see, if you are aware of spiritual processes, like those in ordinary life, using a typewriter creates a very definite impression. After I have been typing during the day (as you see, I am really not against it, and I'm pleased when I have time for it), it continues to affect me for quite a while afterward. In itself, this does not disturb me, but the effects are noticeable. When I finally reach a state of inner quiet, the activity of typing—seen in *imaginative* consciousness—is transformed into seeing myself. Facing oneself standing there, one is thus able to witness outwardly what is happening inwardly. All this must occur in full consciousness, which enables us to recognize that appearance, as form as an outer image, is simply a projection of what is or has been taking place, possibly much earlier, as inner organic activity. We can clearly see what is happening inside the human body once we have reached the stage of clairvoyant *imagination.* In objective seeing such as this, every stroke of a typewriter key becomes a flash of lightning. And during the state of *imagination,* what one sees as the human heart is constantly struck and pierced by those lightning flashes. As you know, typewriter keys are not arranged according to any spiritual principle, but according to frequency of their use, so that we can type more quickly. Consequently, when the fingers hit various keys, the flashes of lightning become completely chaotic. In other words, when seen with spiritual vision, a terrible thunderstorm rages when one is typing.

Such causes and effects are part of the pattern of life. There is no desire on our part to deride technical innovations, but we should be able to keep our eyes open to what they do to us, and we should find ways to compensate for any harmful effects. Such matters are especially important to teachers, because they have to relate education to ordinary life. What we do at school and with children is not the only thing that matters. The most important thing is that school and everything related to education must relate to life in the fullest sense. This implies that those who choose to be educators must be familiar with events in the larger world; they must know and recognize life in its widest context. What does this mean? It means simply that here we have an explanation of why so many people walk about with weak hearts; they are unable to balance the harmful effects of typing through the appropriate countermeasures. This is specially true of people who started typing when they were too young, when the heart is most susceptible to adverse effects. If typing continues to spread, we will soon see an increase in all sorts of heart complaints.

In Germany, the first railroad was built in 1835, from Fürth to Nuremberg. Before this, the Bavarian health authorities were asked whether, from a medical point of view, building such a railroad would be recommended. Before beginning major projects such as this, it was always the custom to seek expert advice. The Bavarian health authorities responded (this is documented) that expert medical opinion could not recommend building railroads, because passengers and railroad workers alike would suffer severe nervous strain by traveling on trains. However, they continued, if railroads were built despite their warning, all railroad lines should at least be closed off by high wooden walls to prevent brain concussions to farmers in nearby fields or others likely to be near moving trains.

These were the findings of medical experts employed by the Bavarian health authority. Today we can laugh about this and similar examples. Nevertheless, there are at least two sides to every problem, and from a certain point of view, one could even agree with some aspects of this report, which was made not so long ago—in fact not even a century ago. The fact is, people have become more nervous since the arrival of rail travel. And if we made the necessary investigation into the difference between people in our present age of the train and those who continued to traveled in the old and venerable but rather rough stagecoach, we would definitely be able to ascertain that the constitutions of these latter folks were different. Their nervous systems behaved quite differently. Although the the Bavarian health officials made fools of themselves, from a certain perspective they were not entirely wrong.

When new inventions affect modern life, we must take steps to balance any possible ill effects by finding appropriate countermeasures. We must try to compensate for any weakening of the human constitution through outer influences by strengthening ourselves from within. But, in this age of ever-increasing specialization, this is possible only through a new art of education based on true knowledge of the human being.

The only safe way of introducing writing to young children is the one just advocated, because at that age all learning must proceed from the realm of the will, and the inclination of children toward the world of rhythm and measure arises from the will. We must satisfy this inner urge of children by allowing them controlled will activities, not by appealing to their sense of observation and the ability to make mental images. Consequently, it would be inappropriate to teach reading before the children have been introduced to writing, for reading represents a transition from will activity to abstract observation. The first step is to introduce writing artistically and imaginatively and then to let children read what they have written. The last step, since modern life requires it, would be to help children read from printed texts. Teachers will be able to discern what needs to be done only by applying a deepened knowledge of the human being, based on the realities of life.

When children enter class one, they are certainly ready to learn how to calculate with simple numbers. And when we introduce arithmetic, here, too, we must carefully meet the inner needs of children. These needs spring from the same realm of rhythm and measure and from a sensitive apprehension of the harmony inherent in the world of number. However, if we begin with what I would call the "additive approach," teaching children to count, again we fail to understand the nature of children. Of course, they must learn to count, but additive counting as such is not in harmony with the inner needs of children.

It is only because of our civilization that we gradually began to approach numbers through synthesis, by combining them. Today we have the concept of a unit, or oneness. Then we have a second unit, a third, and so on, and when we count, we mentally place one unit next to the other and add them up. But, by nature, children do not experience numbers this way; human evolution did not develop according to this principle. True, all counting began with a unit, the number one. But, originally, the second unit, number two, was not an outer repetition of the first unit but was felt to be contained *within* the first unit. Number one was the origin of number two, the two units of which were concealed within the original number. The same number one, when divided into three parts, gave number three, three units that were felt to be part of the one. Translated into contemporary terms, when reaching the concept of two, one did not leave the limits of number one but experienced an inner progression within number one. Twoness was inherent in oneness. Also three, four, and all other numbers were felt to be part of the all-comprising first unit, and all numbers were experienced as organic members arising from it.

Because of its musical, rhythmic nature, children experience the world of number in a similar way. Therefore, instead of beginning with addition in a rather pedantic way, it would be better to call on a child and offer some apples or any other suitable objects. Instead of offering, say, three apples, then four more, and finally another two, and asking the child to add them all together, we begin by offering a whole pile of apples, or whatever is convenient. This would begin the whole operation. Then one calls on two more children and says to the first, "Here you have a pile of apples. Give some to the other two children and keep some for yourself, but each of you must end up with the same number of apples." In this way you help children comprehend the idea of sharing by three. We begin with the total amount and lead to the principle of division. Following this method, children will respond and comprehend this process naturally. According to our picture of the human being, and in order to attune ourselves to the children's nature, we do not begin by adding but by dividing and subtracting. Then, retracing our steps and reversing the first two processes, we are led to multiplication and addition. Moving from the whole to the part, we follow the original experience of number, which was one of analyzing, or division, and not the contemporary method of synthesizing, or putting things together by adding.

These are just some examples to show how we can read in the development of children what and how one should teach during the various stages. Breathing and blood circulation are the physical bases of the life of feeling, just as the head is the basis for mental imagery, or thinking. With the change of teeth the life of feeling is liberated and, therefore, at this stage we can always reach children through the element of feeling, provided the teaching material is artistically attuned to the children's nature.

To summarize, before the change of teeth, children are not yet aware of their separate identity and consequently cannot appreciate the characteristic nature of others, whose gestures, manners of speaking, and even sentiments they imitate in an imponderable way. Up to the seventh year, children cannot yet differentiate between themselves and another person. They experience others as directly connected with themselves, similar to the way they feel connected to their own arms and legs. They cannot yet distinguish between self and the surrounding world.

With the change of teeth new soul forces of feeling, linked to breathing and blood circulation, come into their own, with the result that children begin to distance themselves from others, whom they now experience as individuals. This creates in them a longing to follow the adult in every way, looking up to the adult with shy reverence. Their previous inclination was to imitate the more external features, but this changes after the second dentition. True to the nature of children, a strong feeling for authority begins to develop.

You would hardly expect sympathy for a general obedience to authority from one who, as a young person, published *Intuitive Thinking As a Spiritual Path* in the early 1890s. But this sense for authority in children between the change of teeth and puberty must be respected and nurtured, because it represents an inborn need at this age. Before one can use freedom appropriately in later life, one must have experienced shy reverence and a feeling for adult authority between the change of teeth and puberty. This is another example of how education must be seen within the context of social life in general.

If you look back a few decades and see how proud many people were of their "modern" educational ideas, some strange feelings will begin to stir. After Prussia's victory over Austria in 1866, one often heard a certain remark in Austria, where I spent half my life. People expressed the opinion that the battle had been won by the Prussian schoolmaster. The education act was implemented earlier in Prussia than in Austria, which was always considered to have an inferior educational system, and it was the Prussian schoolmaster who was credited with having won the victory. However, after 1918 [and World War I], no one sang the praises of the Prussian schoolmaster.

This is an example to show how "modern" educational attitudes have been credited with the most extraordinary successes. Today we witness some of the results—our chaotic social life, which threatens to become more and more chaotic because, for so many, their strong sense of freedom is no longer controlled by the will and by morality, but by indulgence and license. There are many who have forgotten how to use real, inner freedom. Those who are able to observe life find definite connections between the general chaos of today and educational principles that, though highly satisfying to intellectual and naturalistic attitudes, do not lead to a full development of the human being. We must become aware of the polar effects in life. For example, people in later life become free in the right way only if, as a child, they went through the stage of looking up to and revering adults. It is healthy for children to believe that something is beautiful, true and good, or ugly, false, and evil, when a teacher says so.

With the change of teeth children enter a new relationship to the world. As the life of their own soul gradually emerges, which they now experience in its own right, they must first meet the world supported through an experience of authority. At this stage, educators represent the larger world, and children have to meet it through the eyes of their teachers. Therefore we would say that, from birth to the change of teeth, children have an instinctive tendency to imitate, and from the change of teeth to puberty, they need to experience the principle of authority. When we say "authority," however, we mean children's natural response to a teacher—never enforced authority. This is the kind of authority that, by intangible means, creates the right rapport between child and teacher.

Here we enter the realm of imponderables. I would like to show you, by way of an example, how they work. Imagine that we wish to give children a concept of the soul's immortality, a task that is much more difficult than one might suppose. At the age we are speaking of, when children are so open to the artistic element in education, we cannot communicate such concepts through abstract reasoning or ideas, but must clothe them in pictures.

Now, imagine a teacher who feels drawn to the more intellectual and naturalistic side of life; how would this teacher proceed? Subconsciously she may say to herself, I am naturally more intelligent than a child who is, in fact, rather ignorant. Therefore I must invent a suitable picture that will give children an idea of the immortality of the human soul. The chrysalis from which the butterfly emerges offers a good metaphor. The butterfly is hidden in the chrysalis, just as the human soul is hidden in the body. The butterfly flies out of the chrysalis, and this gives us a visible picture of what happens at death, when the suprasensory soul leaves the body and flies into the spiritual world. This is the sort of idea that a skillful, though intellectually inclined, person might make up to pass on to children the concept of the soul's immortality. With such an attitude of mind, however, children will not feel touched inwardly. They will accept this picture and quickly forget it.

But we can approach this task in a different way. It is inappropriate to feel, "I am intelligent, and this child is ignorant." We have seen here how cosmic wisdom still works directly through children and that, from this point of view, it is children who are intelligent and the teacher who is, in reality, ignorant. I can keep this in mind and fully believe in my image of the emerging butterfly. A spiritual attitude toward the world teaches me to believe the truth of this picture. It tells me that this same process, which on a higher plane signifies the soul's withdrawal from the body, is repeated on a lower level in a simple, sense-perceptible form when a butterfly emerges from the chrysalis. This picture is not my invention but was placed into the world by the forces of cosmic wisdom. Here, before my very eyes, I can watch a representation of what happens on a higher plane when the soul leaves the body at death.

If this picture leaves a deep impression on my soul, I will be convinced of its truth. If teachers have this experience, something begins to stir between their students and themselves, something we must attribute to the realm of imponderables. If teachers bring this picture to children with an inner warmth of belief, it will create a deep and lasting impression and become part of their being.

If you can see how the effects of natural authority lead to a kind of inner obedience, then in a similar light authority will be accepted as wholesome and positive. It will not be resented because of a mistaken notion of freedom. Teachers, as artists of education, must approach children as artists of life, because, after the change of teeth, children approach teachers as artists as well—as sculptors and musicians. In certain cases, the unconscious and inherent gifts of children are very highly developed, especially in children who later become virtuosi or geniuses. Such individuals never lose their artistic gifts. But inwardly, entirely subconsciously, every child is a great sculptor; they retain these gifts from before the change of teeth. After this, inner musical activities are interwoven with the inner formative activities. As educators, we must learn to cooperate in a living way with these artistic forces working through children.

Proceeding along these lines, it becomes possible to prevent rampant growth in young people, and we enable them to develop their potential in the broadest possible sense.

CHILDREN IN THE TENTH YEAR

January 1, 1922

Once children have completed the ninth year, an important moment then arrives in their development. To appreciate the significant change that takes place during the ninth and tenth years, we must keep in mind that the children's inborn feeling for authority (which began with the change of teeth) was rather general and undifferentiated. Children accepted the dictates of authority as a matter of course and felt an inner need to conform without yet being concerned about the individual character of the adults. With the end of the ninth year, however, children want to feel inner justification for authority.

Do not misunderstand my meaning. Children would never reason inwardly about whether this or that authority is worthy. Yet something arises in the soul and seeks assurance that an adult's authority will stand the test of quality—that it is properly based in life and that it carries a certain inner assurance. At this time of life, children have an acute awareness of these qualities, and this awareness manifests as a subtle, though objective, change in the soul's condition. Any good educator must be able to notice such a change and act accordingly. Up until this time, children have been unable to discriminate fully between themselves and their surroundings; they experienced the world and the self as a unity.

When trying to describe such matters, we must occasionally become rather extreme, and I ask you to accept this with the right attitude. For example, when I say that, before the ninth year, children do not distinguish properly between humans, animals, plants, and rocks, and that everything around them seems alive in a general kind of way, it would be completely incorrect to dogmatically say that children could not appreciate the difference between a person and a lily. Yet, in a certain sense, this statement is correct. A true art of education can appreciate the meaning of such seemingly radical statements without turning them into dogmas. Everywhere, life itself shows us that there are no sharp, rigid contours, so popular among pedantic minds.

The end of the ninth year is also the end of a typical feature that is frequently misinterpreted by child psychologists. For example, when a child accidentally runs into a table, the response is to hit back. Psychologists explain this as "personifying" the table. According to child psychology, children endow an inanimate object with a living soul, which they want to punish. But this interpretation shows only a superficial understanding of children's feelings. In truth, children do not personify tables at all but have not learned yet to discriminate between inanimate objects and living beings. Children respond to the situation this way because they cannot separate themselves yet from their environment.

Toward the end of the ninth year, a whole range of questions arise in children's souls, and they all come from a new feeling of differentiation between self and the outer world, as well as from a feeling of separateness from their teacher as a person. This new way of confronting the world turns this age into a turning point in a child's development. Until now, children were barely aware of whether a teacher was a clumsy sort person who might bump into desks and tables, or one who dropped pieces of chalk on the floor. It would not have occurred to children under nine to react to a situation, as, for example, a congregation once did during a church service. The preacher was in the habit of touching his nose every time he completed a sentence in his sermon, and this habit caused ripples of laughter in church. True, children would notice such an idiosyncrasy even before they completed the ninth year, but it would pass by without making a deeper impression. It would be wrong to think that children do not notice such things, but after the ninth year they become acutely aware of these things. One or two years later, by the tenth or eleventh year, children are far less attentive to such matters. But, at this particular age, such keen observations become wrapped up in an entire system of inner questions that burden their souls. Children may never voice these questions, but they are present nonetheless. Children wonder whether teachers are skillful in everything related to life, whether they know what they want, and, above all, whether they are firmly rooted in life. They are sensitive to the general background of a teacher's personality. Consequently, teachers who are skeptics will make a totally different impression than those who are genuine believers, no matter what they say.

These are the kinds of things that concern children between the ninth and tenth years. Many individual features of adults play an important role. A strict Protestant teacher will arouse an entirely different impression in children than would a Catholic teacher, simply because of differences in their souls. Other factors also need to be considered, such as the fact that this turning point manifests at varying ages according to race and nationality, earlier in one and later in another. In each case this change may appear earlier or later, so that any generalizations might be misleading. All we can say is that it is up to the teacher to perceive this subtle change in the child's soul. As in so many other aspects of education, much depends on a teacher's keen and objective observation of all the students in a class.

This aspect is of special importance to us in the Waldorf school. In our regular teachers' meetings, we discuss each student and try to learn as much as we can through each child's individuality. Naturally, if our numbers continue to grow, we may have to make other arrangements. But it is certainly possible to learn a great deal in these meetings, especially if we endeavor to study the more hidden aspects of the growing human being. And here we can make rather surprising discoveries. For example, for awhile I made careful observations in our coeducational school regarding the effects of whether boys or girls were in the majority in the various classes, or whether their numbers were more or less balanced. Leaving aside more obvious features of the general class life of the students—features that could be explained rationally—I found that classes where the girls were in the majority had a completely different quality than those where there were more boys. Here, imponderables are very much at work in the social sphere. However, it would be very wrong to draw a convenient conclusion and suggest doing away with coeducation. Such a retrograde step would merely increase the problems. The only answer is to learn how to deal with the problems posed by the majority or minority of boys or girls in various classes.

The way in which teachers are able to observe each student as well as the class as a whole is always very important, and it raises deeply philosophical questions. For example, in the Waldorf school, we have observed that teachers made the best progress when they were able to relate in the right way to the lessons they were giving, and also that, with time, their way of teaching had to change. Here again, subconscious elements play a dominant part.

From all that has been said so far, you can see that children at this crucial point will approach teachers with all kinds of inner questions. Neither the substance of those questions nor the answers given are as important as a certain inner awareness that gradually dawns upon a child's soul. This awareness springs from an indefinable element that, at this particular time, must develop between the teacher, as a guide, and the student. The student feels, "Until now I have always looked up to my teacher, but now I can't do this unless I know that my teacher looks up to something even higher, something safely rooted in life." Especially inquisitive children will even pursue their teachers beyond school time, noticing what they do outside school. Everything depends on teachers recognizing the significance of this stage and realizing that a child's tender approach now longs for renewed confidence and trust. And the way a teacher responds to this situation may be a decisive factor for a child's entire life. Whether children develop unstable characters or become strongly integrated into life may depend on whether teachers act with inner certainty and understanding during this crucial time.

If we realize the importance of a teacher's conduct and response during the child's ninth to tenth year, we may wonder in what ways human beings are dependent on their environment. However, we cannot answer this important question unless we include other fundamental factors in our deliberations, ones deeply linked with destiny, or karma—matters that will occupy us more toward the end of this conference. Nevertheless, what has been said here is absolutely relevant and true for any serious discussion on education. What matters is that, at this moment in life, children can find someone (whether one person or several people) whose picture they can carry with them through life.

Only a few people can observe a certain phenomenon of life that I would like to describe to you. During certain periods in a person's life, the effects of childhood experiences surface again and again, and the images that arise from this particular turning point are of great importance. It is tremendously important whether they emerge only dimly in later life; whether they appear in dreams or in the waking state; or whether they are viewed with feelings of sympathy or antipathy. All this is important, not sympathy or antipathy in itself, but the fact that something passed through child's soul that in one case evoked sympathy and in another case antipathy. I am not implying that these reminiscences of this turning point during the ninth to tenth year are experienced in clear consciousness. In some cases they remain almost completely hidden within the subconscious, but they are nevertheless bound to occur. People who have vivid dreams may regularly see a certain scene or even a person or guide who helped in childhood by admonishing, reassuring, and awaking a personal relationship. This is the kind of soul experience that everyone needs to have had between the ninth and the tenth year. It is all part of the objective change taking place in children, who were previously unable to distinguish themselves from their surroundings, and now feel the need to find their own identities, becoming separate individuals who can confront the outer world.

From what has been said, it follows that the material we teach children at this age must be adapted to this particular period in their development. In our time, especially, it will become increasingly necessary to deal with all educational matters through real insight into the human being. Just think for a moment of how many children, after their change of teeth, have the possibility of seeing all kinds of machines at work, such as railroad engines, metro trains, and so on. Here I can speak from personal experience, because as a young child I grew up in a small railroad station where, every day, I could watch countless trains pass by. And I have to say quite definitely that the worst thing for a child before the end of the ninth year is to gain mechanical understanding of a locomotive, a metro transport, or any other mechanical contrivance.

You will understand how such matters can affect the entire constitution right down to the physical body if you observe related phenomena. For example, just think of what it means to the life experience of several generations when a whole nation adopts a new language. Why, for instance, do the Bulgarians appear Slavic? Their racial origin is not Slavic at all, for racially they belong to the family of the Finns, or Huns. According to their race, they belong to the Mongol and Tartar stream. But early in their history they adopted a Slavic idiom, and because of this they gradually became a Slavic nation. All that they have taken in with their new language and culture penetrated their entire inner being. I have met people who considered the Bulgarians to be among the purest of all Slavic elements, which from the anthropological perspective they are definitely not. Too often we fail to realize the potent effects of soul and spiritual influences on children's whole constitution, working right into the physical organization.

So I must make a rather radical comment. After the change of teeth, when children experience conceptual thinking, it is as if spikes were being driven through their whole being, especially when such concepts come from the inorganic, lifeless realm. Anything taken from the soulless realm will in itself estrange a child. Consequently, those whose task is to teach children of this age need an artistic ability that will imbue everything they bring with life; everything must be alive. Teachers must let plants speak, and they must let animals act as moral beings. Teachers must be able to turn the whole world into fairy tales, fables, and legends.

In this context, something else of great significance also must be considered. What would lazy teachers do when faced with such an educational challenge? They would most likely go to a library and look for books of legends, animal stories, and other similar subjects, then they would read through them for use in the classroom. Of course, sometimes you have to make do with inferior arrangements, but this method is far from ideal. Ideally, teachers would prepare themselves so well for this task—which does require thorough preparation—that a conversation between plants, or a fairy tale about a lily and a rose, comes to children as the teacher's own creation. And ideally, a conversation between the sun and moon should be a product of the teacher's unique imagination. Why should it work this way? Let me answer with an image. If you tell students what you found in books—no matter how lively you may be—if you tell them what you have read and perhaps even memorized, you will talk to them like a dry and desiccated person, as though you did not have a living skin but were covered with parchment, for there are always death-like traces in one's own being of what was thus learned from the past. If, on the other hand, you are creative in your work as a teacher, your material will radiate with growing forces, it will be fresh and alive, and this is what feeds the souls of children.

If as teachers you want to reach children at this age, there has to be a creative urge to clothe the world of plants and animals and the sun and moon with living stories. Once you have engrossed yourself in such imaginative work (which demands a great deal of inner effort), you will hurry to school with steps betraying your eagerness to share this offering with your class, and the effects of such an endeavor will be wholesome for all the children. Such teachers know very well that their story will remain incomplete until they have seen the radiant faces of those young listeners.

Until the end of the ninth year, everything children learn about plants, animals, and stones, about the sun, moon, and stars, or about clouds, mountains, and rivers should be clothed in pictures, because children will feel at one with the world. In those young days, a child and the world are one whole.

With the arrival of the great change a new situation arises. Children now begin to experience themselves as self-contained. They learn to distinguish themselves from the environment, which offers the possibility—indeed, the necessity—of introducing them to the world in new terms. Now teaching should emphasize the fundamental difference between the plant world and that of the animals, because children need to be introduced to each of these two natural kingdoms in its own way. It is certainly possible to introduce children, during their tenth to twelfth years, to the plant and animal kingdoms, but these two subjects must be approached from different points of view.

Introducing students at this age to a plant by showing them a specimen pulled from the earth, as if it were complete in itself, is terrible thing to do. Right from the beginning, there should be a feeling that a single plant torn from the earth does not represent reality, like a human hair pulled from the body, which could never exist on its own. Likewise, once a plant has been pulled from the earth, it cannot exist independently. A plant belongs to the surface of the earth, just as a human hair belongs to the head. Plant and earth belong together. We will see in a moment that something else is needed here, but to begin with, we awaken children to a feeling of how plant and earth belong together. We let them experience how a plant is more earth-like in its root; a root adapts itself to the varying nature of the soil. Such an observation, however, must never be abstract, nor should it be taught simply as a fact, but students should gradually develop a feeling for how roots, for example, are different in dry or wet soil, or how they grow when close to towering rocks or near the sea. First of all, children must learn to see the plant as part the earth's soul, and see all sprouting vegetation as arising from the soil.

Then we have to develop a feeling in children for the contrast between the earth-like root and the blossom and fruit, which are closely related to the sun. When talking about blossoms and fruit, we should lead children from the earth to the sun sphere. Students should get a feeling for how the blossom unfolds in the warmth and light of the sun's rays, and how, in blossom and fruit, the plant is emancipated from the fetters of the earth. Earth, plant growth, and the sun's influence all have to be seen as being part of a complete whole. I would even say that a child's idea of the plant should be so steeped in feeling that, if we were to talk about it without speaking of both the earth as a whole and the sun, the child would experience an inner twinge of pain, like seeing the plant being torn from its earthly home.

Here again we must not see the subject we teach merely in the abstract but consider its social implications. Just think of what it means for the development of our civilization that a large portion of our population now lives in urban environments. This has the effect (and people who have left the country to live in towns will confirm this) that generations of city children have grown up who are unable to distinguish wheat from rye. Although this may sound like an exaggeration, in my opinion a person who has not learned to distinguish rye from wheat cannot be considered a full human being. I would even go as far as to say that a city dweller who knows the difference between these grains only through handling them still does not attain the ideal. Only one who has stood on the soil where rye and wheat were growing and learned to recognize them there has the right inner connection with those plants.

Now we can easily make a transition to geography if we present a picture of how plants grow from the earth, as from a living organism, and how plants adapt to various kinds of soil, different climates, and other influences. Other aspects of this subject will fit into the picture quite naturally. And yet, when talking about the earth, what kind of picture is usually presented today? Often, the earth's green mantle, the realm of plants, is completely left out. People talk as though the earth were simply a globe moving through space and controlled by the laws of gravity, which explain the way heavenly bodies affect one another. It is as if this mathematical and mechanical aspect were all that mattered. But who has the right to isolate mathematical and mechanical laws of gravity from what belongs to the earth so intimately, the growing plants? When speaking of the earth as a sphere moving through the universe, one should give at least equal attention to what the earth contributes to the root of the plant and to the mathematical and mechanical relationships of gravity and so on.

As teachers we should avoid collecting specimens to show to our students in class. It would be far better to take the children out into nature, so that out there in the real, living places of earth, sun, and weather they can get an understanding of plant life. This would also give us an opportunity to show them something else important: what a potato really is. The potato is not part of the root, as it may seem; in reality, it is a bulbous stem. The dry soil, in which the potato plant grows, draws what is really part of the green leaves and stems back into the earth. Looking at these green parts of a plant, one should be able to recognize how much the plant's growth is governed by the forces of the earth, and how much the soil makes its impulse felt in the plant. One should be able to experience how potato stalks demean themselves by creeping under the dry ground. Again one should have an eye for the way a moist meadow and the angle of the autumn sunlight create the lilac-colored cups of *colchicum autumnale,* the autumn crocus. It is important to let every lesson be filled with life. And, just as we relate the plant world to the earth's surface, similarly, when introducing zoology, we should link animals to the human being.

When introducing ideas about the plant world as I described, teachers will notice all sorts of questions coming out of class conversations about the whys and wherefores of the world. It is really much healthier if such questions of causality come up while studying plants than if they are stimulated by mechanical concepts or the study of inorganic minerals. We should allow a feeling for causality to develop while studying plants, and similarly we should introduce the study of animals by comparing them with the human being, an analogy that remains valid throughout life. To facilitate a clear understanding of the principles behind the introduction to zoology, I would like to pass certain ideas on to you, ideas that are too often ignored today. However, these ideas are specifically addressed to adults and would have to be adapted for use with students at the ages of ten to twelve.

If we look at the human being in a morphological and physiological way, we see that externally the head appears more or less spherical. Within the head is the brain's grey matter, which is only slightly differentiated from cellular ganglia, and more deeply within this is the fibrous white matter. Now, can we find an analogy to this formation of the human head in the animal world? And if so, where? We must look among the lowest of the animal kingdom. The human head is, of course, a highly complex organ, but its most characteristic feature is this soft mass enclosed within a hard outer shell, and this basic feature can be found in a much more primitive state among the lower animals. Anyone willing to look at nature without preconceptions will recognize in crustaceans the principle of the human head in its most primitive form, and consequently one can relate the human head to a shellfish. From this point of view, the human head resembles an oyster far more than it does an ape. If you look at any of the soft-fleshed animals encased within a hard shell, you see the human head in its simplest form.

Now, if we observe the human chest system, the part of our body that is influenced primarily by the spine, we are led to higher animals, for example fish. And what is the makeup of a fish? In a fish, the head is little more than a continuation of the spine, despite the fact that its head is more differentiated. The fish is essentially a "spine creature." If we look the organization of the fish as a creature at the center of the animal kingdom, we would compare it with the human lymph system, the system at the center of the human being. If we look at still higher animals, the mammals, we must compare the high degree of development in them to the human metabolic-limb system. The whole being of a lion or camel, for example, is dominated by a specially developed organization of limbs and metabolism.

Looking at the animal kingdom from this point of view, a remarkable relationship emerges between the three animal groups and the human makeup:

Head organization:	lower animals
Rhythmic system:	intermediate animals
Metabolic-limb system:	higher animals

This also gives us real insight into the evolution of human beings and animals. Human development began with what finally emerged as the head, and this happened during very ancient times when the outer conditions of earth were entirely different from what they are today. There was still plenty of time and opportunity during those early stages of the head—which was oyster-like and depended on impulses from the environment—to develop into what it has become. Like a parasite, the head sits on top of the rest of the organism and draws, like an oyster, from its environment.

During the course of evolution, human beings replaced the external earthly surroundings by developing the head as part of the human organism. We can follow this development by looking at human embryology and see, with regard to the head, that humankind has undergone a long evolution. The head began during an era still represented by mollusks. Today's mollusks, however, are late arrivals in evolution. Because they have to develop under less favorable outer conditions today, they cannot achieve the density of the human head but remain a soft-bodied animal surrounded by a hard shell. In today's completely different external conditions, they still represent early stages of the human head organization.

The constitution of fish, on the other hand, occurred during a later period of earthly evolution than that of the human being, and even then it met different outer conditions. At that time, human beings had already reached a stage where they could draw impulses from their own rhythmic system that a fish still had to draw from its surroundings. The makeup of the intermediate animal group was added to that of the evolving human being, who by that time had reached a certain stage of development. And finally, the higher animals began to appear on the earth when human beings began to develop the limb and metabolic system as it appears today—when the human metabolism had become differentiated, leaving only a residue in the head and chest organizations.

This perspective will enable you to understand that the current theory of human descent is correct. But it is correct only with regard to the head, since the head stems from forebears who had a remote resemblance to the lowest animals of today. Yet, these forebears were again quite different from our present-day crustaceans, because these creatures exist within such a different environment.

The makeup of the central system in human beings descended from forebears that were definitely on the way toward becoming human and, regarding their physical organization, resembled the fish. However, the fish species itself arrived too late and, consequently, lacked the time it needed to develop the head fully, especially since fish were limited to the watery element.

Thus we obtain a theory of human descent that accords with reality. On the other hand, if we do not consider the human threefold organization, we can gain only a onesided theory that, however ingenious it may be, does not stand up to a thorough investigation. So we can say that, in the ascending order of today's animal species, we see a onesided development of one system of the human organization. The shellfish is a onesided "head animal," the fishes are onesided "chest animals," and the higher mammals are specialized through their development of the metabolic and limb system. We can understand every animal form by looking at each major animal group as having specialized, onesidedly, in one of the three main systems of human physiology.

Around 1900, there were still those who had a natural feeling for such ideas. But because there was insufficient knowledge to work with them thoroughly and realistically, only the underlying feelings were correct. Oken, a German natural philosopher now held much in contempt, was nevertheless an ingenious person.[1] He once made a statement that seems grotesque—of course, it is easy to ridicule this today, but in a certain sense it was said from the right feeling. He said that the human tongue is an octopus. Well, a human tongue is certainly not an octopus, but it is easy enough to conclude such a thing. Behind Oken's statement there was a general feeling that we must look at the lower animals if we want to understand the forms of various organs in the human head.

What I told you is for your own information, but it is possible to present such ideas so that children can understand them

---

1. Lorenz Oken (1779–1851), also known as Okenfuss, was a German morphologist and philosopher influenced by Pythagorean mysticism and a self-proclaimed pantheist, whom New England transcendentalists considered a brilliant thinker.

as well, because they are receptive to a morphological approach to the human being. One can study the various human forms and then find the appropriate analogy to forms in the animal world. In this way it is certainly possible to awaken children to a feeling that the entire animal kingdom could be described as a human being spread out into all the manifold animal forms, or that the human being is a synthesis of the whole animal kingdom.

In this way, teachers link the animal world to the human being, just as the plant world was related to the earth. By introducing each of these two subjects according to its own character, we awaken a healthy feeling for the world in children after the age of nine, when they have learned to distinguish between the inner and outer worlds. The goal is not for students to accumulate a great deal of knowledge, but to prepare the ground so they can acquire the right feeling for the world.

Just think of the things that are done in the name of education, regarding both students and the training of teachers. Awful things are happening in teacher education, wherein candidates are often expected to carry an unnecessary burden of factual knowledge in their heads just to pass examinations. In most instances, exam questions demand the kind of knowledge that one could simply look up in an encyclopedia. Memorized facts have little real value. What really matters is that examiners become convinced of the candidate's ability to teach out of a true knowledge of the human being.

Memory and our attitude about its development in children is another point of great importance. We must not forget that, until the change of teeth, memory, or the ability to remember, is linked directly to children's organic development. What a child of that age remembers so easily is brought about by forces also at work in the child's process of nutrition and growth. Up to the change of teeth, soul-spiritual and physical forces in children are a simple unity. Therefore we would make a great mistake by trying to artificially strengthen the child's memory before the change of teeth.

We must be clear that, before this change, children are also imitators in the way they develop memory. This means that, if we act properly in their presence, children will develop memory according to their predisposition toward physical growth and nutrition. Physical care (which we will speak about later on) and hygiene are the best means for cultivating memory forces in children.

One of the characteristic traits of our materialistic age is that people try to interfere with the natural development of young children by using artificial educational means. By appealing to their soul and spiritual element, people want to train children's memory even before the seventh year. Some want to go even further, which just shows how out of touch a materialistic attitude can become. There are mothers (and I speak from personal experience) who ask how they can teach their children, before the change of teeth, in a way that is suitable only at a later age. Then they go even further by asking how to educate a child before birth. They ask how the embryo should be educated. All one can say is, let a mother look after herself and her conduct. If her life is healthy and she treats herself properly, the child will develop in a healthy way. The baby's growth will have to be left to the creator. This may be an extreme way of putting it, but it is justifiable in view of the questions about sophisticated educational principles that really belong to educating children at an older age.

On the other hand, we must be clear that, with the change of teeth, the soul and spiritual part of children is freed from the physical to the degree that this is the right time to plan educational methods that will help their faculty of remembering. For this faculty, too, is freed at this stage. When children reach school age, it is right to do something about strengthening their memory, but this needs to be done according to a definite plan. If we burden their memory—that is, if we try to strengthen children by overloading them—their faculty of memory will only be weakened. Such misdirected efforts encourage a certain deep-seated rigidity in later life and a tendency toward prejudice that will be difficult to overcome. If, on the other hand, memory development is completely disregarded, children will be deprived of certain means of developing physical strength. If, when a child reaches school age, nothing is done to train the memory, the consequences will be a tendency toward inflammatory conditions in adolescence. Such a person often suffers from inflammations and is more likely to catch colds.

Causal links of this type again show how we have to consider both the physical and the soul-spiritual aspects together. Therefore, memory development demands a certain tact from teachers, who must avoid doing too much or too little. It would be just as wrong to drill children's memory excessively as it would be to overlook the matter of memory altogether. We should neither damage children's living interest by enforcing mechanical memorizing, nor neglect building memory altogether.

Let us look at ways of putting these ideas into practice. We can introduce children to the four rules of arithmetic as described in the previous lecture. We can give them some understanding of number relationships according to whether we subtract, divide, add, or multiply, as shown yesterday. But there is always an opportunity of letting students memorize multiplication tables, as long as these are related in the right way to the four rules. This also helps them deal with more complicated number relationships that will be introduced later.

In this sense, it is easy to err by introducing so-called object lessons. The calculator [abacus] has been introduced. I do not wish to be a fanatic, and the calculator may have its usefulness; from certain points of view, everything in life is justifiable. But much of what might be gained from the use of invented calculating machines can be achieved equally well by using the ten fingers or, for example, by using the number of students in the class. Do not misunderstand if I say that, when I see calculators in classrooms, from a spiritual point of view it strikes me as if I were in a medieval torture chamber. It really is not right to delegate learning processes to mechanical devices, simply to bypass seemingly mechanical memorization. Here we are facing an especially difficult task in the Waldorf school. I have told you that we aim to achieve soul economy in our teaching, and consequently we believe it would be beneficial for students if we restrict learning to the classrooms. This means that we give students as little homework as possible. This principle is prompted by yet another motive.

Certainly we should aim at developing in children a feeling of duty and responsibility, and later on we shall speak about how to bring this about. But it is very damaging to make certain demands on students that they do not then fulfill. And homework—as with any learning done at home—is very conducive to this effect. Parents often complain to us that their children are not given enough homework. But we have to consider the fact—and this is absolutely clear to anyone with sufficient insight—that too much homework causes some students to be overtaxed, while others are tempted to produce slipshod work or simply evade it altogether. Sometimes it is simply beyond their abilities to fulfill a teacher's demands. But the worst thing is when children do not do what the teacher has told them to do. Therefore, it would be better to ask less than to risk letting them get away with not fulfilling their assignments. All expectations and demands regarding memory training as well as those involving homework need to be dealt with very tactfully by teachers. The development of the student's memory depends especially on the sensitive perception of teachers, and the right relationship between them and their classes develops largely as a result of this quality.

Tomorrow we shall go into more details about the right attitude toward memory training.

CHILDREN FROM THE
TENTH TO FOURTEENTH YEARS
Part 1

January 2, 1922

At the end of yesterday's lecture, I tried to speak to you about the development of memory during the early school years. If we now look at the attitude regarding this matter as shown by most contemporary educational theorists, we notice a complete lack of awareness of how certain impulses during the early years of students continue to affect their later lives and how these reappear transformed. This, at any rate, is what a true knowledge of the human being reveals to us. What often happens today is that adults reach certain conclusions when they try to understand the ways of their own physical organism and psyche. Although people may not be conscious of it, they then assume that these conclusions apply also to the varying ages and stages of childhood. This attitude, however, is very misleading, because, as I pointed out, the forces that work throughout childhood development need to be recognized and supported if our education is to be sound. We must meet the inner needs of children, which is what was meant by our example of the importance of authority in the life of young children.

Imagine a man who, in his fortieth year, experiences certain vague events of the soul. External circumstances may suddenly shed light on what has arisen in his soul, and he may recognize that what is in his mind had been accepted at the age of eight or nine simply on the authority of a beloved teacher. At such a tender age, he could only entrust it to memory, since he may not have been able to comprehend it until the maturity of forty years of age. (I say this, though not many will believe my interpretation.) Children, however, cannot always wait until they are forty before understanding what they have been told at the age of eight, and this is the reason they have an inner longing for authority. When, at the age of forty, new light suddenly flashes upon what was accepted at the age of eight, simply on authority, this event brings the experience of new inner life forces, which has a refreshing effect on the whole person. New inner strength (sorely needed in later life) is developed in such a process. People are blessed with revitalizing strength for the rest of life if they have accepted a great deal of material on authority—material that, through outer circumstances, reappears as if by magic from one's organism. Today, many people age prematurely, in both body and soul, because they are denied access to this vivifying force. Too many years have gone by since one's memory was systematically strengthened during the early school years through appropriate and reasonable methods, based on faith and belief in the authority of an adult.

Memory training aside, there are plenty of other opportunities to cultivate children's faculties of comprehension, as I mentioned yesterday. But between the change of teeth and puberty, it is absolutely essential for teachers to work through thoughtful and sensible methods for developing students' memory, because without this they will be deprived of too much in later life.

If my intention were to please my listeners, I should have to speak quite differently about many things. But I wish to convey only a true knowledge of the human being as revealed by decades of anthroposophic research. Consequently, much that I

have to say will sound odd when compared with current opinions. Some of my findings will be seen as old-fashioned, while
others may appear avant-garde; but this is not really the point.
The only thing that matters is whether what I say can stand the
test of a true knowledge of the human being.

If we examine the general picture of the human being as seen
by so many today, we get the feeling that it came about only
through external observation. It is like trying to understand
how a clock works by looking only at its exterior. We can read
the time this way, and we can tell whether a watch is made of
gold or silver, but we will never become a clockmaker. Today,
what people call biology, physiology, or anatomy shows us only
what the human being looks like externally. Human nature
becomes transparent to our understanding only when we learn
to penetrate the human body, soul, and spirit. Only by including these three members in our investigations can we treat people according their true nature. If we use real insight into the
human being to look at a certain question much discussed
lately among educators—the question of fatigue in children—
we have to say this: Experiments are being made to establish
the causes of fatigue in children. The results of those investigations are then used in new teaching techniques intended to
reduce stress in students. This sort of thing is done all over the
world, and yet the whole question is based on the wrong
premise. Real knowledge of the human being would never lead
to such a question in the first place. You need only consider
something pointed out here during our last few meetings.
Recall the strong, repeated plea that all teaching during the
younger years should appeal to the rhythmic and musical element in children, which, first and foremost, works on their
breathing and blood circulation.

And now I ask, can the source of fatigue ever lie in the children's breathing and blood circulation? Can it ever arise from

the middle region of the human being, the very region to which we always give special attention and treatment during the child's school years? Never. Don't we all breathe continuously, during both sleep and waking life, from the moment we are born until we die, without ever feeling tired of breathing? Doesn't our blood circulate tirelessly from birth until death? Never is its flow interrupted by fatigue; if this happened, the consequences would indeed be serious. Doesn't this show us that teachers who work from a real art of education constantly appeal to these very organs, which are never subject to fatigue? This whole question has to be considered from quite a different angle. We must formulate it differently and ask, Where are the real sources of tiredness in a human being? We find them in the head and in the limb system. We must look at these two systems if we want to understand the nature of tiredness in children, which bears a completely different character according to whether it emanates from the head or from the limbs and metabolism.

The forces working from the head downward into the rest of the human organism deposit a very fine metabolic residue that wants to permeate the whole human body with fine salt-like deposits. This process, which also affects the breathing and blood circulation, is the cause of fatigue because of the head's direct contact with the external world and because of its arhythmic, nonmusical relationship to the outer world. The rhythms of breathing and blood circulation, on the other hand, are so strongly connected to the human organism that they retain a state of equilibrium and obey their own laws. And, in the central system, what acts like a self-contained unit is not subject to fatigue, at least not to any significant degree. It is possible, of course, to damage the inner rhythms of both children and adults through the wrong kind of treatment. But there is one thing we can be sure of: that the rhythmic system, which is of such primary importance in any true art of education, never suffers from tiredness or fatigue.

The limbs and metabolism, like the head, do get tired. You can see this by watching a snake after it has eaten. The limb and metabolic system tires, or at least becomes a source of tiredness, affecting the whole human being. Yet this form of tiredness is totally different from that of the head. The head system causes tiredness by depositing salts through a precipitation of mineral substances in the human organism. The limb and metabolic system, on the other hand, always tends to dissolve physical substances through its creation of warmth. Here, too, despite its polar opposite effect from that of the head, the cause of tiredness is found in the relative independence of this system from the inner rhythms of the human organization. This tiredness stems from the limbs' activities in the external world and from the metabolic response to food intake. Eating and drinking usually happen at irregular intervals, since there are very few people who adhere to a strict rhythm of eating and drinking. Therefore, although both head and metabolism share the same cause of tiredness, their effects have opposite natures.

Where does all of this lead? The whole question of fatigue in students needs to be put differently. If children tire easily, we should ask, What have we done wrong? Where did we make mistakes? We have no right to assume that our teaching methods are always correct. We will never reach human nature by testing children for the number errors they make after half an hour of writing, or if we test them after a certain period of reading for their comprehension of meaningless words inserted into a text. We reach human nature only by asking the right question, which, in the case of childhood fatigue, should try to determine whether we have overburdened a child's head or limb system. We must find methods that do not place too much strain on either of these two systems.

It would be erroneous, however, to believe that we could achieve this simply by adjusting the schedule of lessons, since gym lessons in themselves will not balance too much head work, nor will arithmetic work directly into the metabolism, though it does so indirectly. It is impossible to achieve the right balance merely by readjusting the schedule; this can be done only through an artistic presentation of lesson materials—at least during the early school years. This, in turn, means that we must appeal (as I have indicated) above all to the rhythmic system, the one system of the human being that never tires. Thus we also involve the other two systems, the head and the metabolic-limb systems, in the activity of learning. Naturally, this needs to be done correctly.

I hope that by now you realize that certain doubts about new ideas and methods of education, which are frequently expressed by those who are biased, do not apply at all to Waldorf education, because, in every sense, it is based on a true understanding of the human being. And because they also try to shed light on the soul and spiritual nature of the human being, Waldorf methods can lay the foundations for an approach that works on the whole human being.

For example, it is important to see that the human head system bears forces that penetrate the entire human organism (most strongly during childhood and decreasing during successive ages), shaping it, forming it, and giving it strength. The thought-directing capacity of the head is something that, as human beings with all our predispositions, we bring with us into this world at birth or conception. Eventually these forces assume the task of forming the entire human being. If the head were not in direct contact with the external world, and if, as a result, the inner rhythms of the human being were not disturbed all the time, then (if I may say it in this way) what has incarnated at birth in the head would be fully satisfied with the physical human organization. Human beings would flow into their physical organization, which would claim their entire being. We would be completely absorbed by it and would be unable to make any contact with the suprasensory world. Because human beings would thus be separated from the spiritual world, their inner life would become increasingly artificial and false. And, conversely, if through the limb and metabolic system human beings were not in constant touch with the external world, they would be unable to permeate with glowing warmth all that flows down from the head. We would be unable to counteract these forces, which would work toward an increasingly artificial state of perfection.

Here we have two marked polarities. The head always wants to cut us off from the spiritual world by shaping our body in a way that prevents us from gaining the right relationship to the spiritual world. The head and all that belongs to it finished developing a long time ago, during humankind's pre-earthly existence, and the process of materialization, issuing from the head, must always be counteracted by the activities of the human metabolism and limbs, which flow upward from below. In this way, a balance is achieved in our corporeality. And between these two poles is our central system—like a self-contained organism—our rhythmic system of respiration and blood circulation. This system is like a separate world in itself, like a microcosm. But despite its relative independence, it must be protected from the extreme influences of the head, which can affect it under certain circumstances, such as when the lungs are invaded by various foreign organic processes. We can observe this in the hardening of lungs and the new growth in the lungs of those suffering from lung diseases.

As human beings, we need this polarity between the head and the metabolism. The metabolism is always trying to dissolve the hardening processes from the head, and this situation can be utilized medically. If we recognize the interplay between what descends from the head and what ascends from the metabolism, we can cure pathological symptoms in the larynx, trachea, or lungs, for example, by treating the metabolic system, even when the source of illness lies in the head system. Especially in the case of children's diseases, spectacular results have been achieved by treating a patient's metabolism for the symptoms of illness that appeared in the head organization. The human being is a single organic entity and must be treated accordingly. This applies to all aspects of the human being, not just in sound methods of therapy, but especially in the field of education.

If one looks at the advances in general knowledge during the last centuries, one quickly notices how little has been achieved with regard to knowledge of the human being. This is mainly because the methods of investigation consider only the physical, external aspects. It is of utmost importance that anyone involved in the art of education be able to recognize quite realistically what happens in the body, soul, and spirit of growing children, especially between the great turning point at nine and the beginning of puberty. It is essential to be able to see how the physical, soul, and spiritual forces work on and affect one another in the children we educate.

If we observe children of nine to ten with real understanding, we find that everything entering the soul is absorbed and transmuted, so that the musculature, which is permeated by forces of growth, becomes actively involved. At that point in life, the muscles always respond to and work with the soul nature of children, especially where the more intimate forces of growth are active. The inner swelling or stretching of the muscles depends mostly on the development of a child's soul forces. The characteristic feature between the ages of ten and twelve is that the muscles have an especially intimate relationship with respiration and blood circulation. They are attuned to the central system of breathing and blood circulation. Because Waldorf education appeals so strongly to this part of a child's being, we indirectly promote the growth and development of the child's muscles.

Toward the twelfth year a new condition arises. The muscles no longer remain connected as intimately with the respiration and blood circulation but incline more toward the bones and adapt to the dynamics of the skeleton. The growth forces are fully engaged in the movement of limbs while walking, jumping, and grasping—indeed, in every limb activity related to the skeleton. The muscles, previously related closely to the rhythmic system, now become oriented entirely toward the skeletal system. Thus, children adapt more strongly now to the external world than they did before the twelfth year. Formerly, the muscular system was connected more directly with a child's inner being, and the rhythmic system, because of its relative independence, played a dominant role in muscle growth. A child moved in harmony with the muscular system, and the skeleton, embedded in the muscles, was simply carried along. Now, toward the twelfth year, the situation quickly changes; the muscles begin to serve the mechanics and dynamics of the skeletal organization.

You will have gained a deep understanding of how human nature develops once you can see and understand what happens within children before the twelfth year—how the muscles simply carry the bones along and later begin to relate directly to the skeleton and, in doing so, relate also to the external world. Such insights free us from abstract, intellectual modes of investigation, which are so prevalent today and easily creep into the field of education. These insights also move educators toward a truly human approach to children. If we allow such things to work on our soul, we will never impose the sort of treatment on a child that Marsyas had to endure.[1] Naturally, it is possible that some are frightened away when they see how transparent the human being becomes in the light of this knowledge of man. They may feel that the human soul is being dissected, but this is not the case; the anthroposophic approach is simultaneously artistic and an act of knowing. This way of looking at the human being is an art, and it is this that is needed if we want to grasp the importance of this whole period until puberty, or (as we can now describe it) the transition from an intimate affinity between the muscular system and the system of breathing and blood circulation before the twelfth year, and the subsequent relationship between the muscles and bones from the twelfth year until puberty.

Can you see now how an incarnating human being gradually adapts to the world? In very young children, the formative forces are centered in the brain and radiate from there. Then the center of activities shifts to the muscular system, and after the age of twelve a child's being pours itself into the skeleton, so to speak. Only then are human beings ready to enter the world fully. Incarnating human beings must first penetrate the body before establishing a relationship with the external world. First, the head forces are active. Later, these forces are poured into the muscles, then into the skeletal system, and after sexual maturity is reached, adolescents are able to enter the world. Only then can they stand properly in the world.

This gradual process of incarnation needs to be considered if if we want to find the right choice and presentation of class material, especially for this age. Unfortunately, however, today's educators hardly have a sound knowledge of the human being.

---

1. Marsyas was the flute player who engaged in a musical contest with Apollo and, after losing, was flayed alive by the god.

Now I must ask you to forgive me if I present you with something that may seem completely absurd to you. Often I feel compelled to do such a thing, because I have to stand up for anthroposophic truths. Contemporary physiologists, biologists, and anatomists will see what I am going to say as pure heresy, but it nevertheless represents the facts. Imagine that the human brain functions in a similar way. The nerves go from the brain to the sensory organs, the location of sense perception, which is then conducted back to the brain. Here in the brain is the central station, a human "London." Then, imagine there are motor nerves going from the brain to the organs of movement, where they give rise to the will impulses of movement according the thoughts of the brain, which are, in some way, also part of this will activity.

When people speak or think about the human being today, they first turn their attention to the head. Although the head itself always has the tendency to push us into what is material and would want to kill us every day if it were given free rein, it has nevertheless become the focus of attention among the general public today, and this is the unhealthy aspect of our current evaluation of the human being. It is a natural consequence of our modern scientific outlook. The general idea is this: in the head is the brain, which is a kind of absolute ruler over everything we think or do. I wonder how such a theory would have been explained before the telegraph, since this invention offered such a plausible analogy to what happens in our brain.

The theory of the human nervous system was postulated only after the use of telecommunications made that analogy possible. And so the brain was compared to a telecommunication center, stationed, say, in London (Steiner drew on the blackboard). If this is the center in London, then here would be Oxford, and Dover over there. If London is the center, then we could say, Here is a line running from Oxford to London. And here in

London messages coming from Oxford are switched over to Dover. Under certain circumstances, we could very well imagine it like this. Once such a theory has been invented, one can present the facts so that they seem to confirm it. Take any book on physiology, and in it you will find descriptions of how, in different experiments, nerves are cut and how various physical reactions in the human body lead to definite logical conclusions. Unless you maintain strong reservations from the beginning—after all, these things look very plausible—everything seems to fit together beautifully. The only snag here is that it does not stand up to what a penetrating knowledge of the human being has to say about it. There, it is unacceptable.

I will ignore the fact that sensory nerves and motor nerves are anatomically indistinguishable. One may be a little thicker, but their structures are not significantly different. According to anthroposophic research, they are uniform (I can indicate this only briefly, otherwise I would have to give whole lectures on anthroposophic physiology). It is absurd to say that sensory and motor nerves are different. The elements of sensation and will are omnipresent in the human soul, so everyone is free to call these either sensory or motor nerves, but they must be recognized as a single, unified entity, since there is no essential difference. The only difference is in the direction in which they function. The optic nerve (a sensory nerve) is open to light impressions on the eye, and peripheral events affect another nerve in turn, which modern physiology calls a motor nerve. If this nerve goes from the brain to the rest of the organism, its function is to perceive events during physical movement. A correct treatment of tabes dorsalis would confirm this.[2]

---

2. Tabes dorsalis is a condition that results from the destruction of the dorsal columns in the spinal cord, normally responsible for position sense. Loss of position sense causes severe gait and leg ataxia (balance and motor control problems).

It is the function of so-called motor nerves to perceive motor impulses and occurrences during physical movement, but not to initiate such impulses. Nerves, wherever they may be, are organs for transmitting impressions. Sensory nerves transmit external impressions, and motor nerves transmit internal impressions. However, there is only one kind of nerve. Only scientific materialism could have invented an analogy between nerves and a telegraph system. Only materialistic science could believe that, apart from the nerves, which transmit sense impressions during the process of perception, there must also be other nerves, whose special function is to initiate will impulses. But this is not the way it works. Will impulses originate in the soul and spiritual domain, where they begin and work directly into the metabolic-limb system, not via any other kind of nerves. Nerves that enter the metabolism and limbs transmit only the impressions of what a person is doing in response to soul and spiritual impulses. Through them we perceive the consequences of soul-spiritual will processes in the blood circulation, in the remaining metabolism, and in the movement of the limbs. These we perceive. The so-called motor nerves do not initiate physical movement, but allow us to perceive the consequences of our will impulses.

Unless we are clear about these relationships, we will not come to a proper understanding of the human being. On the other hand, if you can see the truth of what I am saying, you will also appreciate why I have to insist on making such seemingly contradictory statements, because they are instrumental in showing us how the human soul and spirit always work on the entire human being.

Until approximately the twelfth year, the effects of what was just described are found in muscular activity, which is so intensely connected with a child's breathing and blood circulation. From the age of twelve until puberty, these are linked more to the forces at work in the skeleton. This means that, before the twelfth year, children perceive with their so-called motor nerves more what lives in muscle activity, whereas after the twelfth year their perceptivity tends more toward the processes taking place between muscles and bones.

Now consider the fact that volition is also involved in every process of thinking. When connecting (or synthesizing) certain mental images, or when separating (or analyzing) them, we also use our will forces, and you have to look for this will element in the appropriate area of the organism, into which it works from the domain of the human soul and spirit. The will forces involved in the process of thinking are connected with the organism as just described. Consequently, when entering the twelfth year, children develop the kind of thinking that, in the will nature, takes place in the bones and the dynamics of the skeleton. At this point, an important transition is taking place from the soft muscular system to the hard bony system that, as I like to put it, places itself into the world like a system of levers. And here is where the heresy lies, the paradox I have to place before you: When we think about something belonging to external, inorganic nature, we do so primarily with our skeleton. Anyone accustomed to the currently accepted ideas of physiology will most likely laugh when someone living in Dornach maintains that we think abstractly with our bones. But this is how it works. It would be more comfortable not to say this, but it must be said, since correct knowledge of the human being is needed so much today.

Thoughts in our brain are only pictures of what actually occurs during the process of thinking. The brain is only an instrument that produces passive mental images of the real processes going on during the activity of thinking. To become conscious of our thinking, we need these mental pictures. But the images that our brain reflects for us lack the inner force inherent in pure thinking; they lack the element of will. The real nature of thinking has no more to do with the brain's mental images than a certain gentleman's picture on a wall has to do with the man himself. We must distinguish a picture from the actual person. Similarly, the actual processes during thinking must be distinguished from the mental images derived from them. When thinking is directed toward outer physical nature, the entire human organism is involved to a certain extent, but especially the skeleton. In the twelfth year, a child's thinking enters the realm of the skeleton. This is the signal for us to move on to a new range of subjects, leaving behind the subjects described yesterday—the plant in relation to the earth and the animal kingdom in relation to the human being.

Our awareness of what happens in the soul and spiritual domain of children must lead to the appropriate choices and lesson plans. The way the soft muscular system plays its part in relation to respiration and blood circulation indicates that children, from the tenth to twelfth years, should be introduced to plants and animals as described. These subjects relate more directly to our inner human nature than do more distant subjects such as mineralogy, dynamics, physics, and so on. Thus, as the twelfth year approaches, teaching, which previously had a mainly pictorial character and included living plants and sentient animals, should now appeal more to an intellectual grasp of inorganic nature.

Now we reach the point when young adolescents can place themselves as earthly beings into the world of dynamics and mechanics and experience their forces. Now the possibility arises for introducing them to the basic principles of physics and chemistry, which are subject to specific natural laws, and to the mineral realm. If these subjects were taught at an earlier age, we would interfere with evolving human nature and unconsciously damage healthy development in our students.

The ability to grasp historical connections—to gain an overall view of historical developments and the underlying impulses and social implications—represents the other side of the stage where students are able to comprehend the physical and mineral aspects of life. Only toward the twelfth year are they mature enough for both of these aspects. Historical ideas and impulses, which are expressed outwardly in definite historical periods and directly affect social life and forms, are like the skeleton of history, although—seen in a purely historical context—they may also be something quite different. The flesh, or muscles, so to speak, are represented by the lives of historical personages as well as by concrete historical events. Therefore, to introduce history between the tenth and the twelfth year, we must bring it as images that engender a warmth of feeling and inwardly uplift the students' souls. This is possible through telling the children of biographical events and by characterizing certain concrete events that form a whole. But we must not introduce the abstract ideas and impulses behind certain historical eras. Students should meet these in their twelfth year, which is when they begin to take a stand in the outer world. Here again you can see how an inner development gradually extends outward. Now students are ready to grasp how historical impulses, manifesting in outer events, affect the lives of people.

It is important to realize this, because otherwise there is the danger of approaching children from an adult point of view. When educating young people, it is too easy to draw parallels to an adult study of the sciences, beginning with simpler content in physics and chemistry and moving gradually to more difficult parts. One may think that we should teach subjects at school in a similarly graduated way. But this does not accord with the nature of children. An adult may see something as the simplest of material, such as we find in the mineral kingdom and inorganic physical world, but children can grasp this only after they have penetrated the realm of their skeletal system, moving in the outer world according to the dynamics of the skeleton as though conforming to the principles of the lever.

Many today have grown accustomed to looking at almost every aspect of life as though it should belong to the domain of natural laws. We find historians who try to interpret the social phenomena of historical impulses as if they, too, should be subservient to the laws of nature. This attitude is encouraged even in childhood, when physical and chemical laws are taught before the twelfth year and before other subjects more closely allied to human life are studied in lessons. If school subjects are introduced in the wrong order, students project their own experiences and understanding of purely physical laws into the social sphere and into their understanding of history. And since this way of seeing the world has deeply penetrated educational practice, the general public is quite willing to look for natural laws in practically every area of life, so that one may no longer suggest that historical impulses originate in the spiritual world. Again, this is reflected in the current principles of education. Children are encouraged to develop a firm belief in what they have been taught in physics and chemistry, so that later on, as adults, they will maintain this limited view in their outlook as a whole.

What I have written on the blackboard comes from America: "Nature's proceedings in social phenomena."[3] This phrase has

---

3. Steiner refers to the educational ideas of John Dewey (1859–1952), who was an "instrumentalist" related to utilitarian and pragmatic schools of thought. His early works include *The School and Society* (1907). He wrote, "Egoistic desire is gradually coming into harmony with the necessity of the environment, till at last the individual automatically finds happiness in doing what the natural and social environment demands, and serves himself in serving others" (*Human Nature and Conduct*, 1922).

become almost a slogan as an educational principle, postulating that children should be educated so that they will see the processes of society as if they were natural laws. Children are to regard events in community life as they do natural processes.

People have come to me again and again to tell me that this phrase should read differently in English, that it should read "progress of nature" or something similar. However justified their criticism may be from the perspective of language use, what matters is that this quote has become a catchphrase for a specific principle in educational science. Whatever the correct wording is, we must realize that its message needs to be corrected, and this is what I wish to do from a worldwide point of view. Correcting the wording is not good enough, for the meaning implies that we find only natural laws working through social impulses. And this is the kind of attitude that we inculcate in our children. We must begin to experience natural laws at work in the processes of nature, and higher, spiritual laws within the social sphere. But this is not happening. We ruin our students' future worldviews when we introduce them prematurely to subjects such as chemistry, mineralogy, physics, dynamics, and so on. As I have pointed out so many times already, we have to keep an eye on the entire milieu of our culture to know where to promote the impulses of the art of education. Forgive me if I have again raised an argument against common practice, but in my opinion it is justified.

If we approach modern science with the knowledge and insight gained by following paths outlined in *How to Know Higher Worlds,* we get the impression that the world described by natural science—according to mineral and physical law only—is not one in which we can live as human beings of flesh and blood. Theirs is a different world altogether. When we look, with eyes opened by *imaginative* knowledge, at the world described by modern natural science, and when we see how their picture of the world is meant to affect people today, we do not find human beings of flesh and blood there at all. We see only walking skeletons, little bone men and bone women. Theirs is a strange world indeed.

I once made an interesting experiment. The younger people here won't remember a certain Swiss philosopher called Vogt— known as "Fat Vogt"—a typical thinker of recent times who in the 1850s somehow managed to knock together a rough-and-ready materialistic world philosophy that, like a specter, still haunts many worldviews today.[4] I tried to imagine what would happen if real flesh-and-blood human beings were to find their way into this world of walking skeletons. Any healthy person of flesh and blood could not bear to live in such a world. But what would happen, I asked myself, if someone with at least a modicum of flesh and blood were to stray into this world of walking bones? The effects of living in a world as described by a purely materialistic view, and its intentional influences on people, would make a real person suffer the worst kinds of neurasthenia and hysteria. One could never be free of all the surrounding influences. Essentially, today's natural science describes a world where we would all become neurasthenic and hysterical. Mercifully, the world of the natural scientist is not real or the one we live in. Very different forces, undreamed of by such people, are at work in the real world. Nevertheless, we need to extricate ourselves from this falsely uniform world of illusion, from which we receive almost everything that contributes to the general civilization of today. We must reach a true and real knowledge of the human being, and only then will we be able to educate in the right way.

---

4. Karl Vogt (1817–1895), Swiss professor who rejected all dualism and the acceptance of an immaterial soul substance. He stressed the dependence of psychological functions on the brain.

Children from the Tenth to Fourteenth Years
Part 2

January 3, 1922

From what you have heard so far, you may have gotten the impression that the art of education based on anthroposophic knowledge of the human being is intended to nurture, above all, a healthy and harmonious development of the physical body of children. You may have noticed that certain questions could be seen as guidelines for our educational aims. For example, How can we help free the development of formative forces flowing from the head, affecting and shaping the young organism? How can we work in harmony with the child's developing lungs and blood circulation during the middle years? What must we do to cultivate, in the broadest sense, the forces working throughout a child's musculature? How do we properly support the processes of muscle growth in relation to the bones and tendons, so that young adolescents can attain the proper position in the outer world?

These questions imply that whatever we do to enhance the development of a child's soul and spirit is directed first toward the best possible healthy and normal development of the physical body. And this is indeed the case. We consciously try to aid and foster healthy development of the physical body, because in this way the soul and spiritual nature is given the best means of unfolding freely through a child's own resources. By doing as little harm as possible to the spiritual forces working through children, we give them the best possibility of developing in a healthy way. This is not to be done through any preconceived ideas of what a growing human being should be like. Everything we do in teaching is an attempt to create the most favorable conditions for the children's physical health. And because we must pay attention to the soul and spiritual element as well, and because the physical must ultimately become its outer manifestation, we must also come to terms with the soul and spiritual aspect in the way best suited for the child's healthy development.

You may ask which educational ideal such an attitude comes from; it arises from complete dedication to human freedom. And it springs from our ideal to place human beings in the world so that they can unfold individual freedom, or, at least, in such a way that physical hindrances do not prevent them from doing so.

When we emphasize the physical development of children in our education, we are especially trying to help them learn to use their physical powers and skills fully in later life. Waldorf education is based on the knowledge and confidence that life in general has the best chance of developing when allowed to develop freely and healthily. Naturally, all this has to be taken in a relative sense, which, I hope is understood.

Children who, through educational malpractice during the school years, have been prevented from breathing properly and from using their system of bones and connective tissue properly, will not grow up to become free individuals. Likewise, students whose heads have been crammed with fixed ideas and concepts deemed important for later life will not become inwardly free. Children will not grow into a free human beings

unless their childhood needs, as imposed by physical development, were both understood and catered to through the appropriate educational principles and methods. Naturally, the soul
and spiritual needs of children must also be recognized and met
with the right educational methods. Far from leading to any
kind of false or lofty idealism, anthroposophy wishes to prove
itself by enabling its followers to deal with the practical problems of life between birth and death, the span of time in which
we should develop the physical body in accord with the soul
and spirit.

So you see that we have no influence over the development
of what belongs to the realm of soul and spirit, even if we as
educators wanted it. The soul and spiritual part of the human
being exists in its true being only from the moment we fall
asleep until the time of awaking. This means that, if we want to
educate people's soul and spirit, we must do so while they sleep.
In fact, it is impossible for us to do this. Today, we encounter a
strong belief that we must educate the soul and spirit and
indoctrinate people with certain concepts. All we can really do
is help people toward the free use of physical capabilities
through the soul and spirit.

I have often said that it is impossible to deal with educational matters without fully considering the entire life situation
of our time, taking into account the general milieu into which
education is placed. I will refrain from introducing any extraneous matter into our considerations here, but what I want to
say now definitely belongs to our theme.

News has come to us that in Eastern Europe a new pedagogy
is being worked out for the benefit of those who are still recognized there, those who belong to the Radical Socialist Party.
Because nothing that was acceptable prior to the Revolution is
now considered correct, new educational methods are being
worked out there. This is being done by purely outward means.

We are told that one of the leaders in modern Russia has been commissioned to write the history of the Communist Party. The new government has given him one month to complete his task. During this month, he will also have to do some practical work at the Moscow Center. As a result of these activities, a book is to be published that will become the official model for reeducating all those being recognized as proper Russians. Another party member has been commissioned to write a history of the workers' movement in the West and a history of international communism. While compiling his authoritative account, he, too, has been given other work to do, and after six weeks he is supposed to have this work completed. All true Soviet Russians are supposed to study this book. Forgive me, I believe that the second writer was actually given two months. A third person was commissioned to publish a theory of Marxism, and it was he who was given six weeks to deliver the book. With this book, every true Russian will become familiar with the new conditions in the East. According to these same methods, several other persons have been assigned to write new Russian literature. They have all been allotted a fixed time schedule in which to complete their orders. And they have all been told what other work they must do during the time of writing. The party member selected to write the book about Marxism has also been made coeditor of *Pravda*.

Why do I bring this up today? Because, basically, what is happening in Soviet Russia today is the ultimate consequence of what lives in all of us, insofar as we represent today's civilization. People will not admit that events in Russia are merely the ultimate consequences of our own situation, taken to extremes in Eastern Europe. The absurdity of communist ideology is that it has determined and officially declared what a citizen must know; it does not ask what people can do to become real human beings who are properly integrated into the world's fabric.

Teachers are called on to bring the utmost respect for soul and spirit to their lessons. Without this they will fail, as though they lacked the most fundamental artistic and scientific understanding. Therefore, the first prerequisite of Waldorf teachers is reverence for the soul and spiritual potential that children bring with them into the world. When facing the children, teachers must be filled with an awareness that they are dealing with innately free human beings. With this attitude, teachers can work out educational principles and methods that safeguard the children's inborn freedom so that in later life, when they look back at their school days, they will not find any infringement on their personal freedom, not even in the later effects of their education.

To clarify the implications of these statements, we can ask ourselves, what becomes of those whose physical idiosyncrasies are not dealt with properly during childhood? Childish idiosyncrasies continue into later life, and if you wonder what sort of effect they will have when children become adults, I will answer by saying something that may seem rather odd and surprising. Peculiar physical habits in early childhood, if left untreated, degenerate and become the causes of illnesses later on. You must realize, in all seriousness, that characteristic physical tendencies in childhood, if allowed to continue unchanged, become causes of illness. Such knowledge will give you the right impulse for a proper care that in no way conflicts with the deepest respect for human freedom.

By comparison, imagine someone who, down to the deepest fibers of her being, is enthusiastic about the inner human freedom. Imagine she falls ill and must call a doctor. The doctor cures her by using the best means available today for the art of healing. Would such a person ever feel that her personal freedom had been interfered with? Never. What meets a person in this way would never impinge upon one's inner freedom.

A similar feeling must be present in those who are engaged in the art of education. They should have the willingness and the ability to see the nature of their own calling as being similar to that of a doctor in relation to patients. Education naturally exists in its own right, and it certainly is not simply therapy in the true sense of the word. But there is a certain relationship and similarity between the work of a doctor and that of a teacher that justifies comparison.

When students leave school in their mid-teens, it is time for us to examine again whether, during their school years from the change of teeth to the coming of puberty, we have done our best to help and equip them for later life. (During the coming days, we will deal with the esthetic and moral aspects of education and look more closely at the stage of puberty. For now, we will consider the more general human aspects.) We must realize that, during their past school years, we have been dealing mainly with their ether body of formative forces, and that the soul life (of which more will be said later) was just beginning to manifest toward the approach of graduation.

We must consider the next stage, which begins with the fourteenth to fifteenth years and continues until the beginning of the twenties, a time when a young man or woman must face the task of fitting more and more into outer life. We have already seen how children gradually take hold of the body, finally incarnating right into the skeleton, and how, by doing so, they connect more and more with the external world and adapt to outer conditions. Fundamentally, this process continues until the early twenties, after which comes a very important period of life. Although, as teachers, we no longer have any direct influence over the young person at this stage, we have in fact already done a great deal in this way during the previous years, and this will become apparent during the early to the late twenties.

After leaving school, young people must train for a vocation. Now they no longer receive what come, mainly from human nature itself, but rather what has become part of the civilization we live in, at least in terms of the chosen trade or profession. Now the young person has to be adaptable to certain forms of specialization. In our Waldorf school, we try to prepare students to step into life by introducing practical crafts such as spinning and weaving to our students of fourteen and fifteen. Practical experience in such crafts is not important only for future spinners or weavers but for all those who want to be able to do whatever a situation may demand. It is nevertheless important to introduce the right activities at the right time.

What has been cultivated in a child's ether body during early school years emerges again in the soul sphere of young people during their twenties, the time when they must enter a profession. The way they were treated at school will play a large role in whether they respond to outer conditions clumsily, reluctantly, full of inhibitions, or skillfully and with sufficient inner strength to overcome obstacles. During their twenties, young people become aware of how the experiences of their school years first went underground, as it were, while they trained for a trade or profession, only to surface again in form of capacities, such as being able to handle certain situations or fit oneself into life in the right way. Teachers who are aware of these facts will pay attention to the critical moments in their students' lives between the change of teeth and puberty.

I have often spoken about the important turning point that appears during the ninth to tenth years. Toward the twelfth year, another important change takes place, which I have also mentioned. Children of six or seven, when entering school, are "one great sensory organ," as I have called them. At this stage, much has already been absorbed through imitation. Children have also been occupied with the inner processes of molding and sculpting the organs, and they bring the results to school. Now, everything that teachers do with the children, until the turning point around nine, should have a formative effect, but in a way that stimulates them to participate freely and actively in this inner shaping. I indicated this with my strong appeal for an artistic approach during the introductions to reading, writing, and arithmetic. The artistic element is particularly important at this age.

All teaching during the early school years must begin with the child's will sphere, and only gradually should it lead over toward the intellect. Those who recognize this will pay special attention to educating the child's will. They will know that children must learn to drive out the will forces from their organism, but in the right way. To do this, their will activities must be tinged with the element of feeling. It is not enough for teachers to do different things with the children; they must also develop sympathy and antipathy according to what they are doing. And the musical element, apart from music per se, offers the best means for achieving this. Thus, as soon as children are brought to us, we ought to immerse them in the element of music, not just through singing but also by letting them make music with simple instruments. Thus, young students will not only nurture an esthetic sense, but most of all (though indirectly), they will learn how to use and control will forces in a harmonious way.

Children bring many inborn gifts to school. Inwardly they are natural sculptors, and we can draw on these gifts as well as their other hidden talents. For instance, we can let children do all kinds of things on paper with paints (even though this might be inconvenient for teachers), and in this way we introduce them to the secrets of color. It is really fascinating to observe how children relate to color when left alone to cover a white surface with various colors. What they produce in a seemingly haphazard way is not at all meaningless, but in all the blotches and smears we can detect a certain color harmony resulting from an inborn relationship to the world of color. We must be careful, however, not to let children use the solid blocks of color that are sold in children's paint boxes, with which they are supposed to paint directly from the blocks onto paper. This has a damaging effect, even in the case of painting as art. One should paint with liquid colors already dissolved in water or some other suitable liquid. It is important, especially for children, to develop an intimate relationship with color. If we use thick paints from a palette, we do not have the same intimate relationship to color as we do when we use liquid colors from bottles.

In a painting lesson, you might say to a child, "What you have painted is really beautiful. You put red in the middle, and all the other colors around it go well with the red. Everything you painted fits well with the red in the middle. Now try to do it the other way round. Where you have red, paint blue, and then paint around it all the other colors so that they also go well with the blue in the middle." Not only will this child be tremendously stimulated by such an exercise, but by working out a transposition of colors—possibly with help from the teacher—the child will gain a great deal toward establishing an inner relationship to the world in general.

However inconvenient it may be for the teachers, they should always encourage young students to form all sorts of shapes out of any suitable material they can lay their hands on. Of course, we should avoid letting them get unduly dirty and messy, since this can be a real nuisance. But children gain far more from these creative activities than they would by simply remaining clean and tidy. In other words, it is truly valuable for children, especially during the early years, to experience the artistic element.

Anything required of children must be induced first in a way that is appropriate to their nature. If artistic activities are introduced as described, learning other subjects becomes easier. Foreign languages, for example, will be learned with far greater ease if students have done artistic work beforehand. I already said that children should learn foreign languages at a very early age, if possible as soon as they enter school.

Nowadays, we often encounter somewhat fanatical attitudes; something that in itself is quite right and justifiable tends to become exaggerated to the point of fanatical extremism. And teaching foreign languages is no exception. Children learn their native tongue naturally, without any grammatical consciousness, and this is how it should be. And when they enter school, they should learn foreign languages in a similar way, without grammatical awareness, but now the process of learning a language is naturally more mature and conscious.

During the tenth year, at the turning point of life mentioned several times, a new situation calls for an introduction to the first fundamentals of grammar. These should be taught without any pedantry whatever. It is necessary to take this new step for the benefit of the children's healthy development, because at this age they must make a transition from a predominantly feeling approach toward life to one in which they must develop their I-consciousness. Whatever young people do now must be done more consciously than before. Consequently, we introduce a more conscious and intellectual element into the language that students have already learned to speak, write, and read. But when doing this, we must avoid pedantic grammar exercises. Rather, we should give them stimulating practice in recognizing and applying fundamental rules. At this stage, children really need the logical support that grammar can give, so that they do not have to puzzle repeatedly over how to express themselves correctly.

We must realize that language contains two main elements that always interact with each other—an emotional, or feeling, element and an intellectual, thinking element. I would like to illustrate this with a quote from Goethe's *Faust:*

> Grey, dear friend, is every theory
> And green the golden tree of life.

I do not expect that our you (who have come mainly from the West) should study all the commentaries on Goethe's *Faust,* since there are enough to fill a library. But if you did, you would make a strange discovery. When coming to this sentence in *Faust,* you would most likely find a newly numbered remark at the bottom of the page (at least a four-digit number because of all the many explanations already given), and you would find a comment about the lack of logic in this sentence. Despite the poetic license granted to any reputable author (so the commentator might point out), the colors of the tree in this stanza do not make sense. A "golden tree"—could he mean an orange tree? But then, of course, it would not be green either. If it were an ordinary tree, it would not be golden. Perhaps Goethe was thinking of an artificial tree? In any case (a typical commentary would continue), a tree cannot be golden and green at the same time. Then there is the other problem of a grey theory. How can a theory be grey if it is invisible? In this way, many commentaries point out the lack of logic in this sentence.

Of course, there are other, more artistically inclined commentators who delight in the apparent lack of logic in this passage. But what is really at the bottom of it all? It is the fact that, on the one side, the emotional, feeling element of language predominates in this sentence, whereas on the other, it stresses a more thoughtful aspect of imagery. When Goethe speaks of a golden tree, he implies that we would love this tree as we love gold. The word *gold* here does not have an image quality but expresses the warm feeling engendered by the glow of gold. Only the feelings are portrayed. The adjective *green*, on the other hand, refers to an ordinary tree, such as we see in nature. This is the logic of it. With regard to the word *theory*, a theory is of course invisible. Yet, right or wrong, a mere word may conjure up certain feelings in some people that remind them of London fog. One can easily transfer such a feeling to *theory* as a concept. A pure feeling element of language is again expressed in the adjective *grey*.

The feeling and thinking qualities in language intermingle everywhere. In contemporary languages, much has already become crippled, but in their earlier stages, an active and creative element lived everywhere, through which the feeling and thinking qualities came into being.

As mentioned, before the age of nine, children have an entirely feeling relationship to language. Yet, unless we also introduce the thinking element in language, their self-awareness cannot develop properly, and this is why it is so important to bring them the intellectual aspect of language. This can be done by judiciously teaching grammatical rules, first in the mother tongue and then in foreign languages, whereby the rules are introduced only after children have begun to speak the language. So, according to these indications, teachers should arouse a feeling in students around the age of nine or ten that they are beginning to penetrate the language more consciously. This is how a proper grammatical sense could be cultivated in children.

By the time children reach the age of twelve, they should have developed a feeling for the beauty of language—an esthetic sense of the language. This should stimulate "beauty in speaking" in them, but without ever falling into mannerisms. After this, until the time of puberty, students should learn to appreciate the dialectical aspect of language; they should develop a faculty for convincing others through command of language. This third element of language should be introduced only when they are approaching graduation age.

To briefly summarize the aims of language teaching, children should first develop, step by step, a feeling for the correct use of language, then a sense of the beauty of language, and finally the power inherent in linguistic command. It is far more important for teachers to find their way into an approach to language teaching than to merely follow a fixed curriculum. In this way, teachers quickly discover how to introduce and deal with what is needed for the various ages. After a mostly artistic approach, in which students up to age nine are involved very actively, teachers should begin to dwell more on the descriptive element in language, but without neglecting the creative aspect. This is certainly possible if you choose the kind of syllabus I have tried to characterize during these past few days, in which the introduction of nature study leads to geography, and animals are seen in the context of humankind. The most effective way to include the descriptive element would be to appeal mainly to the children's soul sphere rather than claiming their entire being. This should be done by clothing the lessons in a story told in a vivid, imaginative way. Likewise, at this stage of life, teachers should present historical content by giving lively accounts of human events that, in themselves, form a whole, as already indicated.

Having gone through the stage of spontaneous activity, followed by an appreciation of the descriptive element, students approaching the twelfth year are ready for what could be called an explanatory approach. Cause and effect now come into general considerations, and material can be given that stretches the powers of reasoning.

Throughout these stages, teachers should present mathematical elements in their manifold forms, in a way appropriate to the student's age. Mathematics, as taught in arithmetic and geometry, is likely to cause particular difficulties for teachers. Before the ninth year, this is introduced in simpler forms and subsequently expanded, since children can take in a great deal if we know how to go about it. It is a fact that all mathematical material taught throughout the school years must be presented in a thoroughly artistic and imaginative way. Using all kinds of means teachers must contrive to introduce arithmetic and geometry artistically, and here, too, between the ninth and tenth years teachers must go to a descriptive method. Students must be taught how to observe angles, triangles, quadrilaterals, and so on through a descriptive method. Proofs should not be introduced before the twelfth year.

A boring math teacher will achieve very little if anything at all, whereas teachers who are inspired by this subject will succeed in making it stimulating and exhilarating. After all, it is by the grace of mathematics that, fundamentally, we can experience the harmonies of ideal space. If teachers can become enthusiastic about the Pythagorean theorem or the inner harmonies between planes and solids, they bring something into lessons that has immense importance for children, even in terms of soul development. In this way, teachers counteract the elements of confusion that life presents.

You see, language could not exist without the constantly intermingling elements of thought and feeling. Again I have made an extreme statement, but if you examine various languages, you will discover how feeling and thinking are interwoven everywhere. This in itself, as well as many other factors, could easily introduce chaos into our lives were it not for the inner firmness that mathematics can give us. Those who can look more deeply into life know that many people have been saved from neurasthenia, hysteria, and worse afflictions simply by learning how to observe triangles, quadrilaterals, tetrahedra, and other geometrical realities in the right way.

Perhaps you will allow me a more personal note at this point, because it may help clarify the point I am making. I have a special love for mechanics, not simply because of its objective value, but for personal reasons. I owe this love of mechanics to one of my teachers in the Vienna High School and the enthusiasm he showed for this subject; such things live on into later life. This teacher glowed with excitement when searching for the resultants from given components. It was interesting to see the joy with which he looked for the resultants and the joy with which he would take them apart again in order to fit them back into their components. While doing this, he almost jumped and danced from one end of the blackboard to the other until, full of glee, he would finally call out the formula he had found, such as $c^2 = a^2 + b^2$. Captivated by his findings, which he had written on the board, he would look around at his audience with a benign smile, which in itself was enough to kindle enthusiasm for analytical mechanics, a subject that hardly ever evokes such feelings in people. It is very important that mathematics, which is taught in various forms right through school, should pour out, as it were, its own special substance over all the students.

And so we can speak of the two poles in human development: the rhythmic and artistic pole and the mathematical and conceptual one. If, as indicated, young souls are worked on from within outward, students will gradually grow into the world in the right way.

At the approach of the graduation age, or mid-teens, teachers will again feel an inner need to survey the most significant moments in the development of their students during the last few years, this time in retrospect. Students entered school in class one at the age of six or seven. A few years later they are sent out into the world again and—as I indicated at the beginning of today's lecture—it is the teacher's aim to enable them to adapt to life in the world. When we receive young students in class one, they are like one great sense organ. Inwardly, they carry a kind of a copy of their parents and others who surround them and of society as a whole. It is our task to transform these adopted and specialized features into more general human features. We can do this by appealing, above all, to children's middle system of breathing and blood circulation, which is not connected so much with their more personal side.

Yet, apart from the adopted features that children have unconsciously copied from their environment, they also bear their very own individual characteristics when they enter school. They are less pronounced than similar characteristics found in adults, features that we associate with melancholic, sanguine, phlegmatic, or choleric temperaments. Nevertheless, the children's nature, too, is definitely colored by what could be called their temperamental disposition, so we can speak of children with melancholic, phlegmatic, sanguine, and choleric tendencies. It is essential for teachers to acquire a fine perception of the manifold symptoms and characteristics that arise from children's temperamental dispositions and to find the right way of dealing with them.

Melancholic children are those who depend most strongly on the conditions of the physical body. Because of their special constitution, they tend to feel weighed down by their bodily nature. They easily become self-centered and, in general, show little interest in what is going on around them. Yet it would be wrong to think of melancholic children as simply inattentive, since this is true only with regard to their surroundings and what comes from their teachers. They are, on the other hand, very attentive to their own inner conditions, and this is the reason melancholic children tend to be so moody. Please note that what I am saying about the temperaments applies only to children whose symptoms cannot be automatically transferred to adults of the same temperament.

The relationship of phlegmatic children to their environment is one of complete, though entirely subconscious, surrender to the world at large. And since the world is so vast and full of things to which they have surrendered themselves, they show little interest in what is closer to them. Again, my remarks about this temperament refer only to children, otherwise they might be seen as a compliment to phlegmatic adults, and they are certainly not meant to be that. Making a rather sweeping statement, one could say that, if children with phlegmatic tendencies did not happen to live on earth but out in the heavenly world of the cosmos, such children would be full of the deepest interest in their surroundings. They feel at home in the periphery of the world. Phlegmatic children are open to immensity and anything that is vast and remote and does not make an immediate impact.

To a certain extent, sanguine children display the opposite characteristics of the melancholic or phlegmatic child. Young melancholics are immersed in bodily nature. Phlegmatic children are drawn outward to the spheres of infinity, because they are so strongly linked to their ether body. The ether body always inclines outward toward infinite totality; it disperses into the cosmos just a few days after death. Sanguine children live in what we call the astral, or soul, body. This member of the human being is different from the physical or ether bodies inasmuch as it is not concerned with anything temporal or spatial. It exists beyond the realm of time and space. Because of the astral body, during every moment of our lives we have an awareness of our entire life up to the present moment, although memories of earlier experiences are generally weaker than more recent ones. The astral body is instrumental mainly in directing our dreams. These, as you know, bear little relationship to the normal sequence of time. We may dream about something that happened only yesterday yet, mixed up in the dream, people may appear whom we met in early childhood. The astral body mixes up our life experiences and has no regard for the element of time and space, but in its chaotic ways it has its own dimension that is totally different from what is temporal and spatial.

Sanguine children surrender themselves to their astral body, and this becomes evident in their entire pattern of behavior. They respond to outer impressions as though what lies beyond time and space were directly transmitted to us through the outer world itself. They quickly respond to impressions without digesting them inwardly, because they do not care for the time element. They simply surrender to the astral body and make no effort to retain outer impressions. Or, again, they do not like to live in memories of earlier events. Because they pay so little attention to time, sanguine children live in and for the present moment. They express outwardly something that, in reality, is the task of the astral body in the higher worlds, and this gives sanguine children a certain superficiality.

Choleric children are most directly linked to their I-center. Their physical build shows a strong will that, permeated by the forces of their I-being, is likely to enter life aggressively.

It is truly important for teachers to cultivate a fine perception for these characteristic features of the temperaments in growing children. You must try to deal with them in a twofold way: first, by introducing a social element in the class, based on the various temperaments. When teachers get an idea of their students as a whole, they should place them in groups according to similarity of temperament. There are children of mixed temperaments, of course, and this has to be considered as well. In general, however, it has a salutary effect when children of the same temperament are seated together, for the simple reason that the temperaments rub up against each other. Melancholic children, for example, will have a neighbor who is also melancholic. They become aware of how this neighbor is suffering from all kinds of discomforts arising from the physical constitution. Melancholic students recognize similar symptoms in themselves, and the mere looks of their neighbors will have a healing effect on their own nature.

If phlegmatic children sit next to other phlegmatics, they become so bored with them that, in the end, their phlegmatic nature becomes stirred to the extent that they try to shake off their lethargy.

Sanguine children, when seated among other sanguines, recognize the way they flutter from one impression to the next, being momentarily interested in one thing and then in another, until they feel like brushing them away like flies. Experiencing their own traits in their neighbors, sanguine children become aware of the superficiality of their own temperament.

When choleric children are seated together, there will be such a constant exchange of blows that the resulting bruises they give each other will have an extraordinary healing effect on their temperament.

You must observe these things, and you will find that by introducing, through your choice of seating, a social element in the classroom, you will have a wholesome and balancing effect on each child. In this way, the teacher's relationship to each of the temperaments will also find the appropriate expression. The second point to be kept in mind is that it would not be helpful to treat melancholic children—or any other temperament for that matter—by going against their inherent disposition. On the contrary, we should develop the habit of treating like with like. If, for instance, we forced a choleric to sit still and to be quiet, the result would be an accumulation of suppressed choler that would act like a poison in the child's system. It simply would not work. On the other hand, if, for example, a teacher shows continued interest and understanding for the doleful moods of a melancholic child, this attitude will finally bring about a beneficial and healing effect. When dealing with phlegmatic children, outwardly we should also appear rather phlegmatic and somewhat indifferent, despite our real inner interest in the student. Sanguine children should be subjected to many quickly changing sense impressions. In this way, we increase the tendencies of their own temperament, with the result that they try to catch up with the many fleeting impressions. They will develop a stronger intensity. The sheer number of sense impressions will bring about an inner effort of self-intensification in the child.

By treating like with like, we can come to grips with the different temperaments. As for the choleric children, if conditions at school allow, it would be best to send them out into the garden during the afternoons and let them run about until they are exhausted. I would let them climb up and down the trees. When they reach a treetop, I would let them shout to a playmate sitting on top of another tree. I would let them shout at each other until they are tired. If we allow choleric children to free themselves in a natural way from pent-up choler, we exercise a healing influence on their temperament.

You will learn to work effectively as teachers by getting to know the qualities of the different temperaments. One thing is essential, however. It will do no good at all if teachers enter the classroom with a morose demeanor—one that, even in early life, leaves deep wrinkles carved on their faces. Teachers must know how to act with a tremendous sense of humor in the classroom. They must be able to become a part of everything they encounter in the classroom. Teachers must be able to let their own being flow into that of the children.

ADOLESCENTS AFTER THE FOURTEENTH YEAR

January 4, 1922

By the time students reach their mid-teens, they have already entered puberty. Teachers need to keep this very much in mind well before it actually manifests. We simply need to open our eyes to what happens in growing children, both before and during the process of sexual maturity, to appreciate how important it is to be prepared for this challenge.

We have seen in our studies that until the change of teeth children are imitators and that, while there is still no clear differentiation between organic functions and soul activities, children are inwardly given over to the soul and spiritual forces flowing down from the head, which continue work organically and permeate the whole organism. The most characteristic feature of this stage is the way those soul-spiritual forces work together with the bodily forces.

I will need to use the insights of clairvoyant consciousness to give you a clear description of what happens in young children at this stage of life—not because I think we need to form our ideas in a particular way, but it just may be the best way to understand what has been said so far.

When young children sleep, the soul and spiritual members leave the physical sheaths (just as in any adult) and reenter at the moment of awaking. In children, however, there is still no significant difference between conscious experiences while awake and unconscious experiences during sleep. Normally, if no memories of daytime events enter the world of sleep (and this rarely happens in childhood), the sleeping life of children moves within realms far beyond the earthly sphere. From these higher worlds, active forces are drawn that then work during the waking state, from the brain down into a child's whole organism.

During the second dentition, certain soul and spiritual forces in children are released from working entirely in the organic sphere. They begin to assume an independent, soul-spiritual quality. Between the change of teeth and puberty, thinking, feeling, and willing in children begin to work more freely. Children are no longer imitators but, through a natural feeling for authority, they develop the consciousness they need to connect with the world. This faith in adult authority is essential, because outer conditions are not enough to ensure that children connect sufficiently with the world. The way adults confront one another, whether verbally or by other means, is very different from the way children encounter adults. Children need the additional support that a sense of authority provides. Consequently, experiences while awake will enter their soul-spiritual life during sleep. So, teachers have the possibility of reaching children through education between the change of teeth and puberty to the same extent that earthly experiences enter children's sleep and replace those of the spiritual world.

With the onset of puberty, an entirely new situation begins, and emerging adolescents are essentially different from what they were prior to sexual maturity. To describe this, it may be helpful to refer back to what was said at the end of yesterday's lecture. Until the change of teeth, it is normal for children to live entirely within the physical body. However, if this state is extended beyond its natural time, when it would no longer be normal, it results in a very melancholic temperament. During childhood it is natural to have a relationship between the soul-spiritual and physical organization that characterizes an adult melancholic. Bear in mind that what is right and good for one stage of life becomes abnormal in another.

During the second dentition, certain soul-spiritual forces are liberated from previous organic activities, and they flow into what I call the body of formative forces, or ether body. This member of the human being is linked entirely to the outer world, and it is appropriate for children to live in it between the change of teeth and puberty. If, even before the change of teeth, these ether forces were excessive—that is, if the child has lived too much in the etheric sheath before the second dentition—the result is a decidedly phlegmatic temperament. However, children can have a normal and balanced relationship with the ether body, and this is absolutely essential between the seventh and the fourteenth years, between the change of teeth and puberty. Again, if this condition is carried too far into later life, a decidedly phlegmatic temperament develops in the adult.

The true birthplace of the sanguine temperament is the next member of the human being that, under normal circumstances, becomes independent during puberty. Yesterday, I called this the astral body—the member of the human being that lives beyond space and time. If, between the change of teeth and puberty, children draw too much from what should come into its own only with sexual maturity, a sanguine temperament arises. Growing human beings become inwardly mature for sanguinity only with the arrival of puberty. Thus everything in life has a normal period of time. Various abnormalities arise when something that is normal for one period of life is pushed into another. If you survey life from this point of view, you begin to understand the human being more deeply.

What really happens as children mature sexually? During the past few days we have already illuminated this somewhat. We have seen how children continue, after the change of teeth, to work inwardly with forces that have to a certain degree become liberated soul-spiritual forces. During the following stages, children incarnate via the system of breathing and blood circulation, and the tendons and the muscles grow more firmly onto the bones. They incarnate from within out, toward the human periphery, and at the time of sexual maturity young adolescents break through into the outer world. Only then do they stand fully in the world.

This dramatic development makes it imperative for teachers to approach adolescents, who have passed through sexual maturity, quite differently from the way they dealt with the children before. Basically, the previous processes, before puberty, involved emancipated soul-spiritual forces that still had nothing to do with sex in its own realm. True, boys or girls show definite predispositions toward their own sexes, but this cannot be considered sexuality as such. Sexuality develops only after the breakthrough into the external world, when a new relationship with the outer world is established.

But then, at this time, something happens in the realm of an adolescent's soul and bodily nature, and this is not unlike what occurred previously during the second dentition. During the change of teeth, forces were liberated to become active in a child's forces of thinking, feeling, and willing, which were then directed more toward the memory. The powers of memory were then released. Now, at puberty, something else becomes available for free activity in the soul realm. These are powers that previously entered the rhythms of breathing and, subsequently, strived to introduce rhythmic qualities into the musculature and even the skeleton. This rhythmic element is now transformed into an adolescent receptiveness to the realm of creative ideas and fantasy. Fundamentally, true powers of fantasy are not born until puberty, because they come into their own only after the astral body is born. The astral body exists beyond time and space and links together past, present, and future according to its own principles, as we experience it in our dreams.

What is it that adolescents bring with them when they break through into the outer world via the skeletal system? It is what they originally brought with them from pre-earthly existence; it was gradually interwoven with their whole inner being. And now, with the onset of sexual maturity, adolescents are, as it were, cast out of the spiritual world. Without exaggerating, we can express it that strongly, because it represents the facts; with the coming of puberty, young people are cast out of the living world of spirit and thrown into the outer world, which they perceive only through the physical and ether bodies. Although adolescents are not aware of what is happening inside them, subconsciously this plays a very important role. Subconsciously, or semi-consciously, it makes adolescents compare the world they have now entered with the one they formerly held within themselves. Previously, they had not experienced the spiritual world consciously, but they nevertheless found it possible to live in harmony with it. Their inner being felt attuned to it and prepared to cooperate freely with the soul-spiritual realm. But now, conditions have changed, and the external world no longer offers such possibilities. It presents all sorts of hindrances that, in themselves, create a desire to overcome them. This, in turn, leads to a tumultuous relationship between adolescents and the surrounding world, which lasts from fourteen or fifteen until the early twenties.

This inner upheaval is bound to come, and teachers do well to be aware of it before it arrives. There may be overly sensitive people who believe that it would be better to save teenagers from this inner turmoil, only to find that they have become their greatest enemy. It would be quite incorrect to try to spare them this tempestuous time of life. It is far better to plan ahead in your educational goals, so that what you do before they reach puberty comes to help and support adolescents in their struggles of soul and spirit.

Teachers must be clear that, with the arrival of puberty, a completely different being emerges, born out of a new relationship with the world. It is no good appealing to students' previous sense of authority; now they will demand reasons for all that is expected of them. Teachers must get into the habit of approaching a young man or woman rationally. For example, think of an adolescent boy whom the spiritual world has led into this earthly world and who now becomes rebellious because it is so different from what he expected. The adult must try to show him (and without any pedantry) that everything he meets in this world has "prehistory." The adult must get this adolescent to see that present conditions are the consequences of what went before. You must act the part of an expert who really understands why things have come to be as they are.

From now on, you will accomplish nothing by way of authority. You have to convince adolescents through the sheer weight of your indisputable knowledge and expertise and provide waterproof reasons for everything you do or expect of them. If, at this stage, students cannot see sound reasons in the material you give them, if conditions in the world seem to make no sense to them, they begin to doubt the rightness of their earlier life. They feel they are in opposition to what they experienced during those years that, seemingly, merely led to the present, unacceptable conditions. And if, during this inner turmoil, they cannot find contact with someone who can reassure them, to some extent at least, that there are good reasons for what is happening in the world, then the inner stress may become so intolerable that they might break down altogether.

This newly emerged astral body is not of this world, and these young people have been cast out of the astral world. They willingly enter this earthly world only if they can be convinced of its right to exist.

It would be a complete misunderstanding of what I have been describing to think that adolescents are the least bit aware of what is happening in them. During ordinary consciousness, this struggle arises in dim feelings from the unconscious. It surges up through blunted will impulses. It lives in the disappointment of seemingly unattainable ideals, in frustrated desires, and perhaps in a certain inner numbness to what manifests in the unreasonable events of the world.

If education is to be effective at all during this stage (which it must be for any young person willing to learn), then your teaching must be communicated in the appropriate form. It must be a preparation for the years to come—up to the early twenties and even later in life. Having suffered the wounds of life and having retaliated in their various ways, young people from fifteen to the early twenties must eventually find their way back into the world from which they were evicted during puberty. The duration of this period varies, especially during our chaotic times, which tend to prolong it even longer into adult life. Young people must feel they are accepted again and be able to renew contact with the spiritual world, for without it, life is impossible. However, should they feel any coercion from those in authority, this new link loses all meaning and value for life.

If we are aware of these difficulties well before the arrival of puberty, we can make good use of the inborn longing for authority in children, bringing them to the point at which there is no longer any need for an authoritarian approach. And this stage should coincide with the coming of sexual maturity. By then, however, educators must be ready to give convincing reasons for everything they ask of their students.

Seen from a broader, spiritual perspective, we can observe the grand metamorphosis taking place in a young person during the period of sexual maturity. It is very important to realize that the whole question of sex becomes a reality only during puberty, when adolescents enter the external world as I have described it. Naturally, since everything in life is relative, this, too, must be taken as a relative truth. Nevertheless, you should realize that, until sexual maturity, children live more as generic human beings; it is not until the onset of puberty that they experience the world differently, according to whether they are men or women. This realization (which in our generally intellectual and naturalistic civilization cannot be assumed) allows real insight into the relationship between the sexes for those who work with open minds toward knowledge of the human being. It also helps them understand the problem of women's position in society, not just during our time but also in the future.

Once you appreciate the tremendous transformation that occurs in the male organism during the change of voice (to use one example), you will be able to understand the statement that, until the age of sexual maturity, a child retains a more general human nature, one still undivided into the sexes. Similar processes occur in the female organism, but in a different area. The human voice, with its ability to moderate and form sounds and tones, is a manifestation of our general human nature. It is born from the soul-spiritual substance that works on children until puberty. Changes of pitch and register, on the other hand, which occur during this mutation, are the result of outer influences. They are forced on adolescents from outside, so to speak, and they are the ways that a boy places himself into the outer world with his innermost being. It is not just a case of the softer parts in the larynx relating more strongly to the bones, but a slight ossification of the larynx itself takes place that amounts, essentially, to a withdrawal of the larynx from the purely human inner nature toward a more earthly existence.

This act of stepping out into the world should really be seen in a much wider context than is generally the case. Usually, people think that the capacity to love, which awakens at this time, is linked directly to sexual attraction, but this is not really the whole story. The power to love, born during sexual maturity, embraces everything within an adolescent's entire sphere. Love between the sexes is only one specific, limited aspect of love in the world. Only when we see human love in this light can we understand it correctly, and then we can also understand its task in the world.

What really happens in human beings during the process of sexual maturity? Prior to this, as children, their relationship to the world was one in which they first imitated their surroundings and then came under the power of authority. Outer influences worked on them, because at that time their inner being mainly represented what they brought with them from pre-earthly life. Humanity as a whole had to work on them externally, first through the principle of imitation and then through authority. Now, at puberty, having found their own way into the human race and no longer depending on outer support as a younger child does, a new feeling arises in them, along with a whole new appraisal of humankind as a whole. And this new experience of humankind represents a spiritual counterpart to the physical capacity to reproduce. Physically, they gain the ability to procreate; spiritually, they gain the ability to experience humankind as a whole.

During this new stage, the polarity between man and woman becomes quite obvious. Any realization of human potential on earth is possible only through a real understanding of the other sex by means of social interaction; and this applies to the realm of soul and spirit as well. Both men and women fully represent humankind, but in different ways. A woman sees humanity as a gift of the metaphysical worlds. Fundamentally, she sees humanity as the result of divine abundance. Unconsciously, in the depths of her soul, she holds a picture of humankind as her standard of values, and she evaluates and assesses human beings according to this standard. If these remarks are not generally accepted today, it is because our current civilization bears all the signs of a male-dominated society.

For a long time, the most powerful influences in our civilization have displayed a decidedly masculine nature. An example of this (however grotesque it may sound) may be found in Freemasonry. It is symbolic of our times that men, if they wish to keep certain matters to themselves, isolate themselves in the lodges of Freemasonry. There are also lodges in which both men and women congregate, but Freemasonry has already become blunted in these, and they no longer bear its original stamp. The constitution of Freemasonry is a specific example, but it nevertheless expresses the male-dominated character of our society. Women, too, have absorbed a great deal of the masculine element from our civilization, and because of this they actually prevent the specifically feminine element from coming into its own. This is why we so often get the impression that, in terms of inner substance and outer form, there is very little difference between the ideals and programs of the various women's movements and those of men—even in the tone of the speeches they deliver. Obviously, these movements differ insofar as, on the one side, there are demands to safeguard women's interests, while, on the other, the demands are on behalf of men. But, in terms of their inner substance, they are barely distinguishable.

When you take a good look at modern medicine in all its materialistic aspects, you can see how it fails to understand human nature, especially in terms of its physical elements, so that it depends on experimentation. If you observe modern medicine, you find the product of a distinctly masculine attitude, however strange this may sound to you. In fact, one could hardly find a better illustration of male thinking than in what modern medicine so blatantly reveals to us. For a man, in his innermost being, experiences humanity as something of an enigma. To him it appears unfathomable and poses endless questions whose solutions seem to lie beyond his powers. This typically masculine characteristic is expressed in all the mysterious ceremony and the dry and manly atmosphere of freemasonry. This same male tendency has permeated our culture to such an extent that, although women suffer under it, they nevertheless wish to emulate it and to make it part of their own lives.

If we speak the truth today, people tend to think that we do so merely to present contrary statements to the world. Yet the reality is often unorthodox. Therefore, if we want to speak the truth, we must put up with seeming contrary, however inconvenient this might be.

Women live more in the images they create of humanity, while men experience humanity in more wishful and enigmatic ways. To understand this, we need to be clear about a symptom that is especially significant for the art of teaching today. When people speak of love today, they seldom differentiate between the various types of love. Naturally, we can generalize the concept of love, just as one can speak about condiments in a general way. But when people speculate abstractly about certain matters and then hold forth about them, it always strikes me as if they were talking about salt, sugar, or pepper merely in terms of condiments. We only need to apply such abstractions to practical life by putting salt instead of sugar in our coffee— they are both condiments, after all—to realize such foolishness. Anyone who indulges in general speculation instead of entering the concrete realities of life commits the same folly.

The love of a woman is very different from that of a man. Her love originates in the realm of imagination and constantly makes pictures. A woman does not love a man just as he is, standing there before her in ordinary, humdrum life (forgive me, but men, after all, are not exactly the sort that a healthy imagination could fall in love with). Rather, she weaves into her love the ideal she received as a gift from heaven. A man's love, on the other hand, is tinged with desire; it has a wishful nature. This difference needs to be noted, regardless of whether it is expressed more in an idealistic or a realistic way. Ideal love may inspire longings of an ideal quality. The instinctive and sensuous kind may be a mere product of fancy. But this fundamental difference between love as it lives in a man and as it lives in a woman is a reality. A woman's love is steeped in imagination, and in a man's love there is an element of desire. And because these two kinds of love are complementary, they can become harmonized in life.

Educators need to bear this in mind when faced with sexually mature students. They must realize that one can no longer bring them certain things that belong to the preadolescent stage, and that they have missed the opportunity for doing so. Therefore, to prevent a onesided attitude in later life, we must try to give to prepubescent children enough of the right material to last them through the following stages. Fortunately, coeducation, in both primary and secondary education, is increasingly accepted today, so that boys and girls work side by side and learn to cooperate later on as men and women in society. Consequently, it is especially important to heed what was just said. Through this, a contemporary phenomenon such as the women's movement will have a truly sound and healthy basis.

If we expand these considerations by taking a worldwide perspective, we are led to the fundamental differences that exist between East and West, with Asia on one side and Europe and

America on the other. This difference between East and West is far greater than any other differences we may find when comparing, say, Europe and America. Throughout Asia, there are still traces of ancient, wise civilizations. Externally, they appear completely decadent, but their wisdom nevertheless lives on like a memory. It is revered as a sacred memory, to the extent that, fundamentally, an Asian cannot really understand a European, and vice versa. Those who are under illusions about this fact will delude themselves about the world's greatest historical secret in our time. It is a secret of special significance not only for today, but very much so for the future.

Despite its manifold complexities, life in the West has a more uniform character than life in the East. The main concern of Western people is life in this earthly civilization, a civilization that draws its ideas mostly from what happens between birth and death. The people of the East (at least in their inner religious lives) do not limit their view to the earthly time between birth and death, or life in the outer mechanical civilization. People of the West, however, do live for this earthly time, even in their religious feelings. The people of the East, on the other hand, ask themselves searching questions, such as, Why was I born into this world? Why did I enter this sense-perceptible world at all? Westerners take life in the physical world more or less for granted, even if they end it by suicide. Western people take earthly life for granted, and they have developed an inner receptivity for life after death only because it would be unsatisfying and a disappointment if earthly existence were entirely wiped out.

There is a fundamental difference between these two views. Again, however, we cannot get to the bottom of this merely through abstract descriptions instead of entering life fully. The farther we move from East to West, the more we find that the Western woman, despite her outer consciousness, cherishes a longing for the spirituality of the East. The man of the West, however, presents a totally different picture. He, too, has his secret longings, but not for anything vague and misty. His longings spring from what he experiences inwardly. From cradle to grave, he is enmeshed in the activities and pressures of his civilization, but something in him longs to get away from it all. We can perceive this mood of soul in all the civilized countries around us, from the River Vistula in Eastern Europe through Germany, France, and Britain, and right across the American continent to the shores of the Pacific Ocean. In all these lands, we find this attribute in common. Educators who deal with adolescents also experience this, perhaps to their despair and without recognizing the underlying causes. Only a teacher wearing blinders could possible overlook this.

During our previous meetings I mentioned that we really ought to throw away every school textbook, because only a direct and personal relationship between teachers and students should affect children. When it comes to teaching adolescents, however, every available textbook and, for that matter, almost our whole outer civilization become great sources of pain. I know that there are many who are unaware of this, because they do not go into real life with their eyes open wide enough. Here, again, in our outer civilization we find a notably lopsided masculine quality. Any book on history—whether a history of civilization or anthropology—will confirm this trend. As representatives of Western civilization, people long to escape the physical world in which they are caught up, but they lack the necessary courage to do so. People cannot find the bridge from the sensory world into the spiritual world. And so, everywhere in our civilization we find a yearning to get away from it all, and yet an inability to act accordingly.

It is hard enough to establish the right environment for teaching prepubescent children. But those who have to teach adolescents could almost feel helpless, because the means available for meeting their needs are so inadequate. This alone should kindle a real longing in such teachers for a deeper understanding of the human being. Of course, this longing may already be there in the teachers of younger children, but it is a prerequisite for anyone of sound pedagogical sense who teaches adolescents.

A woman's nostalgia for the ways of the East and a man's wish to be free of the bondage of Western life represent fundamental features of our time. This difference between the sexes is less apparent in preadolescent children, who still bear more general human features. Yet, as soon as we are confronted by adolescents, we meet many difficulties that arise quite concretely.

Imagine, for example, that a German literature teacher wants to recommend to her adolescent student a book that presents a German perspective of Goethe. She would really find herself in a quandary, since there are no suitable books available. If she chooses an available one, her scholar would not get the right picture of Goethe. If she chooses a biography of Goethe written by, say, Lewes, her German scholar would learn the more outward features of Goethe better than from any of the German books on the subject, but again he would not become familiar with the specifically German characteristics of Goethe.[1] This is the situation today, for we simply do not have adequate literature for teaching adolescents. To remedy this, everything depends on women taking their proper place in culture. They should be allowed to contribute their specifically feminine qualities, but they must at the same time be careful not to introduce anything they have adopted from our male-dominated civilization.

---

1. George Henry Lewes (1817–1878), *The Life and Works of Goethe* (1855).

During the 1890s, I had a conversation with a German feminist. She expressed her views in radical terms, but I could not help feeling that, instead of enriching society with what only womanhood offers, she was trying to force her way into our onesidedly masculine culture by employing masculine tactics. My meaning must not be taken in a crude or biased way. I felt that I had to say to this free and uncompromising lady, "Your movement does not yet offer what the world really needs. The world does not need women who 'wear the pants' [forgive me, I believe in England that such a remark is unforgivably rude]. Rather, both masculine and feminine qualities make specific contributions toward the general enhancement of our society."

As teachers, whenever we approach growing human beings, we must note the striking contrast between the prepuberty and postpuberty years. Let us take a concrete example: There is Milton's *Paradise Lost,* which would be good to use in our lessons. The question is, when? Those of you who have thought through what has been said so far and have understood my remarks about the right time to introduce narrative and descriptive elements will find that this work by Milton (or epic poetry in general) would be suitable material after the tenth year. Also, Homer will be appreciated best when taught between the tenth and the fourteenth years. On the other hand, it would be premature to use Shakespeare as study material at this stage, since, in order to be ready for dramatic poetry, students must at least have entered puberty. To absorb the dramatic element at an earlier age, students would have to drive something out of themselves prematurely, which, later on, they would definitely miss.

What I tried to describe just now can be experienced vividly when, for example, you have to give history lessons to boys and girls after they enter puberty. Both masculine and feminine forces work during historical events, though in a different form than they do today. Yet all of the historical accounts available for teaching adolescents bear a decidedly masculine quality, as though they had been compiled by Epimetheus.[2] Girls who have reached sexual maturity show little inclination toward such an approach. Boys may find it somewhat boring, but in their case it is not impossible to use this Epimethean way, which judges and holds onto what can be ascertained and established. But there is also a Promethean way of looking at history, which not only records events that occurred, but also shows their transformation into the ideas of the present time. This approach to history shows how the impulses that led the past have become the current thinking of today, and how impulses, in turn, continue to lead present time further. A Promethean way of looking at history, in particular, appeals strongly to the feminine element.

However, it would be very onesided to teach history in the Promethean style at a girls' school, or in an Epimethean style at a boys' school. The minds of the young men would simply flow back into the past and become even more rigid than they are already. If the Promethean way of teaching history were to be only one applied in a girls' school, the students would be tempted to fly off into futuristic speculations. They would always be attracted to the impulses that they happened to like naturally. We can achieve a more balanced society only if we add a historical view that bears the prophetic marks of Prometheus to the more predominant Epimethean way, which until now has been just about the only one available. Then, if both attitudes are alive in our lessons, we will at last achieve the right approach to history for students who have reached the age of sexual maturity.

---

2. Prometheus ("Forethought") and Epimetheus ("Afterthought") were brother Titans in Greek mythology.

ESTHETIC EDUCATION

January 5, 1922

The human organization and its various bodies, or members, as I have described them to you, helps in understanding the whole human being. It's an image that can be presented from many different viewpoints, and it is these manifold aspects that enable us to go further into what lies behind the human constitution. I have spoken about the human astral body as being the member of the human being that, using spatial and temporal relationships in its own way, breaks all bounds of space and time, as it were. I have tried to describe how we can experience something of this quality in our dreams, which emanate largely from the astral body and weave together incidents of our lives, otherwise separated by time, into continuous dream imagery.

We can characterize the astral body from many aspects, one of which is based on events in the human being during the process of sexual maturity. If we observe the relevant phenomena and their underlying forces, we arrive at a picture of the astral body, because puberty is the time of its birth, when it can be freely used by a human being.

St. Augustine (354–430), the medieval writer, tried to approach the human astral body in yet another way. I wish to point out that, in his writings, we find a description of the invisible members of the human being that agrees with the one

spiritual science provides. His findings, however, were the outcome of an instinctive clairvoyance, once the common heritage
of all humankind, and not the result of conscious investigation
into the spiritual realm, as practiced in anthroposophy.

St. Augustine's description of the astral body gaining independence at puberty is truly characteristic of human life. He
says that, because of the fundamental properties of the astral
body, people can understand all the human inventions that
affect human life. If we build a house, make a plough, or invent
a spinning machine, we do so by using forces directly connected to the astral body. It is a fact that, through the astral
body, human beings learn about everything in their environment that is produced by human activity. It is therefore fully
consistent with a true knowledge of the human being when, as
educators, we introduce adolescents to the practical side of life
and the results of human ingenuity. This, however, is a far
more complicated process today than in St. Augustine's time,
when life was much simpler.

Only by applying what I have called soul economy in teaching can we hope to succeed in planning an education for students between fifteen and twenty (or even older) that will
gradually introduce them to the manifold contrivances surrounding them today. Just think for a moment of how much we
fall short of this in our present civilization. You just need to ask
yourselves how many people regularly use the telephone, public
transportation, or even a steam ship without having the faintest
idea of how they work. In our civilization, people are practically
engulfed by a technology that they do not understand. Those
who believe that it is only our conscious experiences that are
truly important will dismiss these remarks as irrelevant.

Certainly, it is easy to enjoy life consciously when one has
successfully bought a train ticket to get where one chooses to
go, or if one receives a telegram without having any real idea of

how the message reached its destination or having the slightest notion of what a Morse apparatus is like. Ordinary consciousness is unconcerned about whether it understands the processes or not, and from this point of view it can be argued whether these things matter or not. But when we look at what is happening in the depths of the unconscious, the picture looks entirely different. To use modern technology with no knowledge of how things work or how they were made is like being a prisoner in a cell without windows through which one could at least look out into nature and to freedom.

Educators need to be fully aware of this. When adolescents experience differentiation between the sexes, the time is ripe for understanding other differentiations in modern life as well. Students now need to be introduced to the practical areas of life, and this is why, as puberty approaches, we include crafts such as spinning and weaving in our curriculum. Naturally, such a plan brings with it many difficulties, certainly in terms of the schedule. When planning our curriculum, we must also keep in mind the demands of other training centers, such as universities, technical colleges, or other institutions our students may wish to enter. This requires that we include subject material that, in our opinion, has less value for life. It really requires a great deal of trouble and pain to attain a balanced curriculum that depends entirely on strict soul economy in teaching. It is a very difficult task, but not impossible. This can be done if teachers develop a sense of what has real importance for life, and if teachers can communicate simply and economically to their students so that, eventually, they understand what they are doing while using a telephone, conveyance, or other modern invention. We must try to familiarize our students with the ways of today's civilization so they can make sense of it. Even before the age of puberty, teachers must prepare the chemistry and physics lessons so that, after the onset of

puberty, they can build on what has been given and then
extend it as a basis for understanding the practical areas of life.

Here we must consider yet another point; students are now
entering an age when, to a certain extent, they need to be
grouped according to whether they will follow a more academic or practical career later on. At the same time, we must
not forget that an education based on a real knowledge of the
human being always strives for balance in teaching, and we
need to know how this is done in practice. Naturally, we must
equip students of a more academic disposition with what they
will need for their future education. At the same time, if we are
to retain the proper balance, any specialization (later on also)
should be compensated by some broadening into otherwise
neglected areas. If, on the one hand, we direct their will
impulses more toward the academic side, we must also give
them some concrete understanding of practical life so they do
not lose sight of life as a whole. Thus, we actually fulfill the
demands of the human astral body; when it guides conscious
will impulses in one direction, it also feels the need for appropriate counter-impulses. A concrete example may help.

As an extreme example, it would be incorrect for a statisti-
cian to gather statistics on soap consumption in certain dis-
tricts without the least notion of how soap is manufactured.
No one could understand such statistics without at least a general knowledge of how soap is made. But life has become so
complex that it seems there is no end to all the things we must
consider. Consequently, the principles of soul economy in
teaching have become more important than ever. In fact, it is
the only way to deal with this large problem in education. And
making it even more difficult is the fact that we ourselves are
clogged with erroneous, outmoded forms of education we
receive during our own education, mistakes resulting from educational traditions that are no longer justifiable today.

An ancient Greek would have been surprised to see young people of the time being introduced, before going out into life, to the ways of the Egyptians, Chaldeans, or other previous civilizations. Yet, this is more or less how it works in grade schools today. It is impossible to talk freely about these issues, however, because we have to consider how our students will fit into society as it exists.

Those of our students who are likely to follow an academic career should gain at least some experience of practical work involving manual skills. On the other hand, students who are likely to apprentice in a trade should become familiar with the sort of background one needs for a more academic career. All this should be part of the general school curriculum. It is not right to send boys and girls straight into factories to work alongside adults. Instead, various crafts should be introduced at school, so that young people can use what they have learned as a kind of model before finding their way into more professional skills. Nor do I see any reason why older students should not be given the task of manufacturing certain articles in school workshops, which can then be sold to the public. This has already been done in some of our prisons, with the prisoners' products being sold outside.

Young people should remain in a school setting as long as possible and as long as school is constructive and healthy. It is in keeping with inner human nature to enter life gradually and not be flung into it too soon or too quickly. Today's world youth movement has become strong because the older generation showed so little understanding of the younger generation's needs, and older people at least understand its justification. There are deep reasons for the emergence of this movement, which should not only be recognized but channeled in the right directions. But this will be possible only when the principles of education are also channeled in the right directions.

A primary objective of Waldorf education is to prepare students for life as much as possible. Thus, when they reach their early twenties and their I-being enables them to take their full place in society, they will be able to develop the right relationship to the world as a whole. Then, young people should be able to feel a certain relationship with their elders, since it was, after all, their generation that provided the means for the younger generation. Young people should be able to appreciate and understand the achievements of the older generation. Thus, when sitting in a chair, they should not only realize that the chair was made by someone of their father's generation but should also know something about how it was made.

Naturally, today there are many opinions that argue against introducing young people to practical life as described, but I speak here from a completely practical viewpoint. We can honestly say that, of all the past ages of human development, our present materialistic age is, in its own way, the most spiritual. Perhaps I can explain myself better by telling you something about certain theosophists I once met who were working toward a truly spiritual life. And yet they were, in fact, real materialists. They spoke of the physical body and its density. And the ether body was seen as having a certain density and corporeality, though far more rarefied. They described the astral body as infinitely less dense than the ether body, yet still having a certain density. And this is how they talked about all sorts of other mysterious things as well, believing they were reaching into higher and more spiritual spheres, until the substances they imagined would become so thin and attenuated that one would no longer know what to make of it all. All their images bore the stamp of materialism and, consequently, never reached the spiritual world at all. Strangely, the most materialistic views I ever encountered were among some members of the Theosophical Society. For instance, after giving a lecture to theosophists in Paris, I once asked a member of the audience what impression the lecture had made upon him. I had to put up with the answer that my lecture had left behind good vibrations in the room. It sounded as though one might be able to smell the impressions created by my talk. In this way, everything was reduced to the level of a materialistic interpretation.

On the other hand, I like to tell those who are willing to listen that I prefer a person with a materialistic concept of the world—one who is nevertheless capable of the spiritual activity of thinking—to a theosophist who, though striving toward the spiritual world, falls back on materialistic images. Materialists are mistaken, but even their thinking contains spirit—real spirit. It is "diluted" and abstract, but spirit nevertheless. And this way of thinking compels people to enter the realities of life. Therefore I have found materialists who are richer in spirit than those who are anxious to overcome materialism but do so in an entirely materialistic way. It is characteristic of our time that people absorb spirit in such diluted forms and can no longer recognize it. The most spiritual activity in our time, however, can be found in technological innovation, where everything arises from spirit—human spirit.

It does not require great spiritual accomplishment to put a vase of beautiful flowers on a table, since nature provides them. But to construct even the simplest machine does in fact require spiritual activity. The spirit plays a part, though it goes unnoticed, since people do not observe themselves in the right way. Spirit remains in a person's subconscious during such activities, and human nature finds this difficult to bear unless one has mastered the necessary objectivity. Only by finding our way into practical life do we gradually learn to bear the abstract spirit, which we have poured out through today's civilization.

I can assure you that, once an art of education based on spiritual science has gained a firm foothold, it will put people into the world who are far more practical than those who have gone through our more materialistically inclined educational systems. Waldorf education will be imbued with creative spirit, not with the dreamy kind that tempts people to close their eyes to outer reality. I will call it a true anthroposophic initiative when we find spirit without losing the firm ground under our feet.

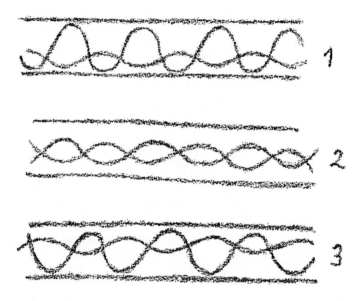

Any teacher who wishes to introduce adolescents to the practicalities of life could easily become discouraged by the lack of manual skills that is symptomatic of our time. We really have to ask ourselves whether there is any possibility of encouraging children between their second dentition and puberty to become more practical and skilful. And if we look at life as it really is—guided by life and not by abstract ideas or theorizing—we find that the answer is to bring children as close as possible to beauty. The more we can lead them to appreciate beauty, the better prepared they will be at the time of puberty to tackle practical tasks without being harmed for the rest of their lives. Our students will not be able to safely understand the workings of conveyances or railroad engines unless an esthetic appreciation of painting or sculpture was cultivated at the right age. This is a fact that teachers should keep in mind. Beauty, however, needs to be seen as part of life, not separate and complete in itself. In this sense, our civilization must still learn a great deal, especially in the field of education.

A few simple examples may give you a better idea of what is meant by cultivating a sense of beauty that is not estranged from daily life. Perhaps you have been present when handwork was done, either in a family home or in a school classroom. You may have seen girls sewing patterns into ribbons, maybe something like this (see diagram 2).

I will keep it as simple as possible and draw it merely for the sake of clarification. If you then ask a student, "What are you doing?" the answer may be, "We first sew this pattern around the neck of the dress, then on the waistband, and finally around the hem of the dress." This kind of remark is enough to make one despair, because it shows a total disregard for fitting beauty to a given purpose. If we are sensitive to these matters and see a girl or young lady sewing the same pattern to the upper, middle, and lower parts of a dress, we can't help feeling that when someone wears such a dress, she will appear to have been compressed or telescoped, from top to bottom. We must open our students' eyes to the necessity of adapting a pattern according to where it appears, whether around the neck, the middle, or around the hem. The uppermost ribbon could be varied somewhat like this (diagram 1), and the bottom one in this way (diagram 3). I am keeping the patterns simple, merely for clarification. Now students can safely sew the first pattern around the neck, because the form indicates that the head will rise above it. The second pattern can be sewn into a belt, and the third to the hem, showing that its place is below. There really is a difference between above and below in the human figure, and this needs to be expressed artistically.

I once discovered that pillows had been embroidered in this way (diagram 4). Would you want to rest your head on a pattern with a center that will scratch your face? It was certainly not designed for putting your head on it. This pattern does not express the function of the pillow in the least. This is how it should be done (diagram 5). But now it can be used only if one's face is turned to the left. To solve the problem artistically, we need the same arrangement on the opposite side as well (diagram 6). But this is not the correct solution either. Fortunately, art enables us to create impressions of something that does not really exist, so the pattern should create the feeling that the pillow allows our head to assume any position it chooses.

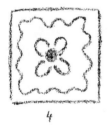  

4   5   6

This leads us right into what I would like to call "reality within the world of appearances" as expressed through art. Only by entering this reality can we develop a faculty that could be viewed as the counter-sense of what is merely practical. Only when our sense of beauty enters the fullness of life are we able to experience the practical realm in a right and balanced way.

It has recently become fashionable to embellish pompadours with all sorts of ornamentation.[1] When I see one of these knitting bags, I often wonder where to look for the opening. Surely the pattern on these bags should indicate the top and bottom, as well as where to put the wool. These things are generally ignored completely, just as book covers are often designed with no indication of where the pages should be opened. Such designs are chosen at random and often encourage one to leave the book closed rather than read it.

These examples merely indicate how a practical sense of beauty can be developed in young people. Unless this has been accomplished, we cannot move on to the next step, which is to fit them into the practicalities of life.

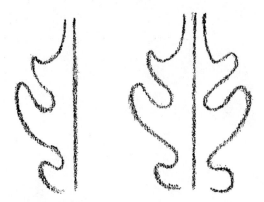

What children need is a sense of reality. Again I will choose a very simple example to show you what I mean. One could draw a pattern such as this (see diagram). Teachers must be able to evoke a feeling in children that such a pattern is intolerable

---

1. Pompadours are small knitting bags for ladies, named for the Marquise de Pompadour of the court of King Louis XV.

because it does not represent reality, and a little practice with students who react in healthy ways will soon enable you to do so. Teachers should intensify this healthy feeling—not through suggestions, but by drawing it out of the students—to the extent that, if they see such a pattern, it will be as though they were seeing a person with only half a face or one arm or foot. Such a thing goes against the grain, because it does not represent reality. This is the kind of reaction teachers should induce in students, for it is all part of an esthetic sensibility. In other words, teachers should allow the students to feel that they cannot rest until they have completed a pattern by drawing the missing, complementary part. In this way one cultivates in children an immediate, living sense of beauty. In German, the word *schön* ("beautiful") is related to the word *Schein* ("shine" or "glory"). Such an approach stimulates the child's astral body to become flexible and to function well as a living member of the human being.

It is important for teachers to cultivate an esthetic sense also in themselves. Teachers quickly see how this enlivens the children. Thus, they also nurture an artistic approach to the other activities, as I have already stated in these lectures. I pointed out that everything teachers bring to children when they enter class one should be permeated by an artistic element. And when talking to children about their surroundings, teachers should do so with real artistry, since otherwise they might easily slip into anthropomorphism, restricting everything to narrow human interests. For instance, when using fairy tales or legends to clothe their lessons, teachers may be misled into telling a class that certain kinds of trees spring from the ground just so people can make corks from the bark and seal their bottles. A pictorial approach must never be presented in such terms. The pictures used at this particular age must be created from a sense of beauty. And beauty demands truth and clarity,

XIX. *Anthroposophische Pädagogik und ihre Voraussetzungen,* 5 lectures, Bern, 1924 (GA 309). *The Roots of Education* (Anthroposophic Press, 1997).

XX. *Der pädagogische Wert der Menschenerkenntnis und der Kulturwert der Pädagogik,* 10 public lectures, Arnheim, 1924 (GA 310). *Human Values in Education* (Rudolf Steiner Press, 1971).

XXI. *Die Kunst des Erziehens aus dem Erfassen der Menschenwesenheit,* 7 lectures, Torquay, 1924 (GA 311). *The Kingdom of Childhood* (Anthroposophic Press, 1995).

XXII. *Geisteswissenschaftliche Impulse zur Entwicklung der Physik. Erster naturwissenschaftliche Kurs: Licht, Farbe, Ton—Masse, Elektrizität, Magnetismus,* 10 lectures, Stuttgart, 1919–20 (GA 320). *The Light Course* (Anthroposophic Press, 2001).

XXIII. *Geisteswissenschaftliche Impulse zur Entwicklung der Physik. Zweiter naturwissenschaftliche Kurs: die Wärme auf der Grenze positiver und negativer Materialität,* 14 lectures, Stuttgart, 1920 (GA 321). *The Warmth Course* (Mercury Press, 1988).

XXIV. *Das Verhältnis der verschiedenen naturwissenschaftlichen Gebiete zur Astronomie. Dritter naturwissenschaftliche Kurs: Himmelskunde in Beziehung zum Menschen und zur Menschenkunde,* 18 lectures, Stuttgart, 1921 (GA 323). Available in typescript only as "**The Relation of the Diverse Branches of Natural Science to Astronomy.**"

XXV. *The Education of the Child and Early Lectures on Education* (a collection; Anthroposophic Press, 1996).

XXVI. Miscellaneous.

LECTURES AND WRITINGS BY
RUDOLF STEINER ON ANTHROPOSOPHY

Anthroposophical Leading Thoughts: Anthroposophy As a Path of Knowledge, The Michael Mystery, London: Rudolf Steiner Press, 1998 (GA 26).

At Home in the Universe: Exploring Our Suprasensory Nature, Great Barrington, MA: Anthroposophic Press, 2000 (GA 231).

Autobiography: Chapters in the Course of My Life, 1861–1907, Great Barrington, MA: Anthroposophic Press, 1999 (GA 28).

Christianity as Mystical Fact, Great Barrington, MA: Anthroposophic Press, 1996 (GA 8).

Founding a Science of the Spirit, London: Rudolf Steiner Press, 1999 (GA 95).

From the History & Contents of the First Section of the Esoteric School, 1904–1914, Great Barrington, MA: Anthroposophic Press, 1998 (GA 264).

How to Know Higher Worlds: A Modern Path of Initiation, Great Barrington, MA: Anthroposophic Press, 1994 (GA 10).

Intuitive Thinking As a Spiritual Path: A Philosophy of Freedom, Great Barrington, MA: Anthroposophic Press, 1995 (GA 4).

An Outline of Esoteric Science, Great Barrington, MA: Anthroposophic Press, 1998 (GA 13).

The Spiritual Guidance of the Individual and Humanity, Great Barrington, MA: Anthroposophic Press, 1991 (GA 15).

Theosophy: An Introduction to the Spiritual Processes in Human Life and in the Cosmos, Great Barrington, MA: Anthroposophic Press, 1994 (GA 9).

A Way of Self-Knowledge, Great Barrington, MA: Anthroposophic Press, 1999 (GA 16, 17).

which speaks directly to human feeling. Beauty in nature does not need anthropomorphism. If we encourage prepubescent students toward an appreciation of beauty in everything they encounter, after puberty they will take human qualities with them into the practical life, harmonizing their views of the world with the practical tasks that await them.

All this has an important bearing on the social question, which must be tackled from many different angles. Few people are aware of this today. If we could cultivate the sense of beauty that lives unspoiled in every child, it is certainly possible that we could transform all the ugliness that surrounds us in almost every European city within a few generations—and you can hardly deny that, esthetically, we are surrounded by all sorts of atrocities in virtually every large city.

Today we look at the human being from the outside and see the physical body. And we observe the inner human being in terms of the personality, or self. Between the I-being and the physical body are the astral and ether bodies, which are becoming more and more stunted today. Essentially, they are properly developed only in Asians. In the West, they are becoming atrophied and do not develop properly. By awakening an overall feeling for beauty, however, we can nurture the free development of those two bodies. During the school years, growing human beings are most receptive to an the appreciation of beauty. We should thus do everything possible to awaken and cultivate a sense of beauty in children, especially between the second dentition and the beginning of puberty so that it will live on into later life.

This is especially important with regard to speech. Languages arose from a direct human response to inner experiences. If we immerse ourselves in the quality of spoken sounds, we can still hear the important role those inner responses played in forming certain words. In our abstract life, however, the logic of language plays the leading part, and our perception of the artistic element has been almost lost. It's true that logic is inherent in language, but it represents only the skeleton, which is dead. There is much besides logic in language, but unless you have been touched by the creative genius of language, you cannot feel its breath and pulse.

In this sense, try to feel the way words try to project themselves into outer life. I will give a typical example, and I hope you will understand it, although it is from the German language. In the word *Sucht* ("sickness"), you can detect the word *suchen* ("to seek"). When the body has a *Sucht,* it is looking for something that normally it would not. Certain other words point to what the body seeks. For example, *Gelbsucht* ("jaundice") or *Fallsucht* ("epilepsy"). The word *Sucht* enables the human soul to experience what the body is seeking through certain forms of sickness.

The farther west we go, the more we find that people have lost the ability to appreciate the artistic element in language, which Asians can still experience. It is very important for us to regain at least some basic experience of the living genius of language. This will especially promote worldwide social understanding.

Forgive me if I use another example—near and dear to me—to explain what I mean. But please be very careful not to misunderstand what I am about to say. On page eighty-eight in the English translation of my book *Die Kernpunkte der sozialen Frage*—translated as *The Threefold Commonwealth*—I find this: "The freedom of one cannot prosper without the freedom of all."[2] This sentence makes no sense when weighed by a deep feeling for words. As I said, you must not misunderstand me, but this English sentence is simply nonsense, because it says

---

2. A more recent translation is *Towards Social Renewal.*

something very different from the original German words, which read, *"Die Freiheit des Einen kann micht ohne die Freiheit des Anderen gedeihen."* This sentence really tries to say something completely different.

To convey its meaning correctly, the translator would have to circumscribe it completely. The translation of any book should read as if it were written directly from the genius of the new language; anything else is unacceptable. I know for certain that Bentham's hair would stand on end if, in the astral world, he were to encounter "The freedom of one cannot prosper without the freedom of all."[3] It simply does not stand up to clear thinking, and for a particular reason. If you encountered such a sentence, you would immediately respond that, yes, freedom exists, but the author talks about something that does not apply to England, especially if you relate it to education. In the original German, however, this is not the situation. There it does make sense. But when translated as quoted, the real meaning of the original cannot be understood. Why is this?

I will demonstrate by focusing on the significant word in the sentence. In English, the word is *freedom*. If we match the quality of this word with the corresponding German word, one would have to use *Freitum*—the ending "dom" in English corresponds to the ending "tum" in German. If such a word existed, we could use *freedom* with impunity. *Freitum* would then be translated as "freedom," and there would be no misunderstanding. But the word used in the original text is *Freiheit*—the ending "heit" corresponds to the English ending "hood." To show you that the translation of *Freiheit* as "freedom" does not harmonize with the genius of language, I will use another German word, *Irrtum* ("error"), which expresses a definite fact that happens only once. If we wanted to give this word the

---

3. Jeremy Bentham (1748–1832), founded a philosophy called utilitarianism.

ending "heit," we would have to form the word *Irreheit*. You won't find this word in any German dictionary, but it would not go against the genius of the language to invent it. It would be quite possible to use it. *Irreheit* immediately leads us to the inner human being. It expresses a quality of inner human nature. There are no words in the German language ending with "heit" that do not point to something flexible within a person. Such words carry their meaning toward a person. Indeed, it is a pity that we do not use the word *Freitum* in German, because, if it existed, we could express the meaning of the English word *freedom* directly, without circumscribing it.

This kind of thing leads us right into the depths of language itself and makes us aware of the genius of language. Consequently, when I write a book in German, I try to choose words that can be translated correctly into other languages—and my German readers do not hesitate to call it poor style. But this is not always possible. If, for example, a book is addressed to the culture of Germany, it may be necessary sometimes to consider the German situation first. And this is why I have repeatedly used the word *Freiheit*, which should never be translated as "freedom." My book *Die Philosophie der Freiheit* should never be titled in English *The Philosophy of Freedom*. A correct English title for this book has yet to be found.[4]

It is also very interesting to look at these things from a statistical point of view. In doing so, I am being neither pedantic nor unscrupulous, but my findings are the results of deliberate investigation. If I were to write a book about education in German, the word *Freiheit* would appear again and again in certain chapters. To find out whether the corresponding word *freedom* could be also used in an English book on education, I carefully

---

4. Various English translations have been titled *The Philosophy of Freedom; The Philosophy of Spiritual Activity;* and *Intuitive Thinking As Spiritual Activity.*

looked through the likely chapters of such a book, and discovered that the word *freedom* did not appear at all, not once. This is the sort of thing for which we should develop a fine perception, because it is the very thing we need for greater world understanding. And it should be considered during the school years as well. I am keenly aware of this when writing books, as I mentioned. Consequently I am very cautious in the choice of certain words. If, for example, I use the German word *Natur* in various sentences, I can be certain that it will be translated as the word *nature* in English. There is no doubt at all that *Natur* would be translated as *nature*. And yet, the English word *nature* would awaken a very different concept than would the German word *Natur*. This is why, when anticipating translations, I have paraphrased certain words in some of my writings. I do this to avoid the wrong interpretation of what I want to say. Of course, there have been numerous times when I used the word *Natur,* but when it was important to match the German concept with a foreign one, I paraphrased *Natur* with "the sensory world" (*die sinnliche Welt*), especially if the book was likely to be translated into Western languages. To me, "the sensory world" seems to match, more or less, the concept of *Natur* as used in German. Obviously, I expected *sinnliche Welt* to be translated as *nature* in English, only to find that, again, it was translated literally into "the sensory world." It really is very important to be aware of the living genius of language, especially where an artistic treatment of language is concerned.

Apart from the fact that the genius of language was not recognized in the translation of the sentence I quoted (I simply mention this in passing), you will also find the following wording: "The freedom of one cannot prosper without the freedom *of all.*" Again, this makes no sense in German. It was neither written nor implied. The original sentence says, "The freedom of one cannot prosper without the freedom *of the other*"—in other words, our fellow human beings, or neighbors. That is the real point.

I ask you again not to misunderstand my intentions. I chose this example, near and dear to me, to show how we have reached a stage in human development where, instead of experiencing the realities of life, we tend to skim over them, and language offers a particularly striking example of this. Our civilization has gradually made us rather sloppy. Now we must make an effort to go into language again and to live with the words. Until we do this, we will not be able to meet the request I made earlier—that children, after being introduced to grammar and then to the rhetoric and beauty of language, should eventually be brought to an appreciation of the artistic element of language. We must open the eyes and hearts of students to the artistic element that lives in language. This is also important in nurturing a stronger feeling of community with other nations. And it is equally important to look, in very new and different ways, at what is usually called the social question.

PHYSICAL EDUCATION

January 6, 1922

What I have to say today concerns primarily the physical education of children. It is in the nature of this subject that I can talk about it only aphoristically, mainly because people tend to have already formed their opinions in these matters. When it comes to talking about physical development, everyone seems to have definite likes and dislikes that too often strongly color people's theories on this subject. But anything arising from personal sympathies or antipathies easily leads to fanaticism, which is far from the real goals and activities of spiritual science. Any form of fanaticism or agitation for some particular cause is entirely alien to the nature of the anthroposophic movement, which simply wants to point out the effects of various attitudes and actions in life and leave everyone free to relate personal sympathies and antipathies to the matter.

Just consider the fanaticism that argues for or against vegetarianism today, each using unassailable, scientific proofs. And yet we cannot help noticing that never before has superficiality flourished so much as when people defend various movements of a similar nature. It is a fact that anthroposophy does not have the slightest leaning toward extremism in any form. It cannot go along with ardent vegetarians who wish to enforce their views on others whose attitudes differ, and who, in their fanaticism, go so far as to deny meat eaters a fully human status in society. If fanaticism occasionally creeps into the anthroposophic movement, it does not at all reflect the true nature of spiritual science.

Now, there is another aspect we must consider within the context of these lectures. Perhaps you have noticed that until now we have emphasized appropriate educational methods in the realm of children's soul and spirit, which also allows the best possibility for physical development in a natural, healthy way. One could say that we are studying an educational system that—if it is practiced correctly and effectively—offers the best means toward healthy physical development. So the fundamentals of a sound physical education have already been presented. Nevertheless, it will be useful to review and summarize them again, although we must do this aphoristically because of a shortage of time. To do justice to this subject I would have to devote a whole lecture cycle to it.

Our theme falls naturally into three main parts: the way we feed children; the way we relate children to warmth or coldness; and our approach to gymnastics. Fundamentally, these three categories comprise everything important for the physical education of children.

Modern methods of knowledge, based as they are on an intellectualistic approach, do not offer the possibility of coming to terms with the complex nature of the human organism. Despite the scientific attitude that people are so proud of today, we need to acquire a certain instinctive knowledge of what nurtures or damages health and includes the whole spectrum between these two poles. A healthy instinct for such matters is immensely important. After all, isn't it true that our natural science is generally becoming more dyed-in-the-wool materialistic? Consider how many secrets have been drawn from nature through research under the microscope or by dissecting various lower animals to investigate the functions of their parts. How many times has human behavior been determined by observing animal behavior, without considering the fact that the human organization in its most important characteristic differs radically from that of all lower animal species? In any case, there has not been enough emphasis placed on this significant difference, primarily because science today depends on investigating every detail separately, thus getting only a partial view of life.

Let me try to illustrate this by a comparison. Imagine that I meet two people at nine o'clock one morning. They are sitting on a bench, and I stop for a while to talk to them about various things, thus gaining a general impression of their characters. Then I go on my way again. At three o'clock in the afternoon I see them still sitting on that bench. Now, there are various possibilities of what may have happened in the meantime. It may be that they have been sitting there talking the whole time. Or, according to the different ways that people of various ethnic groups or nationalities behave, other things may have happened. Perhaps they sat together in silence. Or, unknown to me, one of them might left right after I did, while the other stayed on the bench. The first may have returned just before I reappeared, and so on. Externally, nothing appears to have changed between 9 A.M. and 3 P.M., despite the fact that the two seemed very different in temperament and lifestyle.

Life will never reveal its secrets if we observe only outer appearances. Yet, with today's scientific methods, this happens far more frequently than is generally realized, as anyone can discover. Present scientific attitudes can indeed lead to a situation such as I witnessed not long ago. In my youth, I had a friend whom I knew lived a normal and healthy life. Later, we went our different ways and did not meet for many years. Then, one day, I visited him again. When he sat down to his midday meal, the food was served in an unusual way, and a scale was placed on the table. He weighed the meat and the vegetables, because he had begun to eat "scientifically." He had complete faith in a science that prescribed the correct amounts of various foods one eats to be healthy. Needless to say, such a method may be perfectly justified under certain conditions, but it thoroughly undermines one's healthy instincts.

An instinct for what is wholesome or damaging to health is an essential quality for any teacher worthy of the calling. Such teachers surely know how to elaborate and use all that was given in the previous lectures, and this includes the physical education of children.

We have seen, for instance, that before the change of teeth children live entirely in the physical organism. This applies especially to babies, particularly with regard to nourishment. As you know, when babies begin to take in food, they are completely satisfied with a totally uniform diet. If we, as adults, had to live every day on exactly the same kind of food for breakfast, lunch, and any other meal, we would find it intolerable, both physically and mentally. Adults like to vary their food with a mixed diet. Babies, on the other hand, do not get a change of food at all. And yet, only a few people realize the bliss with which babies receive their "monotonous" diet; the whole body becomes saturated with intense sweetness from the mother's milk. Adults have the possibility of tasting food only with the taste buds and adjacent organs. They are unfortunate, since all their sensations of taste are confined to the head and thus they are very different a baby, whose entire body becomes one great organ for the sense of taste.

At the end of the baby stage, tasting with the whole body ceases and is soon forgotten for the rest of life. People who live with ordinary degrees of consciousness are completely unaware of how different their sensations of tasting food were during infancy. And, sure enough, later life does its best to wipe out this memory. For example, I once took part in a conversation between an "abstainer" and a person of the opposite position. (I won't tell you the whole story, since it would take us too far from our theme.) The abstainer, like so many of these people, was inclined to be a fanatic and tried to convert the gourmand, who replied, "But I was completely temperate for two full years." Greatly surprised, the abstainer asked him when this was, to which the other answered, "During the first two years of my life." In this humorous, though rather frivolous way, important facts of life were discussed. Few people have a deeper and correct knowledge of these things.

Babies are related to the physical body in such a way that they can eat only with their entire physical organization, deriving the greatest benefit and pleasure from this condition. The gradual transition to the next stage involves forces that begin to concentrate in the head and finally lead to the change of teeth. These forces are so powerful that they can force out the milk teeth as the second teeth push through. This slow and gradual process takes place between birth and second dentition, affecting various other regions. After babyhood, the sense of taste withdraws into the head. Children no longer eat only with their physical organization, but with their soul forces as well. They learn to distinguish various tastes through their soul forces. At this stage it is important to watch carefully children's reactions to different foods. Their likes and dislikes are valuable indicators of their inner health. But, to judge such matters, we need at least an basic knowledge of nutrition.

When talking about this today, people typically think of the aspect of weight. But this is not so important. What really matters is the fact that each kind of food contains a certain amount of forces. Each item of food holds a specific amount of forces through which it has adapted to the conditions of the outer world. But what takes place within the human organism is something entirely different. The human organism must completely transform the food it takes in. It must transform the processes that various foods have gone through while growing—forces that will become active within the human organism. What occurs there is a continual conflict, during which the dynamic forces in food are completely changed. We experience this inner reaction to the substances we eat as stimulating and life sustaining. Consequently, it is no good to merely ask how many ounces of this or that we should eat. Rather, we should ask how our organism will react to even the smallest amounts of a certain food. The human organism needs forces that generate resistance to outer natural processes.

Though somewhat modified, processes in certain areas of the human organism (between the mouth and the stomach) can still be compared to forces in the external world. However, those in the stomach and in the subsequent stages of digestion are very different from what we find outside the human being. When it comes to what happens in the head, however, we find exactly the opposite processes from those in outer nature. This shows how the human organism, in its totality, must be stimulated in the right way through the food we eat.

I must be brief, so there is no time to get into the terminology of the deeper aspects of this subject. For now, however, a less specialized and more popular terminology will do. As you know, in ordinary life there are foods we consider rich in nutrition, and others considered poor in nutrients. It is possible to live on food of poor nutritional value—just think of how many people are fed mainly on bread and potatoes, both of which are certainly low in nutritional value. On the other hand, you have to remember that, in cases of ill health, one must take great care not to overburden the digestion with foods having little nourishment. Bread and potatoes make great demands on the digestive system, with the effect that very little energy is left for the remaining functions. Consequently, a diet of bread and potatoes is not likely to promote physical growth. So we look for other foods that do not put unnecessary strain on the digestive system, foods that work the digestive system very little. If these things are taken to extremes, however, an abnormal activity begins in the brain, which in turn begins other processes that have absolutely no resemblance to those of outer nature. These again affect the rest of the human organism, and as a result the digestive system will become sluggish and too slack. All this is extremely complicated, and it is very difficult to understand all the ramifications of what happens. It is one of the most difficult tasks of a thorough scientific investigation—not the kind so common today—to know what really happens when, for instance, a potato or a piece of roast beef is taken into a human mouth. Each of these two processes is very complex, and each is very different from the other. To investigate the subsequent stages of digestion with scientific precision, a great deal of specialized knowledge is needed.

A mere indication of what happens there must be enough. Imagine that a boy eats a potato. First the potato is tasted in his head, the location of one's organs of taste, and then the sensation of taste induces further responses. Although the sense of taste no longer permeates the boy's whole organism, it nevertheless affects it in certain ways. A potato does not have an especially stimulating taste and, consequently, leaves the organism somewhat indifferent and inactive. The organs are not particularly interested in what happens with the potato in the child's mouth. Then, as you know, the potato passes into the stomach. The stomach, however, does not receive it with alacrity either, because it has not been stimulated by the sensation of taste. Taste always determines whether the stomach takes in food with sympathy or aversion. In this case, the stomach will not exert itself to incorporate the potato with its dynamic forces. Yet, this must happen, since the potato cannot be left there in the stomach. If the stomach has the strength, it will absorb the dynamic forces of the potato and work on them with a certain distaste. It allows the potato to enter without developing any significant response to it, because the potato has not stimulated it. This process continues through the rest of the digestive tract, in which the remains of the potato are again worked on with a certain reluctance. Very little of what was once the potato reaches the head organization.

These few indications—which ought to be deepened considerably for any proper understanding—are intended as a mere suggestion of the complex processes that occur in the human organism. Nevertheless, educators should acquire a working knowledge of these things, and to do this I believe it is necessary to go into the whys and wherefores. I can imagine that some listeners might think it good enough just to be told what they should give children to eat and which foods to avoid. But this is not enough, because to do the right things—especially when physical matters are involved—teachers must have sufficient understanding of the problems. There are so many approaches to these things that one needs guidance to see what each case requires. And for this, teachers need at least a simplified picture of how children should be fed.

In physical education, we see in particular how far educational principles have deviated from prevailing social conditions. Unless students happen to live in boarding schools, where it is possible to practice what I have been indicating, it will be necessary to win the cooperation of parents or others in charge of children, and, as we all know, this can cause considerable difficulties. It may not be possible to implement measures one deems right and beneficial for students until tremendous resistance has been overcome.

Let me give you an example. Imagine you have a student in your class who has an excessively melancholic disposition. Extreme symptoms of this kind always indicate an abnormality in the physical organization. Abnormalities in the soul region always originate with physical abnormalities of one kind or another, and physical symptoms are a manifestation of the soul and spiritual life. So let us imagine such a child in a day school. In a boarding school, of course, one would deal with such a problem in cooperation with the dormitory. So what would I have to do? First I must contact the child's parents and—if I am absolutely certain about the real causes of the problem—I may ask them to increase the child's sugar consumption by at least 150 percent, or in some cases by as much as 200 percent, compared to what one gives a child who behaves normally. I would advise the parents not to withhold this additional sugar, which could be given, for instance, as sweets.

Why would I do this? Perhaps the opposite example will make it clearer to you. Imagine that I have to deal with a pathologically sanguine child. If I am to make sense, we must assume this is an excessively sanguine child. Again, the symptoms betray an abnormality in the physical organization, and here I would have to ask the parents to decrease the amount of sugar given to the child. I would ask them to greatly reduce the amount of sweets given to the child.

What are my reasons? One discovers whether to increase or decrease the amount of sugar only by becoming aware of these facts; all milk and milk products, but mother's milk in particular, spread their effect uniformly throughout the entire human organism, so that each organ receives what it needs in a harmonious way. Other foods, however, have more influence on a particular organic system. Please note that I am not saying other foods exercise an exclusive influence, but that they influence some organs more than others. The way a child or an adult responds to a specific taste or a certain food depends on the general condition of a particular organic system. In this respect, certain luxury foods play as important a part, as do ordinary foods.

Milk affects the entire human being, whereas other nutrients affect a particular organic system. With regard to sugar, we must look at activity in the liver. So, what am I doing by giving an abnormally melancholic child lots of sugar? I diminish the activity of the liver, because sugar, in a certain sense, takes over the activity of the liver. This causes the liver to direct its activity more toward something extraneous, and thus the activity is reduced. Under certain circumstances, pronounced melancholic symptoms may be the result of a child's liver activity, so it is possible, purely through diet, to decrease an overly melancholic tendency in a child—which can also manifest as a tendency toward anemia. And why, in the case of an overly sanguine child, do I recommend a reduction of sugar intake? Here I try to decrease the stimulating effect of sugar and cause the liver to become a little more active on its own. In this way, I stimulate the child's I-being, which helps the child overcome the physical symptoms of an excessively sanguine temperament.

If we pay close attention over a period of time, we generally discover the necessary preventive measures. As a rule, this faculty develops only when it has become second nature in alert and dedicated teachers to spot even slightly unusual symptoms in students. Obviously, we must never allow abnormalities to deteriorate too much before taking action. To achieve this ability, teachers must be willing to continually deepen their understanding and to overcome numerous personal hindrances. Otherwise, I am afraid that teachers will not gain the necessary thoroughness until they reach retirement.

This example illustrates the possibility of counteracting certain abnormalities if we observe the human physical organization as a whole. Thus, the whys and wherefores are important. Naturally, we must always contend with countless details, but it is not impossible to relate these to the broader aspects that generally lead to polarities. Truly good teachers (even better than those who already exist), through close contact with their students, know instinctively and beforehand how to handle children when specific circumstances present themselves. In any case, if they are to take the appropriate action, it is extremely important for teachers to perceive any deviation from the normal, healthy behavior of children.

We must watch very closely how children—as beings of body, soul, and spirit—show an interest not only in themselves, but also in their environment. We have to develop an instinctive awareness of the children's interest, or their lack of it. This represents the one side. The other is a teacher's awareness of the first signs of fatigue in students.

What is the source of each child's characteristic interest? It arises in the metabolic and limb system, but mainly in the metabolism. I will know that there is a problem of improper diet if I see that a child is losing interest, for example, in mental activities (and this is the most obvious sign); or if a child shows little interest in outer activities and no longer wants to participate in games or similar pursuits; or if I see that a child has lost interest in food (which is the worst sign of all, since children are naturally interested in various tastes and should learn to distinguish between the various flavors); or if a child suffers from lack of appetite (since a lost appetite also means a lack of interest in food). Here, food demands too much of the child's digestive system. So, I must find out what food this child is being given that has relatively little nutritive value, since such food burdens the digestive system. Just as I can determine the weather by reading the barometer, similarly I can deduce an improper diet when I see a marked lack of interest in a child.

Interest and apathy are the most important indicators with regard to a correct diet for children.

Now let's take a look at the opposite pole. If I notice that a child tires too quickly because of mental or physical activities, again I can trace the cause to physical conditions. In this case, a child may eat with a normal appetite, but after eating, such a child may become drowsy, not unlike a snake after feeding. If a child has an abnormal desire to curl up on the sofa after eating, it shows an inability to cope with digestion, which causes the child to become tired. It is a sign that a child has been given too much of the sort of food that does not stimulate the digestion enough, with the result that the unfulfilled demands of the digestive system now enter the child's head region, causing fatigue.

So, I must give food having concentrated nutritional value to a child who shows a noticeable lack of interest. But there is no need to become a fanatic about these things. Fanatical vegetarians will say that this lack of interest in children is caused by a diet of meat, and that they must now get used to a diet of raw fruits, so they can recover a normal interest in the world. This may be true. But those who believe in giving meat to children will maintain that, if they tire too easily, we must stimulate them with a meat diet.

These things should not provoke too much discussion, simply because it is possible to balance various foods through appropriate combinations that, in this case, might very well take the place of meat. Nor is it essential to turn children into vegetarians. The important thing is to recognize that, on the one hand, children who lack a healthy interest can be helped by an improved diet, one that contains especially nutritious foods and, on the other, that a tendency toward fatigue can be overcome by working in the opposite direction. This is one way to simplify and easily understand a very complex subject. If, for example, I find that a child tires too easily, I must realize that the digestion is not sufficiently engaged, and so I alter the diet accordingly. We must develop a kind of human symptomatology that helps us in a concrete and practical way. It is not always necessary to go into all the details. In matters of nutrition, if we interpret certain symptoms correctly, we begin to see through the situation and recognize what steps to take.

Closely related to all this (though opposite in a certain sense) is the whole question of warmth in childhood. Here, external phenomena guide us even more clearly than does nutrition; we just need the correct interpretation. On the other hand, they easily lead to extremes and become harmful. I am referring to "hardening," or "toughening." Under certain circumstances, this can be good, and much has been done in its favor. Yet, if we are well grounded in our knowledge of the human being, we cannot help feeling a sense of alarm when we see adults who were systematically hardened as children, and now cannot cross a hot and sunlit square without feeling oppressed by the heat. This can reach a point where both their psychological and physical makeup prevents them from ever crossing a sunny, open square. Surely, hardening is inappropriate if does not enable a person to endure any kind of physical hardship.

When considering the question of warmth or cold, two facts need to be kept in mind. First, nature has given us a clear directive; we have a sense of well-being only so long as we are unaware of the temperature surrounding us. If we are exposed to too much heat or cold, we quickly lose our sense of well-being. Obviously, we need our sensory perception of outer temperatures, but this must not adversely affect our whole organism. To protect ourselves from heat and cold, we neutralize their effects by the use of clothing. When exposed to too much cold, a person loses the ability to maintain normal functioning in certain inner organs. If, on the other hand, outer temperatures are too high, the body reacts with an excessive functioning of those organs. So we can say that, if a person is exposed to very low temperatures, the inner organs tend to coat themselves with a layer of mucus, giving rise to the type of ill-nesses I would call (in the vernacular) internal mucositis. Organs become lined with metabolic excesses, and this results in a hypersecretion of mucus. If, on the other hand, a person is exposed to too much heat, those organs respond by drying up. A tendency develops to form crusts, while the organs them-selves ossify and become quite anemic.

This way of looking at the human organism provides the correct indications for moving ahead in matters of education. Every symptom and phenomenon teaches us something. For example, as human beings, it is safe to expose our faces to much colder temperatures than we could other parts of our bodies. And because the face is exposed to colder temperatures, it prevents other organs from drying out by stimulating them. There is a continuous interplay between the face, which readily accepts certain degrees of cold, and the other members of the human physical organization. However, we must not confuse the face with a very different part of the human anatomy. For-give me for putting it so crudely, but we must not confuse peo-ple's faces with their calves. This is the sort of mischief we encounter so frequently today, because in cold weather children are allowed to walk around with their legs bare up to their knees, and sometimes even higher. This truly confuses the two ends of the physical human body. If people were only aware of the hidden connections here, they would realize how many cases of appendicitis develop later on because of this confusion between the two human extremities.

On the other hand, it also needs to be said that we should not be too sensitive to minor changes of temperature, and that children should be brought up to bear them with equanimity.

When children overreact to slight changes of temperature, again we must know that we can help by making corresponding changes in the diet. These things show us that warmth and nutrition must work together, for eating and keeping warm complement each other. Those who are oversensitive to temperature changes should be given food with a high caloric content, which generates the inner strength needed to withstand these changes. Again, you can see how a real knowledge of the human being also helps in such situations, and how, fundamentally, not only must everything in the human organism work harmoniously together, but mostly those entrusted with educating young people must be able to recognize this cooperation among the various organs.

The third major aspect of physical education involves various forms of movement. The human makeup is such that we must be active in more than our bodily functions; we must also participate in the outer world. People must be able to experience a connection with the outer world. It is true that not one human organ can be understood when considered only in a state of rest. We must relate it to the inherent activities and movements of its functions; then we can understand an organ even in a state of rest. This is true whether it is an outer organ—whose form, even at rest, indicates its normal movements—or an inner organ, whose shape and configuration express the function and movement that make it part of the overall human organic processes. All this is considered when we introduce various forms of movement to children in the right way. Again, bear in mind the wholeness of the human being. We must try to give the physical, soul, and spiritual aspects their due. With children, we do this only by allowing them to perform the right kinds of movements, which bring satisfaction because they are in harmony with children's innate intentions. Such movements are always accompanied by a sense of well-being.

In an education based on knowledge of the human being, the first step in this direction is to learn the particular ways children want to move when given freedom. Typical games with their inhibiting rules are quite alien to the nature of young children, because they suppress what should remain freely mobile in children. Organized games gradually dull their inner activity, and children lose interest in such externally imposed movements. We can clearly see this by observing what happens when the free movements of playing children are channeled too much into fixed gymnastic exercises. As I said, I do not wish to condemn gymnastic lessons as such, but in general it must be said that when young students are doing gym exercises, their movements are being determined externally. Anyone working out of a real knowledge of the human being would much rather see young children play freely on parallel bars, on a horizontal bar, or on rope ladders, instead of having to follow the exact commands of a gym instructor shouting "one two three" as the children step on the first, second, and third rungs of a rope ladder or perform precise movements on gym apparatus—movements that tend to impose stereotyped forms on their bodies.

I realize that these remarks go a little beyond the general trend of modern gymnastics, whose advocates are often a bit fanatic. One easily rouses antipathy by shedding light on the kind of gymnastic exercises that are imposed externally, and by comparing them with the natural movements of children arising from their own involvement in free play. Yet it is exactly this free play that we should observe and study. One must get to know children intimately, and then one sees what to do to stimulate the right kind of free play, in which boys and girls should, of course, participate together.

In this way, through the inner flexibility that accompanies children's outer movements, their organic functions work together harmoniously. This method also opens our eyes to what lies behind certain symptoms, such as those indicating anemia in young girls. In most cases such symptoms are simply the result of having been artificially separated from the boys, because it was considered unseemly for them to romp with the boys during free play. Girls, as well as boys, should be allowed to be boisterous when they play, although perhaps in slightly different ways. Conventional notions of what is "ladylike" are often are held up to young girls, but they frequently contribute to anemia in later life. However, I must ask you not to take this remark as a personal criticism of an established way of life, but simply as an objective observation. We can obviate a tendency toward anemia simply by allowing young girls to engage in the right kind of free play. In this way, we safeguard their inner functions from becoming so sluggish that they can no longer form the right kind of blood from their digestive activity.

These days, it has become difficult to fully understand these matters, simply because the kind of knowledge fostered today is not the outcome of observing inner human nature, but comes from collecting detailed data. Through so-called induction, these facts are then turned into a hodge podge of general knowledge. Of course, by following this method it is possible to discover all kinds of interesting facts, but it is more important to observe what has real significance for life. Otherwise, an ardent admirer of modern science might argue by saying, "You told us that anemia can manifest because young girls have not been allowed to play freely; yet I have encountered several cases of anemia in a village where young girls had never been restrained in their play." One would have to look into the causes of anemia in this particular situation; perhaps as a child, one of these girls nibbled an autumn crocus (*Colchicum autumnale*), thus developing a tendency toward anemia in later life.

Another important aspect of our theme concerns the consequences of mental strain in children. If we overburden their mental powers, we definitely exert a harmful influence on their general health. If we prevent children from discovering their natural tendency toward movement and play, the metabolic organization will not be sufficiently stimulated. By burdening children with too much knowledge of the world, we artificially increase metabolic activity in the head. Although human beings have a threefold nature, any activity that dominates one of the three spheres is, to a certain extent, also present in the other two systems. When we overload students with facts about the external material realm instead of with spiritual matters, we divert some of the normal digestive activity from the metabolism into the head, thus causing abnormal activity in the whole metabolic system.

This, too, can cause anemia during puberty. Someone might argue that, in a certain village, students were never subjected to intellectual stress, but there were nevertheless cases of anemia in that town. Again we would have to look at the particular situation. For instance, we might discover that one of the houses in this village was covered by Virginia creeper (*Parthenocissus quinquefolia*), and that a child whose curiosity had been roused by its black, glistening berries had eaten a few that were overripe, in this way increasing an innate tendency toward anemia.

To conclude, I would like to say this: It might be correct to collect separate data from which one then extracts general knowledge. But if we want to gain the kind of knowledge that is closely allied to practical life, we have to observe real life carefully, so that we can discover where and how to tackle problems as they arise. Only a real knowledge of the human being offers educators this kind of insight. It enables them to fulfill their task by guiding children into the right forms of movement and by guarding against stressing the mental capacities of the children in their care. The realization of these possibilities is our first and foremost task.

Of course, we cannot necessarily prevent a child from sucking on an autumn crocus or eating black berries from a Virginia creeper, but we can infuse intuitions into children—and at the right time. And this will enable them to develop physical powers in a well-rounded way and to cultivate greater flexibility.

RELIGIOUS & MORAL EDUCATION

January 7, 1922

In this final lecture of our conference on education based on anthroposophic insight into the human being, I would like to speak about the moral and religious aspect in teaching, two related subjects that naturally belong together. Again, there is time for only a few characteristic observations.

There is hardly any other subject that pervades every aspect and branch of education with such an all-embracing and unifying spirit, born from a real knowledge of the human being. Yesterday I spoke to you about physical education, whereas today's theme must be considered truly spiritual—very much so when we look at it from the spirit of our civilization. I want to emphasize immediately that these two subjects—both physical and spiritual in nature—must flow together and form a unity in the kind of education we are considering here, even though they tend to be treated as two very separate branches in traditional education. It may take time for this to happen in general. But in our Waldorf school, we have tried to make a small beginning in this intimate intermingling of spiritual and physical activities by introducing eurythmy as a required subject in all classes that could be seen as a kind of soul and spiritual form of gymnastics. Eurythmy uses the human physical body as a medium to express whatever it brings. Yet, right down to the smallest detail, every movement is also meaningfully permeated by soul and spirit. Eurythmy depends on the physical organs, as speech depends on the human speech organs, without which there could be no vocal communication. The physical speech organs carry soul and spiritual content.

The spiritual element in language can lead directly into the moral and even religious sphere if we are perceptive enough; there is a reason that the Gospel of St. John begins with "In the beginning was the Word." Thus we can say, This flowing together of body, soul, and spirit is cultivated by teaching eurythmy in every class of the Waldorf school, though it is not a well known subject and, as yet, employs a somewhat instinctive way. Although directly linked to physical movements, eurythmy is one of the subjects that can show, perhaps more clearly than any other, how the unification of body, soul, and spirit can be practiced methodically within class lessons. In the future, many other activities will have to stand alongside eurythmy, offering possibilities as yet undreamed of by people today, and working even more directly into the soul and spiritual realm. Such possibilities are inherent in what has already been given, and waiting to be realized; the way is there. Even if our first efforts in eurythmy are far from perfect and limited in scope, the principles of eurythmy will eventually overcome all imbalance in gymnastics, which is the result of today's materialistic influences.

One really feels an inner urge to speak about the ethical and religious aspects of education, even if this can be done only aphoristically. On the one hand, we wish to appeal most strongly to what all human beings share as a common bond, beyond the limits of race and nationality. On the other, it has become obvious that it is almost impossible to speak of matters so intimately connected with people's inner lives in a way that is both understood and accepted by all nationalities. An example may show how very different moral and religious attitudes are in various regions of the world, and how one thus feels inhibited when trying to reach people on this particular level. In reality, such intimate questions of morality and religion can be approached only through the national and religious background of the people concerned.

In all the previous considerations during our conference, I was able to speak in far more general terms about human affairs than I can today. But the anthroposophic view of the world engenders a strong desire to build bridges across all divisions into nationalities, races, and so on. In its inmost being anthroposophy feels compelled to speak with a voice that is supranational, or international. Nevertheless, we are acutely aware of the difficulties in speaking with a voice of universal humanity about such intimate matters of human life, especially in the contemporary scene, which, after all, is the reality that confronts us. So I must beg you to take what I am going to say with the attitude I just mentioned. It is an example intended to illustrate the deep gulfs dividing humankind.

During these lectures I have mentioned Herbert Spencer, who, regardless of personal opinions of his philosophy, must be considered an exponent of Western civilization. I have indicated that Spencer introduced the world to specific educational principles, one of which may be summarized as follows: It is the goal of humankind to reproduce in kind; consequently, it is in our moral interests to raise and educate our offspring accordingly. We must therefore endeavor to provide suitable parents and educators. Such, approximately, are Spencer's views, which begin with, and aim at, a physical picture of the human being. He follows the development of the human race with an eye on its reproduction and adapts his educational goals accordingly.

Now let us look at another person who, though living a little later, can nevertheless be seen as representing an Eastern worldview. Let us consider the philosophy of Vladimir Solovyov.[1] Although he expresses himself in Western terminology, a true Russian folk soul speaks through his works. And so we find that the ethical and religious aims of Solovyov have a very different message for humankind, one permeated by the spirit of the East. He tells us that, on the one hand, people must strive for perfection with regard to truth, and, on the other, people must partake of immortality. Here Solovyov does not imply an earthly immortality resulting from fame or glory, but the real immortality of the soul, which rightly belongs to every human soul. He goes on to say that, without this effort toward perfection in truth—in other words, without the attainment of real knowledge—human existence would be worthless. Only if we are able to perfect ourselves more and more will our human life gain in value. But if the human soul were denied immortality, then all perfection, all ability to strive toward perfection, would be nothing but a monstrous cosmic deception. Then, all human achievements in the search for truth would be submerged, and humankind would be cheated of its most precious aspirations by the very cosmic foundations themselves. However, Solovyov claims, this would be the case if, through earthly development, humankind were to consider human reproduction the final and most important goal. Then humankind's special task in the world would be shunted from one generation to the next, and the human course would be like the spinning of an unchanging wheel, at least in terms of the moral values of existence. In other words, in the spirit of the East, Solovyov clearly rejects the Western ideals of Spencer.

---

1. Vladimir Solovyov (1853–1900), Russian philosopher devoted especially to Sophia. His most popular works are *Lectures on Divine Humanity* (Lindisfarne Books, 1995) and *The Meaning of Love* (Lindisfarne Books, 1985).

This twofold way of experiencing and judging our human task on earth colors all the many divisions with regard to moral and religious issues. If we wish to understand the ethical and moral aims of humankind, we must first free ourselves from prejudice. Then we need to make an honest effort to understand the various diverging philosophies of life. The opposing views of these two thinkers show how the human constitution differs in terms of the intimate subject of today's discussion.

The anthroposophic worldview itself is intended to help people, wherever they live on earth, toward knowledge that is beyond all limits of race or national language. Consequently, spiritual science tries to speak a supranational language (not in any physical sense, of course), a language that can be understood throughout modern civilization. For now, we can realize these goals only to a limited extent. But even these initial steps will enable us to appreciate wider issues as well. Once we have a better understanding of what was just said, we will see how little can be accomplished in moral and religious education as long as we introduce religious dogmas and fixed moral concepts to children. At best we can teach them to become Christians, Jews, Roman Catholics, or Protestants, according to our own religious beliefs. But we must eradicate from a true art of education any attempt to indoctrinate young people into our own particular ideology.

A specific problem in education may help illustrate this point and also help us respect matters of human freedom when dealing with children. And we will quickly realize that we must respect the inherent freedom of children if we also recognized that a dull or a bright student, or even a budding genius, should be treated with equal care. What would happen if teachers were to decide that students should take in only what was near to their own souls? In their bodily nature, those of a lower intelligence are born with a heavy burden. A genius, on the other hand, is born with a winged soul. We must admit to ourselves that we are called to help carry the burden of a disabled person. But we must also admit that, as teachers, we may not be able to follow the flight of a young genius. Otherwise, every school would have to be staffed with great geniuses, and this is probably impossible. Our teaching methods must nevertheless ensure that we do not impede the progress of an inherent genius. We must never clip the wings of a genius's spirit. We can do these things only by developing an art of education that does not interfere with the spiritual forces that must work freely in growing human beings.

All of our previous considerations of this conference were directed to this goal, and once you examine these things in greater depth, you will find it is true. You will also find that the principles of Waldorf education can be implemented in practical life in such a way that teachers need to deal only with what they can develop in children, even in one who will eventually become a genius. Just as a teacher of short stature cannot prevent a student from becoming tall, similarly a teacher's spiritual limitations need not limit a student's innate possibilities for spiritual growth. The later lives of students will remain unimpeded by the inevitable shortcomings of teachers as long as we stand on a knowledge of the whole human being, which emanates from the complete human being just as the forces of physical growth do.

Consequently, I welcome the fact that, in the Stuttgart Waldorf school, something has emerged that could easily go unnoticed by a passing visitor; nevertheless it is a concrete reality. I'm speaking of the spirit of the Waldorf school, which exists independently, irrespective of the personal situations of various staff members, whose soul and spiritual lives thrive as a result of communal efforts to cultivate it. This spirit encourages teachers more and more to educate children, even when they have to help carry the heavy burden of the disabled. The teachers' group study of the human being helps them bear this burden while making every effort to avoid the educational error of hindering a highly gifted student's free development. This is our ideal, and it goes without saying that it does not exist just in the clouds of cuckooland, because the teachers make concerted efforts to bring it into daily life at the Waldorf school.

When dealing with the moral and religious aspects of education, we cannot draw material from existing ideologies, religious institutions, or established ethics. Our task is to reach the students' inner being so that, in keeping with their destinies, they will be able to work freely with others in the social sphere. Consequently, we do not begin teaching by appealing to their conceptual faculties. Although knowledge provides meaning, it does not make it possible to go into the intimate regions of the soul in a living way. When imparting knowledge—and we are bound to do this in our school—when addressing the faculty of thinking as one of the three soul faculties, we must realize that thinking, too, must be channeled toward ethical aims. However, when dealing with the moral and religious aspects of education, we must appeal first and foremost to the feeling life of students. We cannot address the will directly, because human activities immediately connect people socially, and social activities are determined largely by the prevailing conditions and demands of the social milieu.

So we cannot turn directly to thinking, which always wants to turn in a certain direction, nor to willing, which must take its impulses from prevailing social conditions. We can, however, always appeal to feeling, which to a certain extent is the private domain of each individual. If we appeal to this element when teaching, we meet forces of the human soul that have a moral and religious quality. Yet, we must go beyond cultivating the students' thinking, feeling, and willing as though each were a separate faculty. We must try to train the soul forces together. Obviously, it would be wrong to concentrate on training thinking in a lopsided way, just as it would it be wrong to concentrate only on the will. Rather, we must let feeling flow into both thinking and willing.

With thinking, only knowledge of the world and the human being—based on spiritual science—really helps us, because it allows us to build on a physical foundation. With such knowledge, we can safely turn to subjects such as physics and chemistry without the danger of being unable to rise to the level of metaphysics, or spirit. If we reach the suprasensory world along the way, we engage not only thinking but also feeling. The very moment we lift knowledge of the world to a suprasensory level, we begin to achieve a moral relationship with the ground of the world and to suprasensory beings themselves.

The element of feeling is the first of three soul faculties to which we must turn in moral and religious education. If fostered correctly, feeling will be transformed into gratitude. Right from the very beginning of school life, we must systematically develop a mood of gratitude in children—something that modern education allows in only a limited and relatively unconscious way. We must try to engender a mood of gratitude for everything children receive, with every concrete example we take from life itself.

When this feeling is developed properly, it can rise to the highest realms of cosmic laws available to cognition. At such a moment, people feel how the sensory world surrounds them. They come to understand natural laws and see themselves within the sensory realm. They begin to understand that whatever they discover through the senses alone will never make them fully human. Gradually they find a way of knowing the human being that points beyond the limits of the sensory world but, nevertheless, is accessible by scientific methods.

They then not only experience the activity of universal cosmic laws in themselves, but divine the existence of spiritual beings. Such awareness changes knowledge into a deep feeling of gratitude toward the suprasensory beings who placed them into the world. Knowledge broadens into gratitude toward divine beings. We know we have given young people knowledge of the world in the right way if it eventually wells up in them as a feeling of gratitude toward the suprasensory world.

Thus, a feeling of gratitude is the first quality within the three human soul faculties that leads into the moral and religious sphere and that we must cultivate in young people. Gratitude itself includes a certain quality of knowing, since we must understand why we are grateful. It is characteristic of this feeling that it is closely related to our powers of comprehension. In the Waldorf school, we do not appeal to faith as handed down by tradition; this is left to our visiting religion teachers. After the ground has been prepared by class teachers, religious teachers are invited to relate what they can give to life in general.

With the students' faculty of thinking, we first try to create a mood of gratitude. When we turn to feeling, what we find takes us beyond ourselves and out into the world. With the experience of gratitude, we find ourselves facing other beings. And, if we can identify with other beings to the extent of experiencing them as ourselves, then something begins to develop in our feeling life that we call love in the true sense of this word. Love is the second mood of soul that needs to be nurtured in moral and religious life, the kind of love we can nurture at school by doing whatever we can to help students love one another. We can provide a firm foundation for this kind of love by helping children make a gradual transition from the stage of imitation and authority, in the ninth or tenth year, to a genuine feeling of love for their teachers, whose bearing and general behavior at school must naturally warrant it.

In this way we lay the foundations of a twofold human quality; we instill the essence of the ancient call to love your neighbor as you love yourself, while helping to develop a feeling of gratitude that points more to a comprehension of the world. "Love your neighbor as you love yourself" is complemented by the call to "love Divine Being above everything."

Such words of truth have a familiar ring to most people today, for they have sounded through the ages. However, knowing them in theory and repeating them is not the point. It is most important to find ways to put them into practice in the immediate present, thus every age sees a renewal of humankind. We often hear the admonition to love our neighbor as we love ourselves, and God above everything, yet we see little evidence of it. Life at school should try to assure that such things are not just talked about but become infused with new life.

There is only one way that offers a firm foundation for the capacity to love in a mature way, and that is the natural transformation of the childhood stages of imitation and authority to that of love. If we work in harmony with children's natural development toward the attainment of love—whose quality should be self-evident when seen in this light—we will not need to invent the sort of long-winded theories that are fabricated by materialistic thinkers, intended to guide sexually maturing adolescents in their first experiences of love. A whole literature has been written on the subject, all of which suffers from the simple fact that one no longer knows what to do with young people once they reach sexual maturity. The reason for this failure is that children were not prepared properly, because people did not know how to handle the previous stages of childhood. If adolescents have been guided correctly up to this incisive time in their lives, we do not have such difficulties with them.

In children's life of will, we must guide the developing soul so that feelings flow freely into the will in the right way. Chil-

dren must naturally express many different will impulses outwardly, but what asserts itself now? If we were unable to use our
physical powers to express our will impulses, we would not be
human in the physical sense, especially when our actions are
seen in the light of morality and religion. By engendering love,
we pour ourselves out into the world. By willing, we return to
ourselves, and because willing is essential to our lives, we enter
the realm of instincts, drives, and emotions. At the moment we
look for a path to morality and religion, we must realize that
everything that makes us human must now flow into our
instincts and desires. This path reveals itself to us when we
knowingly contemplate the universe and find the human being
there. Ancient tradition put this into words by telling us that
human beings are images of the Godhead.

Volition that has an ethical and religious character arises only
when we can carry this kind of experience into our deliberate
actions—when we can find the image of God even in our
instinctive impulses. Thus we know that our true humanity
remains alive in the domain of the will. What are we doing
when we allow will impulses to enter the world so that, right
down to the level of instincts, people recognize a true human
being in us? By developing a feeling for our own humanity,
which we pour into our will impulses and activities, we reveal
the third of the three soul moods. There is no word in German
for this third element. So, to make my meaning clear, I have to
borrow a word from English—the word *duty*.[2] There is no German word for duty. Those who can experience how words
reveal the genius of language (as described a previous meeting)
will be able to sense my meaning. It is true that anyone who,
without further ado, translates simply according to what one
finds in a dictionary, would translate the word *duty* into the

---

2. Duty refers to what is "due." Latin: *debere* = "to owe."

German word *Pflicht*. But this word does not meet the need at all. As a noun, formed from the verb *pflegen*, it comes from a very different region of the soul.[3] One would have to approach this matter very differently if we were to base it on *Pflicht*. This difficulty of finding the right word presents another example of how differently people are constituted in various parts of the earth. If we aim to be conscientious and correct in our use of language, we cannot translate *duty* with *Pflicht* to express the third mood of soul, because it would not reflect the truth. It would be a lie, even if only a technical one.

1. Gratitude
2. Love
3. Duty

Again, it is characteristic that we can use the German words for gratitude (*Dankbarkeit*) and love (*Liebe*), but that there is no German word for expressing the third mood of soul. It is characteristic because we find ourselves entering a definite geographic locale as soon as we step from the area of cognition, which links us to humanity (since thought can be shared by all thinking people), and as soon as we leave the realm of love, which can unite people everywhere, and enter the sphere of individual volition. Here we are called on to form our lives and become aware of the individuality being developed in us by our having been placed into a definite location on earth.

However, if we approach students through their life of feeling during their ninth or tenth year, when previous powers of imitation and the inborn sense of authority have gradually changed into new faculties, our teaching will, by its very

---

3. The verb *pflegen* has a double meaning; 1) to nurture or nurse; 2) to be accustomed to, or to be in the habit of. *Er pflegte spazieren zu gehen* = "He used to go for a walk."

nature, lead to a moral and religious experience on their part. And when human beings are permeated by the feeling that they want to be truly human, that they must conduct their lives so that, right down to the level of instincts, they themselves and others will recognize true humanity in them, they immediately become messengers, angels of the divine world. Moral life will be pervaded by a religious mood.

If students have been guided properly up to the twelfth year, the introduction of new subjects will lead them into what lies beyond the human realm. This makes them realize that, by observing outer nature, they are entering another world, limited by the senses and obedient to the laws of a lifeless, inorganic world. (We have already described this period and indicated the right pedagogical approach.) At that moment, children feel, deep down, that they want to be truly human, even in their lower nature, at the level of instincts and drives. And then the third mood of soul arises, which is a sense of duty. Thus, through our education and in conformity with the children's nature, we have guided them to experience the three moods of soul. Naturally, the ground had to be prepared during the previous school years.

At the stage of development toward the twelfth year, a certain loss of inner harmony will manifest in our students' religious experiences. I mean that, in their religious life, a most important moment has arrived. Naturally, students have to be prepared for this turning point so that they can pass through it in the right way. Educators must not simply accept the "fact" that certain conflicts caused by modern civilization are inevitable.

In our time, people have their moral and ethical views, which are deeply rooted in the human soul and without which they cannot imagine human dignity and human values. On the other hand, they find themselves surrounded by the effects of natural laws that, in themselves, are completely amoral, laws that affect human lives regardless of any moral issues and can be dealt with only if questions of morality are left entirely out of consideration.

In educational circles today, there is a widespread tendency to conveniently bypass this issue when children reach this critical point in their lives. In our present civilization, however, this conflict in the human soul is both deep-seated and tragic. This must be resolved one way or another before adulthood. Unless students can reconcile the moral and natural orders of the world so they are seen as part of a unity, they may suffer an inner conflict that has the strength to tear their lives apart. Today such a conflict exists in the lives of nearly all thinking people, but they remain unaware of it. People prefer to fall back on traditional religious creeds, trying to bridge what remains unbridgeable unless they can rise from the sensory world to the spiritual world, as anthroposophy endeavors to do.

For adults, such a conflict is indeed tragic. If it arises in childhood before the eleventh year, it brings disturbances in its wake that are serious enough to ruin the soul life of a child. A child should never have to say, "I study zoology and find nothing about God. It's true that I hear of God when I study religion, but this does not help explain zoology." To allow children to be caught in such a dilemma would be awful, since this kind of questioning can completely throw them off their proper course in life. Of course, the education we have been considering during the last few days would never allow such a schism to develop in a child's soul, because it fully considers the importance of the eleventh to twelfth years and all that follows. Only then (not before) is it time for the student to become aware of the disharmony between life as seen in terms of nature and life seen from the moral point of view. We should not overprotect children by glossing over certain facts of life—such as the fact that, apart from gratitude, love, and duty, the world is a duality seen with human eyes. However, if education is based on the principles elaborated here, students will be able to resolve this seeming disharmony in the world, especially at this particular age. Certain problems will deepen and enrich our students' religious lives far more than if they were fed only the traditional sorts of religious instruction, which have to be accepted on faith. Such real meaning assures students that a bridge can be built across the abyss they have experienced for the first time, because it is a reality.

Our civilization requires that we let our ethical and religious views play their proper role in life as it is. And in our religious teaching we must take our cue from the critical moments of the students' developing life of feeling. The difficulties of finding the kind of bridge I have described are highlighted by a book published in London toward the end of the eighties. It is called *Lux Mundi,* and among its contributors are several authors who represent the official views of the High Church of England.[4] It attempts to take what has crystallized in the Church and integrate it more into social life. Even members of the High Church are at pains to build such a bridge—needless to say, from their point of view. You find people discussing this everywhere, and it could well become the substance of our religious life.

Can we really offer something that is being debated so much today as a subject for growing children? Are we in a position to lead young people into Christianity, while theologians increasingly argue about the reality of Christ? Should it not be our task to find ways to help each person relate to Christianity as a free individual? We must not teach accepted dogmas or fixed formulas as ethical and religious instruction; rather, we must learn to nurture the divine spiritual element that lives in the

---

4. Charles Gore, ed. *Lux Mundi: A Series of Studies in the Religion of the Incarnation* (1889).

human soul. Only then shall we guide children correctly, without impinging on their inner freedom to eventually choose their own religious denomination. Only then will students be spared inner uncertainty on discovering that one adult is a member of the High Church while another may be a Puritan. We must succeed in enabling students to grasp the real essence of religion. Likewise, through the cultivation of the three moods of soul, we must succeed in allowing morality to develop freely in the souls of children instead of trying to inculcate them by means of set moral precepts. This problem is at the very heart of the social question, and all the talk or social work related to it will depend on whether we provide the right basis for the moral education of young people. A significant part of the whole social question is simply a question of education.

It was possible to present only a few rough outlines of the moral and religious aspect of Waldorf education, which we have been studying during the last few days. If our educational aims are rooted in a true knowledge of the human being, and as long as we realize that we must refrain from introducing dogmas, theories, or moral obligations into our teaching, we will eventually succeed in laying the right foundation for the moral and religious life of our students.

So we must continue to work toward a true art of education that conforms to the needs of our time. Perhaps I may hope that what I presented to you during the last few days will show that I an not at all against the achievements of general education. Broadly speaking, our present civilization is not lacking in good educational aims and principles, and during the nineteenth century, they were stated in abstract terms by the great educators of various countries around the world. Waldorf education has no intention of opposing or belittling their findings, but it believes it knows that these ideas can be implemented only through the appropriate measures, and that such measures can grow only from a real and deep experience of the human being and the world. Fundamentally, Waldorf education tries to bring about what most people are looking for, though their goals may be somewhat abstract or ill-defined. We are seeking ways to achieve something that everyone would really like to see in education, and if this is the feeling that has arisen among those who have shown genuine interest in an anthroposophically based education as practiced in the Waldorf school, then the right kind of response has been evoked here.

Ladies and gentlemen, it has meant a great deal to me to be permitted to speak to you in this spirit. It is more important to me that you appreciate the spirit from which I have spoken than that you hear the details of what I brought. Details might have to be modified or adapted in one way or another. What matters are not the details but the spirit behind them. If I have succeeded in evoking some experience of the tolerant and humane, yet *active* spirit behind our education based on spiritual science, then perhaps just a little of what I wanted to bring in these lectures has been achieved.

In conclusion, I wish to emphasize once more my firm conviction that it is of utmost importance to speak from this spirit during our time. I would like to thank you for the interest you have shown during these lectures. I would also like to thank you for spending your time at this conference, especially during this festive season, and I hope that, as you leave, you feel at least some justification for your journey to Dornach. If this is the case, I would like to give you my heartiest farewell in the hope that we may meet again, in the sense in which I spoke to you at the opening of this lecture course.

APPENDIX:
QUESTIONS & ANSWERS

From a Discussion on January 1, 1922

Rudolf Steiner: Because so many questions have been handed in, perhaps it would be best to begin by trying to answer some of them.[1] If there are other matters you wish to discuss, we could meet at another time during this conference.

First Question:

It is certainly possible to believe that spreading a main lesson subject over a longer period of time could have drawbacks.[2] Neither can one deny that it is difficult to engage the attention of children on the same subject for a longer time. Other opinions, representing official contemporary educational theory, also seem to speak against such an extension of a subject into block periods. Nevertheless, it was decided to introduce this method in the Waldorf school. The point is that the results of recent psychological experiments (the main reason for disapproval of our methods) do not represent the true nature of the human being. These methods do not penetrate the deeper layers of the human being.

---

1. Many of the questions were not recorded.
2. In Waldorf schools, a main lesson, or block, period of a single subject lasts approximately four weeks.

Why are psychological experiments done at all? I do not object to them, inasmuch as they are justified within the proper sphere. Within certain limits, I am quite willing to recognize their justification. Nevertheless the question remains: Why perform experiments on the human psyche today?

We experiment with the human soul because, during the course of human evolution, we have reached a point where we are no longer able to build a bridge, spontaneously and naturally, from one soul to another. We no longer have a natural feeling for the various needs of children, of how or when they feel fatigued and so on. This is why we try to acquire externally the kind of knowledge that human beings once possessed in full presence of mind, one soul linked to the other. We ask, How do children feel fatigued after being occupied with one or another subject for a certain length of time? We compile statistics and so on. As I said, in a way we have invented these procedures just to discover in a roundabout way what we can no longer recognize directly in a human being.

But for those who wish to establish a close rapport between the soul of a teacher and that of a child, there is something far more important than asking whether we claim too much of our students' powers of concentration by teaching the same subject for a longer period of time. If I understand the question correctly, it implies that, if we were to introduce more variety into the lesson by changing the subject more frequently, we would gain something of value. Well, something would be gained, all right; one cannot deny that. But these things affect students' whole lives, and they should not be calculated mathematically. One ought to be able to decide intuitively. Do we gain something valuable when seen against the whole life development of an individual? Or is something lost in the long run?

It is an entirely different matter whether we teach the same subject for two hours (as in a main lesson) or teach one subject for an hour and then another for the second hour—or even change subjects after shorter periods of time. Although students will tire to a certain extent (for which teachers must make allowances), it is better for their overall development to proceed in this concentrated way than to artificially limit the lesson time just to fill the students' souls with new and different material in another lesson.

What we consider most important in the Waldorf school is that teachers use their available lesson time in the most economical way—that they apply soul economy in relation to their students' potential. If we build lessons along major lines of content that students can follow without becoming tired, or at least without feeling overcome by tiredness, and if we can work against any oncoming tiredness by introducing variations of the main theme, we can accomplish more than if we followed other methods for the sake of advantages they may bring.

In theory it is always possible to argue for or against such things, but it is not a question of preference. The only thing that matters is finding what is best for the overall development of children, as seen from a long-term viewpoint.

There is one further point to be considered. It is quite correct to say that children will tire if made to listen to the same subject too long. But nowadays there is so little insight into what is healthy or unhealthy for children that people see fatigue as negative and something to be corrected. In itself, becoming tired is just as healthy as feeling refreshed. Life has its rhythms. It is not a question of holding the students' attention for half an hour and then giving them a five-minute break to recover from the strain (which would not balance their fatigue in any case) before cramming something else into their heads. It is an illusion to think that this would solve the problem. In fact, one has not tackled it at all, but simply poured something different into their souls instead of allowing the consequences of the organic causes of fatigue to fade. In other words, we have to probe into the deeper layers of the human soul to realize that it has great value for the overall development of children when they concentrate for a longer period on the same subject.

As I said, one can easily reach the opinion that more frequent changes of subjects offer an advantage, but one must also realize that a perfect solution will never be found in life as it is. The real issue is, relatively speaking, finding the best solution to a problem. Then one finds that short lessons of different subjects do not offer the possibility of giving children content which will unite deeply enough with their spiritual, soul, and physical organizations.

Perhaps I should add this; if a school, based on the principles I have been describing, were ever condemned to put up with boring teachers, we would be forced to cut the length of the lesson time. I have to admit that, if teachers were to give boring and monotonous lessons, it would be better to reduce the length of each lesson. But if teachers are able to stimulate their students' interest, a longer main lesson is definitely better.

For me, it is essential not to become fixed or fanatical in any way but always consider the circumstances. Certainly, if we expect interesting lessons at school, we must not engage boring teachers on the staff.

Second Question:
There may be good reasons for seeing eurythmy as a derivation of another art form rather than as a new form of art. But whenever one deals with an artistic medium or with the artistic side of life, it is not the *what* that matters, but the *how*. To me, there is no real meaning in the statement that sculpture, music, speech, rhythm, and so on are merely a means of expression, whereas the underlying ideas are the real substance. There seems

to be little point in making such abstract distinctions in life. Naturally, if one is interested in finding unifying ideas in the abstract, one can also find different media through which they are expressed. But in real life, these media do represent something new and different. For example, according to Goethe's theory of plant metamorphosis, a colored flower petal is, in the abstract, essentially the same as a green plant leaf. Goethe sees a metamorphosed green leaf in a flower petal. And yet, from a practical point of view, a petal is altogether different from a leaf.

Whether eurythmy is a new form of expression or a new version of another art form is not the point at all. What matters is that, during the course of human evolution, speech and singing (though singing is less noticeable) have increasingly become a means of expressing what comes through the human head. Again, this is putting it rather radically, but from a certain point of view it represents the facts. Today, human language and speech no longer express the whole human being. Speech has become thought directed. In modern cultures, it has become closely connected with thinking, and through this development, speech reveals what springs from egoism.

Eurythmy, however, goes back again to human will, so it engages the whole human being. Through eurythmy, human beings are shown within the entire macrocosm. For example, during certain primeval times, gesture and mime always accompanied speech, especially during artistic activities, so that word and gesture formed a single expression and became inseparable. But today, word and gesture have drifted far apart. So one senses the need to engage the whole human being again by including more of the volition and, thus, reconnecting humankind to the macrocosm.

There seems to be way too much theorizing these days, whereas it is so important to consider the practical aspects of life—especially now. Those who observe life from this point of view, without preconceived ideas, know that for every "yes" there is a "no" and that anything can be proved both right and wrong. Yet the real value does not lie in proving something right or wrong or in finding definitions and making distinctions; it is a matter of discovering ways to new impulses and new life in the world. You may have your own thoughts about all this, but spiritual scientific insight reveals the development of humankind, and today it is leaning toward overcoming the intellectuality of mere definitions, being drawn instead toward the human soul realm and creative activity.

And so, it does not really matter whether we see eurythmy as a version of another art form or as a new art. A little anecdote may illustrate this. When I studied at Vienna University, some of the professors there had been given a much coveted title of distinction; they were called "Privy Councillors" *(Hofrat)*. In Germany I found that such professors received the title of "Confidential Councillors" *(Geheimrat)*. In certain quarters, the distinction between these two titles seemed important. But to me, it was the person behind the title that mattered, not the title itself. This seems similar to the situation in which people engage in philosophical arguments (forgive me, for I really don't wish to offend anyone) to determine the difference between an art form that has been transferred to a different medium or, for want of a better word, one referred to as a new dimension in the world of art.

Third Question:

I am not quite clear what this question means, but it seems to express a somewhat evangelical attitude. At best, discipline, as I have already said, can become a natural byproduct of ordinary classroom life. I have also told you how, during the last two years of the Waldorf school, discipline has improved remarkably, and I have given examples to substantiate this.

With regard to this "sense of sin,"[3] it seems that one's moral attitude led to a belief in awakening this feeling in children for their own benefit. But let's please look at this point without any religious bias. An awakening of an awareness of sin would pour something into the soul of children that would remain there in the form of a kind of insecurity throughout life. Putting this in psychoanalytical terminology, one could say that such a method could create a kind of vacuum, an inner emptiness, within the souls of children, which, in later life, could degenerate into a weakness rather than a more active and energetic response to life in general. If I have understood the question rightly, this is all I can say in answer to it.

Fourth Question:

In my opinion this question has already been answered by what I said during the first part of my lecture this morning. In general, we cannot say that at this particular age boys have to go through yet another crisis, apart from the one described this morning. There would be too many different grades of development if we were to speak of an emerging turbulence that affects all boys at this age. Perhaps some people are under delusions about this. If the inner change I spoke of this morning is not guided correctly by the teachers and educators, children (and not just boys) can become very turbulent. They become restless and inwardly uncooperative, so that it becomes very difficult to cope with them.

Events at this age can vary a great deal according to the temperament of the adolescent, a factor that needs to be taken into account. If this were done, one would not make generalizations of the sort that appears here in the first sentence. It would be more accurate to say that, unless children are guided in their

---

3. Here Steiner used the English words.

development—unless teachers know how to handle this noticeable change around the ninth and tenth years—they become uncooperative, unstable, and so on. Only then does the situation arise that was mentioned in the question. It is essential for teachers and educators to fully consider this turning point in the children's development.

Fifth Question:

What has been written here is perfectly correct and I believe that one needs to simply say "yes." Of course, we need a certain amount of tact when talking about the human being with students between ten and twelve. If teachers are aware of how much they can tell students about the nature of the human being, then I certainly agree that we have to enter the individual life of the person concerned.

Sixth Question:

With regard to this question I would like to say that we must count on the possibility of a continually increasing interest in new methods for understanding the secrets of human nature, because spiritual research into the human being is more penetrating than the efforts of natural science. Of course, the possibilities of this study will not be available in every field, but where they do exist, they should be used. It is beneficial not only for teachers and educators, but also for, say, doctors, to learn to observe the human being beyond what outer appearances tell us. I think that, without causing any misunderstandings, we can safely say that only prejudice stands in the way of such methods, and that their development is to be desired. It really is true that much more could be achieved in this way if old, intellectual preconceptions did not bar the way to higher knowledge. My book *How to Know Higher Worlds* describes just the initial stages of such paths.

Seventh Question:

In the Waldorf school, mathematics definitely belongs to the main lesson subjects, and as such it plays its role according to the students' various ages and stages. In no way is this subject relegated to classes outside the main lesson. This question is based on a misunderstanding.

Rudolf Steiner:

Because of the impending departure of various conference members, there is a wish that the practical application of Waldorf principles be discussed first. Thus, it is surely appropriate for me to speak of the Waldorf school. Nevertheless, I want to broaden this subject, because I believe we need a great deal of strength and genuine enthusiasm in the face of present world conditions before our educational goals can be put into practice. It seems to me that, until we recognize the need to move toward the educational impulses described here, it will be impossible to achieve any sort of breakthrough in education.

I am convinced that if you are willing to observe the recent development of humankind with an open mind, you must realize that we are living in the middle of a cultural decline and that any objection to such an assessment is based on illusions. Of course it's very unpleasant and seems pessimistic, though in fact it is meant to be optimistic to speak as I do now. But there are many indications of a declining culture in evidence today, and the situation is really very clear. And the whole question of education arises properly in hearts and souls only when this is fully recognized. In view of this, I see the establishment of the Waldorf school as only the first example of a practical application of the education we have been talking about.

How did the Waldorf school come about? It owes its existence—this much can surely be said—to the realization of educational principles based on true knowledge of the human being. But what made it happen? The Waldorf school is an indirect result of the total collapse of society all over Central Europe in 1919. This general collapse embraced every area of society—the economic, sociopolitical, and spiritual life of all people. Perhaps we could also call it a collapse of economic and political life and a complete bankruptcy of spiritual life. In 1919 the stark realities of the situation made the entire public very much aware of this. Roughly halfway through 1919, there was a general and complete awareness of it.

Today there is much talk, even in Central Europe, about how humankind will recover, how it will eventually pull itself out of the trough again, and so on. But such talk is a figment of an all too comfortable way of thinking, and in reality such thoughts are only empty phrases. The fact is that this decline will certainly accelerate. Today, the situation in Central Europe is not unlike those who have known better days, when they bought plenty of good clothes. They still have those clothes and wear them down to their last threads. The fact that they cannot buy new clothes is certainly clear. And, although they realize they cannot replenish their stock, they nevertheless live under the illusion that all is well and that they will be adequately provided for. Similarly, the world at large fails to realize that it is no longer possible to obtain "new clothes" from its cultural past.

During the first half of 1919, the people of Germany were ready for a serious reassessment of the general situation. At that time, however, a Waldorf school had not yet begun, but it was the time when I gave lectures on social and educational issues, which addressed what I have been describing during this conference (though only in rough outline).[4] Some people saw sense in what was said, and this led to founding the Waldorf school.

---

4. *Geisteswissenschaftliche Behandlung sozialer und pädagogischer Fragen* (lectures in Stuttgart, May 11 and 18 and June 1, 1919; G.A. 192).

I emphasize this point, because the prerequisite for a renewal of education is an inner readiness and openness to assess the real situation, which will itself clearly indicate what needs to be done. At the founding of the Waldorf school, I remarked how good it is that this school will serve as a model, but this in itself it is not enough. As the only school of its kind, it cannot solve today's educational problems. At least a dozen Waldorf schools must be started during the next three months if we are to take the first steps toward a solution in education. However, since this has not happened, we can hardly see our achievement in Stuttgart as success. We have only a model, and even this does not yet represent what we wish to see. For example, apart from our eurythmy room, which we finally managed to obtain, we badly need a gymnasium. We still do not have one, and thus anyone who visits the Waldorf school must not see its current state as the realization of our goals. Beyond all the other problems, the school has always been short of money. Financially it stands on extremely weak and shaky legs.

You see, hiding one's head in the sand goes nowhere in such serious matters. Therefore, I must ask you to permit me to speak freely and frankly. Often, when I speak of these things, as well as my views on money, I am told, "In England we would have to go about this in a very different way; otherwise, we would merely put people off." Now, in my opinion, two things must be done. First, the principles of this education—based as they are on a true picture of the human being—should be made widely known, and the underlying ideas need to be thoroughly taken in and understood. Everything possible should be done in this direction.

If we were to leave it at that, however, there would be little progress. Unless we make up our minds to overcome certain objections, we will never move forward at all. For instance, people say, "In England, people must see practical results."

This is precisely what the civilized world has been saying for the past five or six hundred years. Only what people see with their own eyes has been considered truly valuable, and this drags us down. And if we insist on this stance, we will never pull ourselves out of this chaos.

We are not talking about small, insignificant matters. It is absolutely necessary that we grasp our courage and give a new impulse. Well-meaning people often think that I cannot appreciate what they are saying when they state, "In England, we would have to do things very differently." I understand this only too well, but this does not get to the root of the issue at all.

If the catastrophic conditions of 1919 had not hit the people of Central Europe so hard—though this ill fortune was really a stroke of good luck in terms of beginning the Waldorf school—if that terrible situation had not opened people's eyes, there would be no Waldorf school in Central Europe, even today. In Central Europe, and especially in Germany, there is every need for a new impulse, because there is an innate lack of any ability to organize and so little sense of structured social organization. When people outside Central Europe speak so highly of German organization, it does not reflect the facts. There is no assertive talent for organization in Germany. Above all, there is no articulated social organization; rather, real culture is carried by individuals, not by the general public. Look, for example, at German universities. They do not represent the real character of the German people at all. They are very abstract structures, and do not at all express what is truly German. The real German spirit lives only in individuals. Of course, this is only a hint, but it shows what would probably happen if we appealed to the national mood in Germany; one meets a void and a lack of understanding for what we have been speaking of here. In other words, the Waldorf school owes its existence to an "unlucky stroke of luck."

Now, with regard to the second point, the most important thing, besides the need to build further on what was spoken of here, is that something like a Waldorf school should be established also in countries where the populations have not been jolted into action by abysmal, cataclysmic conditions, such as Germany experienced in 1919. If, for instance, some sort of Waldorf school could be opened in England, this would mark a significant step forward. Naturally, such a school would have to be adapted to the conditions and culture of that country.

I realized that the Waldorf educational movement was not going to spread its wings, because the original Waldorf school was, in fact, still the only one. So I tried to initiate a worldwide Waldorf school movement. I did this because, during the preceding years, there had been a tremendous expansion of the anthroposophic movement, at least in Central Europe. Today this movement is a fact to be reckoned with in Central Europe. As a spiritual movement, it has made its mark. But there is no organization to direct and guide this movement. It needs to said, and generally understood, that the Anthroposophical Society is not in a position to carry the anthroposophic movement. The Anthroposophical Society is riddled with a tendency toward sectarianism, and consequently it is not capable of carrying the anthroposophic movement as it has developed and exists today.

All the same, I had wanted to make a final appeal to the stronger elements within the Anthroposophical Society, because I was hoping that some individuals might respond by making a final effort to bring about a Waldorf movement. Well, this did not happen. The world school movement is dead and buried, because it is not enough simply to talk about such things; it must be accomplished in a down-to-earth and practical way. To implement such a plan, a larger body of people is needed.

The Waldorf school in Stuttgart is one of the results of the German revolution. It is not itself a revolutionary school, but the revolution was its matrix, so to speak. It would mean a big step forward if something like a Waldorf school were started in another country also (say, in England) because the general world situation was clearly recognized. Perhaps later, when time has been given to the discussion, a little more could be said about this.

Millicent MacKenzie (Professor at University College, Cardiff: At this point, I would like to add that, among the members of this conference, there are several people from England who recognize the needs of humankind and would be in a position to work in this direction. They are in a position to exert considerable influence in an effort to realize this educational impulse. As a first step, they would like to invite Dr. Steiner to come to England some time later this year, and they are eager to create the right attitude and context for such a visit, during which they hope a number of prominent individuals and educators would also be present to welcome Dr. Steiner.[5]

Rudolf Steiner: I wish to add that such a step must be taken only in a practical sense, and that it would be harmful if we talk too much about it. Those of you who are in a position to take a step forward in this direction would have to prepare the ground, so that when the right time has come, the appropriate action may be taken.

I am sure that Mrs. MacKenzie and her friends will agree if there are conference members from other countries who might have ideas on this subject and wish to come forward to add their suggestions.

---

5. This is George Adams's abbreviated translation of the question.

Mrs. K. Haag: Today we have heard a great deal about England. We are pleased about this and have found it useful. But there are various other matters that we, who come from our little Holland, have on our heart. In fact, we have come with a very guilty conscience because the idea of a World school movement was just discussed for the first time in Holland. Somehow we did not do what we might have done about it, partly because of misunderstandings and partly because of a lack of strength. But we have not been quite as inactive as people might think, and I can assure you that we are more than ready to make good on our failure, as far as possible. Despite our shortcoming, I would like to ask Dr. Steiner whether the plan he outlined for England could also be implemented in Holland. And since Dr. Steiner has promised to visit us in April, I would like to ask him if he might be willing to discuss this with a larger group of people who have a particular interest in education.

Rudolf Steiner: There is already a plan for Holland, which, as far as I know, is being worked out.[6] From the fifth to the twelfth of April this year, an academic course will be held there that are similar to courses given elsewhere. It has the task, first and foremost, of introducing anthroposophy in depth.

After the need to work for anthroposophy in Holland was repeatedly pointed out, and after the lectures and performances there during February and the beginning of March last year, it has been somewhat discouraging to see a notable decline, not in an understanding of spiritual science, but certainly in terms of the inner life of the Anthroposophical Society in Holland.

---

6. Steiner lectured at The Hague from April 7–13. See *Die Bedeutung der Anthroposophie im Geistesleben der Gegenwart* (GA 82) and *Das Sonnenmysterium und das Mysterium von Tod und Auferstehung. Exoterisches und esoterisches Christentum* (GA 211).

Therefore it seems to me very necessary, especially in Holland, that the anthroposophic movement make a new and vigorous beginning. From which angle this should be approached will depend on the prevailing conditions, but an educational movement could certainly be the prime mover.

Another question has been handed to me, which has a direct bearing on this point.

Question: According to Dutch law, it is possible to set up a free school if the government is satisfied that the intentions behind it are serious and genuine. If we in Holland were unable to raise enough money to begin a Waldorf school, would it be right for us to accept state subsidies, as long as we were allowed to arrange our curriculum and our lessons according to Waldorf principles?

Rudolf Steiner: There is one part of the question I do not understand, and another fills me with doubts. What I cannot understand is that it should be that difficult to collect enough money for a free school in Holland. Forgive me if I am naive, but I do not understand this. I believe that, if the enthusiasm is there, it should at least be possible to begin. After all, it doesn't take so much money to start a school.

The other point, which seems dubious to me, is that it would be possible to run a school with the aid of state subsidies. For I seriously doubt that the government, if it pays out money for a school, would forego the right to inspect it. Therefore I cannot believe that a free school could be established with state subsidies, which imply supervision by inspectors of the educational authorities. It was yet another stroke of good luck for the Waldorf school in Stuttgart that it was begun just before the new Republican National Assembly passed a law forbidding the opening of independent schools. Isn't it true to say that, as liberalization increases, we increasingly lose our freedom? Consequently, in Germany we are living in a time of progress, whereas it is quite unlikely that we could begin a Waldorf school in Stuttgart today. It was established just in time.

Now the eyes of the world are on the Waldorf school. It will be allowed to exist until the groups that were instrumental in instituting the so-called elementary schools have become so powerful that, out of mistaken fanaticism, they will do away with the first four classes of the Waldorf school. I hope this can be prevented, but in any case we are facing menacing times. This is why I continue to emphasize the importance of putting into action, as quickly as possible, all that needs to be done. A wave is spreading all over the world, and it is moving quickly toward state dictatorship. It is a fact that Western civilization is exposing itself to the danger of one day being inundated by an Asiatic sort of culture, one that will have a spirituality all its own. People are closing their eyes to this, but it will happen nevertheless.

To return to our point: I think it only delays the issue to think it is necessary to claim state help before starting a school. Somehow this does not look promising to me at all. But perhaps others have different views on this subject. I ask everyone present to voice an opinion freely.

Question: He states that, at the present time, it is impossible to establish a school in Holland without interference by the state, which would demand, for instance, that a certain set curriculum be formulated and so on.

Rudolf Steiner: If things had been any different, I would not have decided at the time to form a world school movement, because, as an idea, it borders on the theoretical. But because the situation stands as you have described it, I thought that such a movement would have practical uses. The matter is like this: Take the example of the little school we used to have here in Dornach. For the reason already mentioned several times, we managed to have only a very small school because of our continual "overabundant lack of funds." Children around the age of ten came together in this school. Now, in the local canton of Solothurn, there is a strict law in education that is really not much different from similar laws all over Switzerland. This law is so fixed that, when the local education authorities found out that we were teaching children under the age of fourteen, they declared it completely unacceptable; it was simply unheard of. Whatever we might have done to arrive at some agreement, we would never have received permission to apply Waldorf methods in teaching children under fourteen.

Hindrances of this kind will, of course, be placed in our way all over the continent. I dare not say how this would work in England at the moment. But if turns out to be possible to begin a totally free school there, it would really mean a marvelous step forward. But because we meet resistance almost everywhere when we try to put Waldorf education into practice, I thought that a worldwide movement for the renewal of education might have some practical value. I had hoped that it might make an impression on people interested in education, thus creating possibilities for establishing new Waldorf schools. I consider it extremely important to bring about a movement counter to modern currents, which culminated in Russian Bolshevism. These currents find their fulfillment in absolute state dictatorship in education. We see it looming everywhere, but people won't realize that Lunatscharski is merely the final result of what lies dormant all over Europe.[7] As long as it does not

---

7. Anatol Wassiljewitsch Lunatscharski (1875–1933), political author, Commissar for the Enlightenment of the People (1917–1929).

interfere with people's private lives, the existence of such thinking is conveniently ignored. Well, in my opinion, we should react by generating a movement against Lunatscharski's principle that the state should become a giant machine, and that each citizen should be a cog in the machine. The goal of this countermovement should be to educate each person. It is this that is needed. In this sense, one can make most painful experiences even in the anthroposophic movement.

Today it would also be possible to give birth to a real medical movement on the basis of the anthroposophic movement. All the antecedents are there. But it would require a movement capable of placing this impulse before the eyes of the world. Yet everywhere we find a tendency to call those who are able to represent a truly human medicine "quacks," thus putting them outside the law. As an example, and entirely unconnected with the anthroposophic medical movement, I would like to tell you what happened in the case of a minister in the German government who rigorously upheld a strict law against the freedom of the healing profession, a law that still operates today. However, when members of his own family fell ill, he surreptitiously called for the help of unqualified healers, showing that, for his own family, he did not believe in official medical science, but only in what the law condemned as "quackery."

This is symptomatic of the root causes of sectarianism. A movement can free itself of such causes when it stands up to the world, while remaining fully within the laws of the land, so that there can be no confusion in terms of the legal aspects. And this is what I had in mind with regard to a world school movement. I wanted to create the right setting for introducing laws that allow schools based entirely on the need for educational renewal. Schools will never be established correctly by majority decisions, which is also why such schools cannot be run by the state.

That's all I have to say about the planned world school movement, an idea that, in itself, does not appeal to me at all. I do not sympathize with it, because it would have led to an international association, a "world club," and to the creation of a platform for the purpose of making propaganda. My way is to work directly where the needs of the times present themselves. All propaganda and agitation is alien to me. I abhor these things. But if our hands are tied and if there is no possibility to establish free schools, we must first create the right climate for ideas that might eventually lead to free education. Compromises may well be justified in various instances, but we live in a time when each compromise is likely to pull us still further into difficulties.

Question: How can we best work in the realm of politics?

Rudolf Steiner: I think that we should digress too much from our main theme if we were to look at these deep and significant questions from a political perspective. Unless today's politics experience a regeneration—at least in those countries known to me on the physical plane—they hold little promise. It is my opinion that it is exactly in this area that such definite symptoms of decadence are most obvious, and one would expect society to recognize the need for renewal—the threefold social order. Such a movement would then run parallel to the anthroposophic movement.

Where has the old social order placed us? I will indicate this only very briefly and, thus, possibly cause misunderstandings. Where did the old social order, which did not recognize its own threefold nature, land us? It has led to a situation in which the destinies of whole populations are determined by political parties whose ideological backgrounds consist of nothing but phrases. No one today can maintain that the phrases used by the various political parties contain anything of real substance.

A few days ago I spoke of Bismarck, who in later life became a rigid monarchist, although in his younger years he had been something of a bashful, closet republican.[8] This is how he described himself. This same Bismarck expressed opinions similar to those expressed by Robespierre.[9] People can make all sorts of statements. What matters in the end is what comes to light when the real ideology of a party is revealed.

For some years, I taught at the Berlin Center for the Education of the Working Classes, a purely social-democratic institution.[10] I took every opportunity to spread the truth wherever people were willing to listen, no matter what the political persuasion or program of the organizers of those institutions. And so, among people who were, politically, rigid Marxists, I taught a purely anthroposophic approach to life, both in courses on natural science and on history. Even when giving speech exercises to the workers, I was able to express my deepest inner convictions. The number of students grew larger and larger, and soon the social-democratic party leaders began to take notice. It led to a decisive meeting, attended not only by party leaders but also by all my adult students, who were unanimous in their wish to continue their courses. But three to four party leaders stolidly declared that this kind of teaching had no place in their establishment, because it was undermining the character of the

---

8. Lecture in Dornach, January 1, 1922, *Alt und neue Einweihungsmethoden* (GA 210).

9. Prince Furst Otto von Bismarck (1815–1898), "The Iron Chancellor," credited with the 1871 unification of Germany; Maximilien Robespierre (1758–1794), a leader of the "Committee of Public Safety" who helped oversee the "Reign of Terror" following the French Revolution.

10. From 1899 to 1904; see Steiner's *Autobiography: Chapters in the Course of My Life, 1861–1907* (Anthroposophic Press, 1999), part 3.

social-democratic party. I replied that surely the party wanted
to build for a future and that, since humankind was moving
inevitably toward greater freedom, any future school or educational institution would have to respect human freedom. Then
a typical party member rose and said, "We don't know anything about freedom in education, but we do know a reasonable form of compulsion." This was the decisive turning point
that finally led to closing my courses.

It may seem rather silly and egotistic to say this, but I am
convinced that, had this quickly growing movement among
my students at the end of the nineteenth and beginning of the
twentieth century been allowed to live and expand unhindered,
conditions in Central Europe would have been different during
the 1920s.

So you can see that I do not have much trust in working
with political parties. And you will have the least success in
bringing freedom into education when dealing with socialist
parties. They, above all, will strive in most incredible ways for
the abolition of freedom in education. As for the Christian parties, they are bound to clamor for independent schools, simply
because of the constitution of the present German government.
But if they were placed at the helm, they would immediately
claim this freedom in education only to suit themselves. It is a
simple fact that we will be unable to make progress in public
life unless we first create the necessary foundations for a threefold social order, in which the democratic element prevails
exclusively in the middle sphere of rights. This in itself would
guarantee the possibility of freedom in education. We will
never achieve it through electioneering.

Question: If children of the present generation were educated
according to the principles of anthroposophic knowledge,
would this in itself be enough to stem the tide of decadence

and decay, or would it be necessary to send them out into the world with the stated intent of changing society to bring about a new social organism?

Rudolf Steiner: The ideas I tried to express in *Towards Social Renewal* are not fully understood. The reasons for writing this book are decades old. Humanity has reached a stage when, although someone might show up with the most promising ideas for improving society and people's social attitudes, one could not implement them simply because there is a lack of practical possibilities for such purposes. The first step would be to create the right conditions for the possibility of implementing such ideas and insights into social life.

Consequently, I do not believe it is helpful to ask, If a generation were educated in the way we have described, would the desired social conditions automatically follow? Or, Would a change of the social order one way or another still be necessary? I would say, we must understand that the best we can do in practical life is to help as many people as possible of one generation to make progress through education based on knowledge of the human being. This in itself would obviate the second question, because the thoughts and ideas needed to change society would be exactly those developed by that generation. Since their human conditions would be different from those of the general public today, they would have very different possibilities for implementing their aims.

The point is, if we want to be practical, we have to think in practical terms rather than theories. To think practically means to do what is possible, not attempt to realize an ideal. Our most promising aim would be to educate as many as possible of one generation, working from knowledge of the human being, and then trust that, in their adult lives, they would be able to bring about a desirable society. The second question can be answered only through the actions of those who, through their education, have been prepared for the task you outlined. It cannot be answered theoretically.

Question: How can one make use of what we have heard in this course of lectures to educate profoundly mentally retarded children?

Rudolf Steiner: In answer to this question I should like to give you a real and practical example. When I was twenty-three or twenty-four, I was called to work as a tutor in a family of four boys.[11] Three of the boys presented no educational difficulties, but one, who was eleven at that time, had a particular history. At the age of seven, a private tutor had tried in vain to teach him according to the accepted methods of an elementary school. Bear in mind that this happened in Austria, where anyone was free to teach children, because the only thing that mattered was that they could pass an examination at the end of each year, and students were allowed to take these exams at any state school. No one cared whether they had been taught by angels or by devils, as long as they passed their exam, which was seen as proof of a good education.

Among those four boys, one had four to nearly five years of private tutoring behind him. He was around eleven years old when his latest drawing book was presented to me, which he had brought home from his most recent annual exam. In all other subjects he had remained either completely silent or had talked complete nonsense, but he had not put anything down on paper. His drawing book was the only document he had

---

11. At the recommendation of Karl Julius Schröer, from July 1884 until September 1890, Steiner became a teacher of the four sons of Specht family in Vienna. See Steiner's *Autobiography,* part 1, chapter 16.

handed in during his exam, and all it contained was a big hole in the first page. All he had done was scribble something and then immediately erase it, until only a big hole was left as evidence of his efforts and the only tangible result of his exam. In other respects, it proved impossible—sometimes for several weeks—to get him to say even a single word to anyone. For awhile, he also refused to eat at table. Instead, he went into the kitchen, where he ate from the garbage can. He would rather eat garbage than proper food.

I am describing these symptoms in detail so you can see that we are dealing with a child who certainly belonged to the category of "seriously developmentally disabled." I was told that not much could be done, since everything has been tried already. Even the family doctor (who incidentally was a leading medical practitioner in Vienna and a greatly respected authority) had given up on the boy, and the whole family was very discouraged. One simply did not know how to approach that boy.

I asked that this child's education, as well as that of his three brothers, be left entirely in my hands, and that I be given complete freedom in dealing with the boy. The whole family refused to grant me such freedom, except for the boy's mother. From their unconscious depths, mothers sometimes have the right feeling for these things, and the boy was given into my care. Above all else, when preparing my lessons I followed the principle of approaching such a child—generally called "feeble-minded"—entirely in terms of physical development. This means that I had to base everything on the same principles I have elaborated to you for healthy children. What matters in such a case is that one gains the possibility of looking into the inner being of such a child. He was noticeably hydrocephalic, so it was very difficult to treat this boy. And so my first principle was that education means healing and must be accomplished on a medical basis.

After two and a half years, the boy had progressed enough to work at the curriculum of a grammar school, for I had succeeded in teaching him with the strictest economy. Sometimes I limited his academic work to only a quarter or, at most, a half hour each day. In order to concentrate the right material into such a short time, I sometimes needed as much as four hours of preparation for a lesson of half an hour. To me, it was most important not to place him under any strain whatsoever. I did exactly as I thought right, since I had reserved the right to do so. We spent much time on music lessons, which seemed to help the boy. From week to week, the musical activity was increased, and I could observe his physical condition gradually changing. Admittedly, I forbid any interference from anyone. The rest of the family, with the exception of the boy's mother, registered objections when, time and again, they noticed that the boy looked pale. I insisted on my rights and told them that it was now up to me whether I made him look pale, and even more pale. I told them that he would look ruddy again when the time came.

My guiding line was to base the entire education of this child on insight into his physical condition and to arrange all soul and spiritual measures accordingly. I believe that the details will always vary in each case. One has to know the human being thoroughly and intimately, and therefore I must repeatedly point out that everything depends on a real knowledge of the human being. When I asked myself, What is the boy's real age and how do I have to treat him? I realized that he had remained a young child of two years and three months, and that I would have to treat him as such, despite the fact that he had completed his eleventh year, according to his birth certificate. I had to teach him according to his mental age. Always keeping an eye on the boy's health and applying strictest soul economy, I initially based my teaching entirely on the principle of imitation, which meant that everything had to be systematically built on his forces of imitation. I then went on to what, today, I called "further structuring" of lessons. Within two and a half years, the boy had progressed enough that he was able to study grammar school curriculum. I continued to help when he was a student in grammar school. Eventually, he was weaned of any extra help. In fact, he was able to go through the last two classes of his school entirely on his own. Afterward, he became a medical doctor with a practice for many years. He died around the age of forty from an infection he had contracted in Poland during the World War.

This is just one example, and I could cite many others. It shows that, especially in the case of developmentally disabled children, we need to apply the same principles I elaborated here for healthy children. In the Waldorf school there are quite a number of slightly and profoundly "mentally-retarded children" (to use the phrase of the question). Naturally, more serious cases would disturb their classmates, so we have opened a special remedial class for such children of various ages, whose members are drawn from all our classes. This group is under the guidance of Dr. Schubert.

Whenever we have to decide whether to send a child into this remedial class, I have the joy (if I may say it this way) of having to fight with the child's class teacher. Our class teachers never want to let a class member go. All of them fight to keep such children, doing their best to support them within the class, and often successfully. Although our classes are certainly not small, by giving individual attention, it is possible to keep such children in the class. The more serious cases, however, must be placed in our remedial group, where it is absolutely essential to give them individual treatment. Dr. Schubert, who is freed from having to follow any set curriculum, allows himself be guided entirely by the individual needs of each child.

Consequently, he may be doing things with his children that are completely different from what is usually done in a classroom. The main thing is to find specific treatments that will benefit each child.

For instance, there may be some very dull-witted children in such a group, and once we develop the necessary sense for these things, we realize that their faculty of making mental pictures is so slow that they lose the images while making them. They lose mental images because they never fully make them. This is only one type of mental handicap. We can help these children by calling out unexpected commands, if they are capable of grasping their meaning. We have also children who are unable to follow such instructions, so one has to think of something else. For instance, one may suddenly call out, "Quickly hold your left earlobe between your right thumb and second finger. Quickly grip your right arm with your left hand!" In this way, if we let them orient themselves first through their own body geography and then through objects of the world outside, we may be able to make real progress with them. Another method might get them to quickly recognize what one has drawn on the blackboard (Steiner drew an ear on the board). It is not easy at all to get such a child to respond by saying "ear." But what matters is this flash of recognition. One has to invent the most varied things to wake up such children. It is this awakening and becoming active that can lead to progress, though, of course, not in the case of those who display uncontrollable tempers. They have to be dealt with differently. But these examples may at least indicate the direction in which one has to move. What matters is the individual treatment, and this must spring from a real knowledge of the human being.

From a Discussion on the Evening of January 5, 1922

Rudolf Steiner: Several questions have been handed in and I will try to answer as many as possible in the short time available.

First Question: This question has to do with the relationship between sensory and motor nerves and is, primarily, a matter of interpretation. When considered only from a physical point of view, one's conclusion will not differ from the usual interpretation, which deals with the central organ. Let me take a simple case of nerve conduction. Sensation would be transmitted from the periphery to the central organ, from which the motor impulse would pass to the appropriate organ. As I said, as long as we consider only the physical, we might be perfectly satisfied with this explanation. And I do not believe that any other interpretation would be acceptable, unless we are willing to consider the result of suprasensory observations, that is, all-inclusive, real observation.

As I mentioned in my discussions of this matter over the past few days, the difference between the sensory and motor nerves, anatomically and physiologically, is not very significant. I never said that there is no difference at all, but that the difference was not very noticeable. Anatomical differences do not contradict my interpretation. Let me say this again: we are dealing here with only *one* type of nerves. What people call the "sensory" nerves and "motor" nerves are really the same, and so it really doesn't matter whether we use *sensory* or *motor* for our terms. Such distinctions are irrelevant, since these nerves are (metaphorically) the physical tools of undifferentiated soul experiences. A will process lives in every thought process, and, vice versa, there is an element of thought, or a residue of sensory perception, in every will process, although such processes remain mostly unconscious.

Now, every will impulse, whether direct or the result of a thought, always begins in the upper members of the human constitution, in the interplay between the I-being and the astral body. If we now follow a will impulse and all its processes, we are not led to the nerves at all, since every will impulse intervenes directly in the human metabolism. The difference between an interpretation based on anthroposophic research and that of conventional science lies in science's claim that a will impulse is transmitted to the nerves before the relevant organs are stimulated to move.

In reality, this is not the case. A soul impulse initiates metabolic processes directly in the organism. For example, let's look at a sensation as revealed by a physical sense, say in the human eye. Here, the whole process would have to be drawn in greater detail. First a process would occur in the eye, then it would be transmitted to the optic nerve, which is classified as a sensory nerve by ordinary science. The optic nerve is the physical mediator for seeing.

If we really want to get to the truth of the matter, I will have to correct what I just said. It was with some hesitation that I said that the nerves are the physical instruments of human soul experiences, because such a comparison does not accurately convey the real meaning of physical organs and organic systems in a human being. Think of it like this: imagine soft ground and a path, and that a cart is being driven over this soft earth. It would leave tracks, from which I could tell exactly where the wheels had been. Now imagine that someone comes along and explains these tracks by saying, "Here, in these places, the earth must have developed various forces that it." Such an interpretation would be a complete illusion, since it was not the earth that was active; rather, something was done to the earth. The cartwheels were driven over it, and the tracks had nothing to do with an activity of the earth itself.

Something similar happens in the brain's nervous system. Soul and spiritual processes are active there. As with the cart, what is left behind are the tracks, or imprints. These we can find. But the perception in the brain and everything retained anatomically and physiologically have nothing to do with the brain as such. This was impressed, or molded, by the activities of soul and spirit. Thus, it is not surprising that what we find in the brain corresponds to events in the sphere of soul and spirit. In fact, however, this is completely unrelated to the brain itself. So the metaphor of physical tools is not accurate. Rather, we should see the whole process as similar to the way I might see myself walking. Walking is in no way initiated by the ground I walk on; the earth is not my tool. But without it, I could not walk. That's how it is. My thinking as such—that is, the life of my soul and spirit—has nothing to do with my brain. But the brain is the ground on which this soul substance is retained. Through this process of retention, we become conscious of our soul life.

So you see, the truth is quite different from what people usually imagine. There has to be this resistance wherever there is a sensation. In the same way that a process occurs (say in the eye) that can be perceived with the help of a so-called sensory nerve, in the will impulses (in one's leg, for example), a process occurs, and it is this *process* that is perceived with the help of the nerve. The so-called sensory nerves are organs of perception that spread out into the senses.

The so-called motor nerves spread inward and convey perceptions of will force activities, making us aware of what the will is doing as it works directly through the metabolism. Both sensory and motor nerves transmit sensations; sensory nerves spread outward and motor nerves work inward. There is no significant difference between these two kinds of nerves. The function of the first is to make us aware, in the form of thought processes, of processes in the sensory organs, while the other "motor" nerves communicate processes within the physical body, also in form of thought processes.

If we perform the well-known and common experiment of cutting into the spinal fluid in a case of tabes dorsalis, or if one interprets this disorder realistically, without the usual bias of materialistic physiology, this illness can be explained with particular clarity.[12] In the case of tabes dorsalis, the appropriate nerve (I will call it a sensory nerve) would, under normal circumstances, make a movement sense-perceptible, but it is not functioning, and consequently the movement cannot be performed, because movement can take place only when such a process is perceived consciously. It works like this: imagine a piece of chalk with which I want to do something. Unless I can perceive it with my senses, I cannot do what I want. Similarly, in a case of tabes dorsalis, the mediating nerve cannot function, because it has been injured and thus there is no transmission of sensation. The patient loses the possibility of using it. Likewise, I would be unable to use a piece of chalk if it were lying somewhere in a dark room where I could not find it. Tabes dorsalis is the result of a patient's inability to find the appropriate organs with the help of the sensory nerves that enter the spinal fluid.

This is a rather rough description, and it could certainly be explained in greater detail. Any time we look at nerves in the right way, severing them proves this interpretation. This particular interpretation is the result of anthroposophic research. In other words, it is based on direct observation. What matters is that we can use outer phenomena to substantiate our interpretation. To give another example, a so-called motor nerve may

---

12. Tabes dorsalis, or syphilis in the spinal cord and appendages, is characterized by shooting pains and other sensory disturbances, and, in the later stages, by paralysis; also called locomotor ataxia.

be cut or damaged. If we join it to a sensory nerve and allow it to heal, it will function again. In other words, it is possible to join the appropriate ends of a "sensory" nerve to a "motor" nerve, and, after healing, the result will be a uniform functioning. If these two kinds of nerves were radically different, such a process would be impossible.

There is yet another possibility. Let us take it in its simplest form. Here a "sensory" nerve goes to the spinal cord, and a "motor" nerve leaves the spinal cord, itself a sensory nerve (see drawing). This would be a case of uniform conduction. In fact, all this represents a uniform conduction. And if we take, for example, a simple reflex movement, a uniform process takes place. Imagine a simple reflex motion; a fly settles on my eyelid, and I flick it away through a reflex motion. The whole process is uniform. What happens is merely an interpretation. We could compare it to an electric switch, with one wire leading into it and another leading away from it. The process is really uniform, but it is interrupted here, similar to an electric current that, when interrupted, flashes across as an electric spark. When the switch is closed, there is no spark. When it is open, there is a spark that indicates a break in the circuit. Such uniform conductions are also present in the brain and act as links, similar to an electric spark when an electric current is interrupted. If I see a spark, I know there is a break in the nerve's current. It's as though the nerve fluid were jumping across like an electric spark, to use a coarse expression. And this makes it possible for the soul to experience this process consciously. If it were a uniform nerve current passing through without a break in the circuit, it would simply pass through the body, and the soul would be unable to experience anything.

This is all I can say about this for the moment. Such theories are generally accepted everywhere in the world, and when I am asked where one might be able to find more details, I may even mention Huxley's book on physiology as a standard work on this subject.[13]

There is one more point I wish to make. This whole question is really very subtle, and the usual interpretations certainly appear convincing. To prove them correct, the so-called sensory parts of a nerve are cut, and then the motor parts of a nerve are cut, with the goal of demonstrating that the sensations we interpret as movement are no longer possible. If you take what I have said as a whole, however, especially with regard to the interrupt switch, you will be able to understand all the various experiments that involve cutting nerves.

Question: How can educators best respond to requests, coming from children between five and a half and seven, for various activities?

Rudolf Steiner: At this age, a feeling for authority has begun to make itself felt, as I tried to indicate in the lectures here. Yet a longing for imitation predominates, and this gives us a clue about what to do with these children. The movable picture books that I mentioned are particularly suitable, because they stimulate their awakening powers of fantasy.

If they ask to do something—and as soon as we have the opportunity of opening a kindergarten in Stuttgart, we shall try to put this into practice—if the children want to be engaged in some activity, we will paint or model with them in the simplest way, first by doing it ourselves while they watch. If children have already lost their first teeth, we do not paint for them first, but encourage them to paint their own pictures. Teachers will

---

13. Thomas H. Huxley (1825–1895), *The Elements of Physiology and Hygiene; A Text-Book for Educational Institutions* (1868).

appeal to the children's powers of imitation only when they want to lead them into writing through drawing or painting. But in general, in a kindergarten for children between five and a half and seven, we would first do the various activities in front of them, and then let the children repeat them in their own way. Thus we gradually lead them from the principle of imitation to that of authority.

Naturally, this can be done in various ways. It is quite possible to get children to work on their own. For instance, one could first do something with them, such as modeling or drawing, which they are then asked to repeat on their own. One has to invent various possibilities of letting them supplement and complete what the teacher has started. One can show them that such a piece of work is complete only when a child has made five or ten more such parts, which together must form a whole. In this way, we combine the principle of imitation with that of authority. It will become a truly stimulating task for us to develop such ideas in practice once we have a kindergarten in the Waldorf school. Of course, it would be perfectly all right for you to develop these ideas yourself, since it would take too much of our time to go into greater detail now.

Question: Will it be possible to have this course of lectures published in English?

Rudolf Steiner: Of course, these things always take time, but I would like to have the shorthand version of this course written out in long hand as soon as it can possibly be done. And when this is accomplished, we can do what is necessary to have it published in English as well.

Question: Should children be taught to play musical instruments, and if so, which ones?

Rudolf Steiner: In our Waldorf school, I have advocated the principle that, apart from being introduced to music in a general way (at least those who show some special gifts), children should also learn to play musical instruments technically. Instruments should not be chosen ahead of time but in consultation with the music teacher. A truly good music teacher will soon discover whether a child entering school shows specific gifts, which may reveal a tendency toward one instrument or another. Here one should definitely approach each child individually. Naturally, in the Waldorf school, these things are still in the beginning stage, but despite this, we have managed to gather very acceptable small orchestras and quartets.

Question: Do you think that composing in the Greek modes, as discovered by Miss Schlesinger, means a real advance for the future of music?[14] Would it be advisable to have instruments, such as the piano, tuned in such modes? Would it be a good thing for us to get accustomed to these modes?

Rudolf Steiner: For several reasons, it is my opinion that music will progress if what I call "intensive melody" gradually plays a more significant role.[15] Intensive melody means getting used to the sound of even *one* note as a kind of melody. One becomes accustomed to a greater tone complexity of each sound. This will eventually happen. When this stage is reached, it leads to a certain modification of our scales, simply because the intervals become "filled" in a way that is different from what we are used to. They are filled more concretely, and this

---

14. Kathleen Schlesinger, *The Greek Aulos; A Study of Its Mechanism and of Its Relation to the Modal System of Ancient Greek Music* (1939).
15. See answers to questions, September 29, 1920, in *Eurythmie als sichtbarer Gesang. Ton-eurythmie (Eurythmy as Visible Music,* GA 278), the lecture of February 21, 1924.

in itself leads to a greater appreciation of certain elements in what I like to call "archetypal music" (elements also inherent in Miss Schlesinger's discoveries), and here important and meaningful features can be recognized. I believe that these will open a way to enriching our experience of music by overcoming limitations imposed by our more or less fortuitous scales and all that came with them. So I agree that by fostering this particular discovery we can advance the possibilities of progress in music.

Question: Is it also possible to give eurythmy to physically handicapped children, or perhaps curative eurythmy to fit each child?

Rudolf Steiner: Yes, absolutely. We simply have to find ways to use eurythmy in each situation. First we look at the existing forms of eurythmy in general, then we consider whether a handicapped child can perform those movements. If not, we may have to modify them, which we can do anyway. One good method is to use artistic eurythmy as it exists for such children, and this especially helps the young children—even the very small ones. Ordinary eurythmy may lead to very surprising results in the healing processes of these children.

Curative eurythmy was worked out systematically—initially by me during a supplementary course here in Dornach in 1921, right after the last course to medical doctors.[16] It was meant to assist various healing processes. Curative eurythmy is also appropriate for children suffering from physical handicaps. For less severe cases, existing forms of curative eurythmy will be enough. In more severe cases, these forms may have to be intensified or modified. However, any such modifications must be made with great caution.

---

16. See *Curative Eurythmy* (Rudolf Steiner Press, 1990).

Artistic eurythmy will not harm anyone; it is always beneficial. Harmful consequences arise only through excessive or exaggerated eurythmy practice, as would happen with any type of movement. Naturally, excessive eurythmy practice leads to all sorts of exhaustion and general asthenia, in the same way that we would harm ourselves by excessive efforts in mountain climbing or, for example, by working our arms too much. Eurythmy itself is not to blame, however, only its wrong application. Any wholesome activity may lead to illness when taken too far.

With ordinary eurythmy, one cannot imagine that it would harm anyone. But with curative eurythmy, we must heed a general rule I gave during the curative eurythmy course. Curative eurythmy exercises should be planned only with the guidance and supervision of a doctor, by the doctor and curative eurythmist together, and only after a proper medical diagnosis.

If curative exercises must be intensified, it is absolutely essential to proceed on a strict medical basis, and only a specialist in pathology can decide the necessary measures to be taken. It would be irresponsible to let just anyone meddle with curative eurythmy, just as it would be irresponsible to allow unqualified people to dispense dangerous drugs or poisons. If injury were to result from such bungling methods, it would not be the fault of curative eurythmy.

Question: In yesterday's lecture we heard about the abnormal consequences of shifting what was right for one period of life into later periods and the subsequent emergence of exaggerated phlegmatic and sanguine temperaments. First, how does a pronounced choleric temperament come about? Second, how can we tell when a young child is inclined too much toward melancholic or any other temperament? And third, is it possible to counteract such imbalances before the change of teeth?

Rudolf Steiner: The choleric temperament arises primarily because a person's I-being works with particular force during one of the nodal points of life, around the second year and again during the ninth and tenth years. There are other nodal points later in life, but we are interested in the first two here. It is not that one's I-being begins to exist only in the twenty-first year, or is freed at a certain age. It is always present in every human being from the moment of birth—or, more specifically, from the third week after conception. The I can become too intense and work with particular strength during these times. So, what is the meaning and nature of such nodal points?

Between the ninth and tenth years, the I works with great intensity, manifesting as children learn to differentiate between self and the environment. To maintain normal conditions, a stable equilibrium is needed, especially at this stage. It's possible for this state of equilibrium to shift outwardly, and this becomes one of many causes of a sanguine temperament. When I spoke about the temperaments yesterday, I made a special point in saying that various contributing factors work together, and that I would single out those that are more important from a certain point of view.

It is also possible for the center of gravity to shift inward. This can happen even while children are learning to speak or when they first begin to pull themselves up and learn to stand upright. At such moments, there is always an opportunity for the I to work too forcefully. We have to pay attention to this and try not to make mistakes at this point in life—for example, by forcing a child to stand upright and unsupported too soon. Children should do this only after they have developed the faculty needed to imitate the adult's vertical position.

You can appreciate the importance of this if you notice the real meaning of the human upright position. In general, animals are constituted so that the spine is more or less parallel to the earth's surface. There are exceptions, of course, but they may be explained just on the basis of their difference. Human beings, on the other hand, are constituted so that, in a normal position, the spine extends along the earth's radius. This is the radical difference between human beings and animals. And in this radical difference we find a response to strict Darwinian materialists (not Darwinians, but Darwinian materialists), who deny the existence of a defining difference between the human skeleton and that of the higher animals, saying that both have the same number of bones and so on. Of course, this is correct. But the skeleton of an animal has a horizontal spine, and a human spine is vertical. This vertical position of the human spine reveals a relationship to the entire cosmos, and this relationship means that human beings bear an I-being. When we talk about animals, we speak of only three members—the physical body, the ether body (or body of formative forces), and the astral body. I-being incarnates only when a being is organized vertically.

I once spoke of this in a lecture, and afterward someone came to me and said, "But what about when a human being sleeps? The spine is certainly horizontal then." People often fail to grasp the point of what I say. The point is not simply that the human spine is constituted only for a vertical position while standing. We must also look at the entire makeup of the human being—the mutual relationships and positions of the bones that result in walking with a vertical spinal column, whereas, in animals, the spine remains horizontal. The point is this: the vertical position of the human spine distinguishes human beings as bearers of I-being.

Now observe how the physiognomic character of a person is expressed with particular force through the vertical. You may have noticed (if the correct means of observation were used) that there are people who show certain anomalies in physical growth. For instance, according to their organic nature, they were meant to grow to a certain height, but because another organic system worked in the opposite direction, the human form became compressed. It is absolutely possible that, because of certain antecedents, the physical structure of a person meant to be larger was compressed by an organic system working in the opposite direction. This was the case with Fichte, for example.[17] I could cite numerous others—Napoleon, to mention only one. In keeping with certain parts of his organic systems, Fichte's stature could have become taller, yet he was stunted in his physical growth. This meant that his I had to put up with existing in his compressed body, and a choleric temperament is a direct expression of the I. A choleric temperament can certainly be caused by such abnormal growth.

Returning to our question—How can we tell when a young child is inclined too much toward melancholic or another temperament?—I think that hardly anyone who spends much time with children needs special suggestions, since the symptoms practically force themselves on us. Even with very naive and unskilled observation, we can discriminate between choleric and melancholic children, just as we can clearly distinguish between a child who "just sits" and seems morose and miserable and one who wildly romps around. In the classroom, it is very easy to spot a child who, after having paid attention for a moment to something on the blackboard, suddenly turns to a neighbor for stimulation before looking out the window again. This is what a sanguine child is like. These things can easily be observed, even on a very naive level.

Imagine a child who easily flies into a fit of temper. If, at the right age, an adult simulates such tantrums, it may cause the child to tire of that behavior. We can be quite successful this

---

17. Johann Gottlieb Fichte (1762–1814), German philosopher.

way. Now, if one asks whether we can work to balance these traits before the change of teeth, we must say yes, using essentially the same methods we would apply at a later age, which have already been described. But at such an early age, these methods need to be clothed in terms of imitation.

Before the change of teeth, however, it is not really necessary to counteract these temperamental inclinations, because most of the time it works better to just let these things die off naturally. Of course, this can be uncomfortable for the adult, but this is something that requires us to think in a different way. I would like to clarify this by comparison. You probably know something of lay healers, who may not have a thorough knowledge of the human organism but can nevertheless assess abnormalities and symptoms of illnesses to a certain degree. It may happen that such a healer recognizes an anomaly in the movements of a patient's heart. When asked what should be done, a possible answer is, "Leave the heart alone, because if we brought it back to normal activity, the patient would be unable to bear it. The patient needs this heart irregularity." Similarly, it is often necessary to know how long we should leave a certain condition alone, and in the case of choleric children, how much time we must give them to get over their tantrums simply through exhaustion. This is what we need to keep in mind.

Question: How can a student of anthroposophy avoid losing the capacity for love and memory when crossing the boundary of sense-perceptible knowing?

Rudolf Steiner: This question seems to be based on an assumption that, during one's ordinary state of consciousness, love and the memory are both needed for life. In ordinary life, one could not exist without the faculty of remembering. Without this spring of memory, leading back to a certain point in early childhood, the continuity of one's ego could not exist. Plenty of cases are known in which this continuity has been destroyed, and definite gaps appear in the memory. This is a pathological condition. Likewise, ordinary life cannot develop without love.

But now it needs to be said that, when a state of higher consciousness is reached, the substance of this higher consciousness is different from that of ordinary life. This question seems to imply that, in going beyond the limits of ordinary knowledge, love and memory do not manifest past the boundaries of knowledge. This is quite correct. At the same time, however, it has always been emphasized that the right kind of training consists of retaining qualities that we have already developed in ordinary consciousness; they stay alive along with these new qualities. It is even necessary (as you can find in my book *How to Know Higher Worlds*) to enhance and strengthen qualities developed in ordinary life when entering a state of higher consciousness. This means that nothing is taken away regarding the inner faculties we developed in ordinary consciousness, but that something more is required for higher consciousness, something not attained previously. To clarify this, I would like to use a somewhat trivial comparison, even if it does not completely fit the situation.

As you know, if I want to move by walking on the ground, I must keep my sense of balance. Other things are also needed to walk properly, without swaying or falling. Well, when learning to walk on a tightrope, one loses none of the faculties that serve for walking on the ground. In learning to walk on a tightrope, one meets completely different conditions, and yet it would be irrelevant to ask whether tightrope walking prevents one from being able to walk properly on an ordinary surface. Similarly, the attainment of a different consciousness does not make one lose the faculties of ordinary consciousness—

and I do not mean to imply at all that the attainment of higher consciousness is a kind of spiritual tightrope walking. Yet it's true that the faculties and qualities gained in ordinary consciousness are fully preserved when rising to a state of enhanced consciousness.

And now, because it is getting late, I would like to deal with the remaining questions as quickly as possible, so I can end our meeting by telling you a little story.

Question: What should our attitude be toward the ever-increasing use of documentary films in schools, and how can we best explain to those who defend them that their harmful effects are not balanced by their potential educational value?

Rudolf Steiner: I have tried to get behind the mysteries of film, and whether or not my findings make people angry is irrelevant, since I am just giving you the facts. I have to admit that the films have an extremely harmful effect on what I have been calling the ether, or life, body. And this especially true in terms of the human sensory system. It is a fact that, by watching film productions, the entire human soul-spiritual constitution becomes mechanized. Films are external means for turning people into materialists. I tested these effects, especially during the war years when film propaganda was made for all sorts of things. One could see how audiences avidly absorbed whatever was shown. I was not especially interested in watching films, but I did want to observe their effects on audiences. One could see how the film is simply an intrinsic part of the plan to materialize humankind, even by means of weaving materialism into the perceptual habits of those who are watching. Naturally, this could be taken much further, but because of the late hour there is only time for these brief suggestions.

Question: How should we treat a child who, according to the parents, sings in tune at the age of three, and who, by the age of seven, sings very much out of tune?

Rudolf Steiner: First we would have to look at whether some event has caused the child's musical ear to become masked for the time being. But if it is true that the child actually did sing well at three, we should be able to help the child to sing in tune again with the appropriate pedagogical treatment. This could be done by studying the child's previous habits, when there was the ability to sing well. One must discover how the child was occupied—the sort of activities the child enjoyed and so on. Then, obviously, with the necessary changes according to age, place the child again into the whole setting of those early years, and approach the child with singing again. Try very methodically to again evoke the entire situation of the child's early life. It is possible that some other faculty may have become submerged, one that might be recovered more easily.

Question: What is attitude of spiritual science toward the Montessori system of education and what would the consequences of this system be?[18]
Rudolf Steiner: I really do not like to answer questions about contemporary methods, which are generally backed by a certain amount of fanaticism. Not that I dislike answering questions, but I have to admit that I do not like answering questions such as, What is the attitude of anthroposophy toward this or that contemporary movement? There is no need

18. Montessori education was founded in Rome by Dr. Maria Montessori (1870–1952). The goal of this method, according to its founder, "is not merely to make children understand, and still less to force them to memorize, but to touch their imaginations so as to enthuse them to their innermost core."

for this, because I consider it my task to represent to the world only what can be gained from anthroposophic research. I do not think it is my task to illuminate other matters from an anthroposophic point of view. Therefore, all I wish to say is that when aims and aspirations tend toward a certain artificiality—such as bringing to very young children something that is not part of their natural surroundings but has been artificially contrived and turned into a system—such goals cannot really benefit the healthy development of children. Many of these new methods are invented today, but none of them are based on a real and thorough knowledge of the human being.

Of course we can find a great deal of what is right in such a system, but in each instance it is necessary to reduce also the positive aspects to what accords with a real knowledge of the human being.

And now, ladies and gentlemen, with the time left after the translation of this last part, I would like to drop a hint. I do not want to be so discourteous as to say, in short, that every hour must come to an end. But since I see that so many of our honored guests here feel as I do, I will be polite enough to meet their wishes and tell a little story—a very short story.

There once lived a Hungarian couple who always had guests in the evening (in Hungary, people were very hospitable before everything went upside down). And when the clock struck ten, the husband used to say to his wife, "Woman, we must be polite to our guests. We must retire now because surely our guests will want to go home."

The Foundations
of Waldorf Education

THE FIRST FREE WALDORF SCHOOL opened its doors in Stuttgart, Germany, in September 1919, under the auspices of Emil Molt, director of the Waldorf Astoria Cigarette Company and a student of Rudolf Steiner's spiritual science and particularly of Steiner's call for social renewal.

It was only the previous year—amid the social chaos following the end of World War I—that Emil Molt, responding to Steiner's prognosis that truly human change would not be possible unless a sufficient number of people received an education that developed the whole human being, decided to create a school for his workers' children. Conversations with the minister of education and with Rudolf Steiner, in early 1919, then led rapidly to the forming of the first school.

Since that time, more than six hundred schools have opened around the globe—from Italy, France, Portugal, Spain, Holland, Belgium, Britain, Norway, Finland, and Sweden to Russia, Georgia, Poland, Hungary, Romania, Israel, South Africa, Australia, Brazil, Chile, Peru, Argentina, Japan, and others—making the Waldorf school movement the largest independent school movement in the world. The United States, Canada, and Mexico alone now have more than 120 schools.

Although each Waldorf school is independent, and although there is a healthy oral tradition going back to the first Waldorf teachers and to Steiner himself, as well as a growing body of secondary literature, the true foundations of the Waldorf method and spirit remain the many lectures that Rudolf Steiner gave on the subject. For five years (1919–1924), Rudolf Steiner, while simultaneously working on many other fronts, tirelessly dedicated himself to the dissemination of the idea of Waldorf education. He gave manifold lectures to teachers, parents, the general public, and even the children themselves. New schools were founded. The movement grew.

While many of Steiner's foundational lectures have been translated and published in the past, some have never appeared in English, and many have been virtually unobtainable for years. To remedy this situation and to establish a coherent basis for Waldorf education, Anthroposophic Press has decided to publish the complete series of Steiner lectures and writings on education in a uniform series. This series will thus constitute an authoritative foundation for work in educational renewal, for Waldorf teachers, parents, and educators generally.

LECTURES AND WRITINGS BY RUDOLF STEINER ON EDUCATION

I. *Allgemeine Menschenkunde als Grundlage der Pädagogik: Pädagogischer Grundkurs,* 14 lectures, Stuttgart, 1919 (GA 293). Previously *Study of Man.* **The Foundations of Human Experience** (Anthroposophic Press, 1996).

II. *Erziehungskunst Methodische-Didaktisches,* 14 lectures, Stuttgart, 1919 (GA 294). **Practical Advice to Teachers** (Rudolf Steiner Press, 1988).

III. *Erziehungskunst,* 15 discussions, Stuttgart, 1919 (GA 295). **Discussions with Teachers** (Anthroposophic Press, 1997).

IV. *Die Erziehungsfrage als soziale Frage,* 6 lectures, Dornach, 1919 (GA 296). Previously *Education as a Social Problem.* **Education as a Force for Social Change** (Anthroposophic Press, 1997).

V. *Die Waldorf Schule und ihr Geist,* 6 lectures, Stuttgart and Basel, 1919 (GA 297). **The Spirit of the Waldorf School** (Anthroposophic Press, 1995).

VI. *Rudolf Steiner in der Waldorfschule, Vorträge und Ansprachen,* 24 lectures and conversations and one essay, Stuttgart, 1919–1924 (GA 298). **Rudolf Steiner in the Waldorf School: Lectures and Conversations** (Anthroposophic Press, 1996).

VII. *Geisteswissenschaftliche Sprachbetrachtungen,* 6 lectures, Stuttgart, 1919 (GA 299). **The Genius of Language** (Anthroposophic Press, 1995).

VIII. *Konferenzen mit den Lehrern der Freien Waldorfschule 1919–1924,* 3 volumes (GA 300a–c). **Faculty Meetings with Rudolf Steiner,** 2 volumes (Anthroposophic Press, 1998).

IX. *Die Erneuerung der pädagogisch-didaktischen Kunst durch Geisteswissenschaft,* 14 lectures, Basel, 1920 (GA 301). **The Renewal of Education** (Anthroposophic Press, 2001).

X. *Menschenerkenntnis und Unterrichtsgestaltung,* 8 lectures, Stuttgart, 1921 (GA 302). Previously *The Supplementary Course: Upper School* and *Waldorf Education for Adolescence.* **Education for Adolescents** (Anthroposophic Press, 1996).

XI. *Erziehung und Unterricht aus Menschenerkenntnis,* 9 lectures, Stuttgart, 1920, 1922, 1923 (GA 302a). The first four lectures are in **Balance in Teaching** (Mercury Press, 1982); last three lectures in **Deeper Insights into Education** (Anthroposophic Press, 1988).

XII. *Die gesunde Entwicklung des Menschenwesens,* 16 lectures, Dornach, 1921–22 (GA 303). **Soul Economy: Body, Soul, and Spirit in Waldorf Education** (Anthroposophic Press, 2003).

XIII. *Erziehungs- und Unterrichtsmethoden auf anthroposophischer Grundlage,* 9 public lectures, various cities, 1921–22 (GA 304). **Waldorf Education and Anthroposophy 1** (Anthroposophic Press, 1995).

XIV. *Anthroposophische Menschenkunde und Pädagogik,* 9 public lectures, various cities, 1923–24 (GA 304a). **Waldorf Education and Anthroposophy 2** (Anthroposophic Press, 1996).

XV. *Die geistig-seelischen Grundkräfte der Erziehungskunst,* 12 Lectures, 1 special lecture, Oxford, 1922 (GA 305). **The Spiritual Ground of Education** (Anthroposophic Press, 2003).

XVI. *Die pädagogische Praxis vom Gesichtspunkte geisteswissenschaftlicher Menschenerkenntnis,* 8 lectures, Dornach, 1923 (GA 306). **The Child's Changing Consciousness as the Basis of Pedagogical Practice** (Anthroposophic Press, 1996).

XVII. *Gegenwärtiges Geistesleben und Erziehung,* 14 lectures, Ilkeley, 1923 (GA 307). **A Modern Art of Education** (Anthroposophic Press, 2003) and **Education and Modern Spiritual Life** (Garber Publications, 1989).

XVIII. *Die Methodik des Lehrens und die Lebensbedingungen des Erziehens,* 5 lectures, Stuttgart, 1924 (GA 308). **The Essentials of Education** (Anthroposophic Press, 1997).

XIX. *Anthroposophische Pädagogik und ihre Voraussetzungen,* 5 lectures, Bern, 1924 (GA 309). *The Roots of Education* (Anthroposophic Press, 1997).

XX. *Der pädagogische Wert der Menschenerkenntnis und der Kulturwert der Pädagogik,* 10 public lectures, Arnheim, 1924 (GA 310). *Human Values in Education* (Rudolf Steiner Press, 1971).

XXI. *Die Kunst des Erziehens aus dem Erfassen der Menschenwesenheit,* 7 lectures, Torquay, 1924 (GA 311). *The Kingdom of Childhood* (Anthroposophic Press, 1995).

XXII. *Geisteswissenschaftliche Impulse zur Entwicklung der Physik. Erster naturwissenschaftliche Kurs: Licht, Farbe, Ton—Masse, Elektrizität, Magnetismus,* 10 lectures, Stuttgart, 1919–20 (GA 320). *The Light Course* (Anthroposophic Press, 2001).

XXIII. *Geisteswissenschaftliche Impulse zur Entwicklung der Physik. Zweiter naturwissenschaftliche Kurs: die Wärme auf der Grenze positiver und negativer Materialität,* 14 lectures, Stuttgart, 1920 (GA 321). *The Warmth Course* (Mercury Press, 1988).

XXIV. *Das Verhältnis der verschiedenen naturwissenschaftlichen Gebiete zur Astronomie. Dritter naturwissenschaftliche Kurs: Himmelskunde in Beziehung zum Menschen und zur Menschenkunde,* 18 lectures, Stuttgart, 1921 (GA 323). Available in typescript only as **"The Relation of the Diverse Branches of Natural Science to Astronomy."**

XXV. *The Education of the Child and Early Lectures on Education* (a collection; Anthroposophic Press, 1996).

XXVI. Miscellaneous.

LECTURES AND WRITINGS BY
RUDOLF STEINER ON ANTHROPOSOPHY

Anthroposophical Leading Thoughts: Anthroposophy As a Path of Knowledge, The Michael Mystery, London: Rudolf Steiner Press, 1998 (GA 26).

At Home in the Universe: Exploring Our Suprasensory Nature, Great Barrington, MA: Anthroposophic Press, 2000 (GA 231).

Autobiography: Chapters in the Course of My Life, 1861–1907, Great Barrington, MA: Anthroposophic Press, 1999 (GA 28).

Christianity as Mystical Fact, Great Barrington, MA: Anthroposophic Press, 1996 (GA 8).

Founding a Science of the Spirit, London: Rudolf Steiner Press, 1999 (GA 95).

From the History & Contents of the First Section of the Esoteric School, 1904–1914, Great Barrington, MA: Anthroposophic Press, 1998 (GA 264).

How to Know Higher Worlds: A Modern Path of Initiation, Great Barrington, MA: Anthroposophic Press, 1994 (GA 10).

Intuitive Thinking As a Spiritual Path: A Philosophy of Freedom, Great Barrington, MA: Anthroposophic Press, 1995 (GA 4).

An Outline of Esoteric Science, Great Barrington, MA: Anthroposophic Press, 1998 (GA 13).

The Spiritual Guidance of the Individual and Humanity, Great Barrington, MA: Anthroposophic Press, 1991 (GA 15).

Theosophy: An Introduction to the Spiritual Processes in Human Life and in the Cosmos, Great Barrington, MA: Anthroposophic Press, 1994 (GA 9).

A Way of Self-Knowledge, Great Barrington, MA: Anthroposophic Press, 1999 (GA 16, 17).

INDEX

breathing, 89–90
Bruno, Giordano, 15
building blocks, 114

C

calculators, 173
calves, exposure of, 262
career, educating with eye toward, 234
causality, laws of, 27
causal process, 23, 166
cause and effect, introducing into teaching, 206
Central Europe, conditions in early 1920s, 294, 296
Central Europeans, different from Westerners, 34
change of teeth, 103–4, 135
    addressing behavioral traits before, 326
    ether body becoming independent during, 106
    forces liberated during, 217
    rhythm and beat of increasing importance after, 136
    significance of, 107
chemistry, 189, 191, 233–34
chest areas, ether body freeing self from, 112
child
    new relationship of thinking, feeling, willing after seventh year, 104
    soul and spiritual life connected to physical processes in early life, 135–36
child nature, higher cognition facilitating understanding of, 75
childhood experience, reemergence of effects, 159–60

childhood illnesses, 108
childhood physical idiosyncrasies, cause of adult illness, 198
childishness, carried into maturity, 54–56, 57–58
child psychology, 156
children
    ages newborn to 2½, 107–12
        2½–5, 113–15
        5–7, 115–16
        under 7, 101–7
        7–10, 135–54
        10, 155–74
        10–14, 175–213
    approaching teachers as artists, 154
    artistic element important to, 201–3
    avoiding interference in their inner activities, 105
    awakening sense of right an wrong in, 116
    beginning school at age seven, 116
    bringing to beauty, 238–39
    characteristic interest, 259
    choleric, 211–13, 325
    confronting teachers, 96
    destiny of caregivers, 103
    differentiating between self an outside world (age 9), 156
    digesting sensory perceptions, 55–56
    dreams of, 94–95
    educating in life's utilitarian aspects, 40
    experiencing selves as self-contained (after change of teeth), 163
    faith in adult authority, 215

DURING THE LAST TWO DECADES of the nineteenth century the Austrian-born Rudolf Steiner (1861–1925) became a respected and well-published scientific, literary, and philosophical scholar, particularly known for his work on Goethe's scientific writings. After the turn of the century, he began to develop his earlier philosophical principles into a methodical approach to the research of psychological and spiritual phenomena.

His multifaceted genius led to innovative and holistic approaches in medicine, science, education (Waldorf schools), special education, philosophy, religion, agriculture (biodynamic farming), architecture, drama, movement (eurythmy), speech, and other fields. In 1924 he founded the General Anthroposophical Society, which has branches throughout the world.